The Contested Removal Power, 1789–2010

American Political Thought
Wilson Carey McWilliams and Lance Banning
Founding Editors

The Contested Removal Power, 1789–2010

J. David Alvis, Jeremy D. Bailey, and
F. Flagg Taylor IV

UNIVERSITY PRESS OF KANSAS

Published by the University Press of Kansas (Lawrence, Kansas 66045),
which was organized by the Kansas Board of Regents and is operated and
funded by Emporia State University, Fort Hays State University, Kansas
State University, Pittsburg State University, the University of Kansas,
and Wichita State University

Library of Congress Cataloging-in-Publication Data
Alvis, J. David.
   The contested removal power, 1789–2010 / J. David Alvis, Jeremy D.
Bailey, F. Flagg Taylor IV.
      pages cm.—(American political thought)
   Includes index.
   ISBN 978-0-7006-1922-1 (hardback)
1. Executive power—United States. 2. United States—Officials and
employees—Dismissal of. I. Bailey, Jeremy D., 1974– II. Taylor, F.
Flagg III. Title.
   KF5053.A754 2013
   342.73'062—dc23

                                                2013020174

British Library Cataloguing-in-Publication Data is available.

Printed in the United States of America

10 9 8 7 6 5 4 3 2 1

The paper used in this publication is recycled and contains 30 percent
postconsumer waste. It is acid free and meets the minimum requirements
of the American National Standard for Permanence of Paper for Printed
Library Materials Z39.48–1992.

Contents

Acknowledgments

The idea for this book began at a panel at a conference of the American Political Science Association, where each of us presented a paper on the removal power. After a few years of discussing the removal power during breaks at various conferences, we finally approached Fred Woodward with the idea of writing a book on the topic. Fred told us to send him a proposal, we did, and the book was conceived.

Writing a coauthored book was new for each of us. Each of us contributed the same amount, which in retrospect feels more like we each worked 50 percent rather than 33 percent. Happily, the benefits easily outweighed the costs of the extra work. Each of us had a pretty good grasp of the essential ways to understand the removal power before we collaborated, but each of us has had his mind changed throughout the course of this book. Our collective understanding, and we hope, our collective writing is superior to any contribution we might have made as individuals. Whatever merit or flaws this book might have should be divided equally.

Portions from the sections on Hamilton in Chapters 1 and 3, as well as a few sentences in Chapter 5, reproduce material from "The New Unitary Executive and Democratic Theory: The Problem of Alexander Hamilton," by Jeremy D. Bailey, *American Political Science Review* 102, 4 (November 2008): 453–465. Permission has been granted by Cambridge University Press. Portions from the section on Hamilton in Chapter 2 also reproduce material from "The Traditional View of Hamilton's Federalist No. 77 and an Unexpected Challenge: A Response to Seth Barrett Tillman," by Jeremy D. Bailey, *Harvard Journal of Law and Public Policy* 33 (2010): 169–184. Permission to reproduce this material has been granted.

We have benefited from the insight and patience of family and colleagues along the way. Collectively, we thank Fred Woodward and University Press of Kansas not only for seeing the potential value of this project but also for putting together the best list out there on the presidency in American political development. We also thank Peter Schramm and the Ashbrook Center for providing us space for us to come together on several summer days in 2011 and 2012. We also thank Mike, Pam, and Rafe at the Jack Miller Center for giving us the intellectual space to think aloud.

We also have our debts as individuals.

David is grateful for all of the assistance he has received from many generous colleagues, including James Ceasar, David and Mary Nichols, Michael Zuckert, Marc Landy, Robert Jeffrey, Bill Demars, and John Farrenkopf. He would also like to thank Meghan Cathey and Paul Jones of the Wofford Library for their patience with his infinite requests for research material. Wofford College generously provided him the means and opportunity to undertake the writing of this book. His children, Patrick, Brigid, Brendan, Maeve, and Finbar have supported him with their affection and encouraged him along during the course of writing this book. Above all, he is deeply indebted to his wife, Megan, for lovingly bearing with this and other conceptions.

Jeremy thanks all those who have helped him think about the removal power in the context of the presidency, especially Richard Bensel, James Ceasar, Benjamin Kleinerman, Daniel Klinghard, Steve Knott, Karren Orren, Stephen Skowronek, and George Thomas. Jeremy would also like to thank Marc Landy, who continues to teach him what it important about executive power and what is not. His biggest debts are to Wyndham and Wilson, who will never get those summer days back.

Flagg thanks David Nichols for encouraging his studies of the presidency and constitutional law. His colleague Pat Ferraioli offered her constitutional law class as a forum for testing his ideas on the removal power. Ron Seyb provided many insights on the book. A pretenure leave, generously granted by Skidmore College, made much of Flagg's work on this book possible. He is very grateful to his family for the patience they have shown as the book took its final shape.

Finally, the authors would like to express their gratitude to those that have helped to prepare this work for publication. Fred Woodward at the University Press of Kansas mentored this project from its first conception to its final form. His guidance and advice have been an invaluable contribution to the book's completion. Jon Howard rendered this work far more readable by virtue of his painstaking efforts of copyediting. We are also grateful for the assistance of Susan Schott and Kelly Chrisman Jacques at UPK for their management of the manuscript. Finally, we thank Skidmore College and the College of Liberal Arts and Social Sciences at the University of Houston for their generous financial support for the cost of the index.

The Contested Removal Power, 1789–2010

Introduction

[The President] shall have Power, by and with the Advice and Consent of the Senate, to make Treaties, provided two thirds of the Senators present concur; and he shall nominate, and by and with the Advice and Consent of the Senate, shall appoint Ambassadors, other public Ministers and Consuls, Judges of the supreme Court, and all other Officers of the United States, whose Appointments are not herein otherwise provided for, and which shall be established by Law: but the Congress may by Law vest the Appointment of such inferior Officers, as they think proper, in the President alone, in the Courts of Law, or in the Heads of Departments.

— United States Constitution, Article II, Section 2, Clause 2

The question of the proper *interpretation* of [Congress's] decision of 1789 is one thing — that of its *finality* another.

— Edward S. Corwin, 1927

Article II of the Constitution includes a parallel silence. It explains how the president can initiate a treaty and hire an executive official, but it does not explain how to end treaties and fire executive officials appointed by the president. As a result, both powers have been — and continue to be — subjects of political controversy and constitutional debate. This book outlines and analyzes the president's removal power as a way to more fully understand how the extent and limits of executive power developed within American political and constitutional history.

The uncertainties surrounding the president's power to remove, in comparison to his powers with respect to foreign affairs, might seem small. And as we will discuss in detail, many scholars consider it to have been settled by the seminal Decision of 1789 passed by the First United States Congress. As a result, there has been little scholarship in political science

1

on the removal power. But we believe the overarching question—about the extent and limits of removal power—is important and unsettled. It is important because it bears on a persisting question of scholarly and journalistic interest—namely, the sources and scope of executive power. Moreover, the removal power often has implications for all three branches of government and therefore is closely intertwined with the core principle of American constitutionalism: separation of powers. It has also been at the center of longstanding political debates about competing constitutional and governmental purposes, sometimes resulting in constitutional crisis. The extent and limits of the removal power remain unsettled because the United States Constitution is less than clear; both sides in the debate have very good reasons for taking their positions. On the one hand, Americans desire accountability and a clear hierarchical chain of command; this promotes policy direction and allows for change based on electoral mandates. On the other, many Americans prize independence; this reflects the need for stable and consistent policy execution informed by technical expertise. A relevant Supreme Court case decided in 2010 (discussed in the section just below) reveals the extent to which the constitutional and political questions surrounding removal power remain unresolved and demand more attention and clarity.

Free Enterprise Fund v. Public Company Accounting Oversight Board

The removal issue last came before the Supreme Court during the fall 2009 term in *Free Enterprise Fund et al. v. Public Company Accounting Oversight Board et al.*[1]

The Public Company Accounting Oversight Board (PCAOB, or the Board) was created by the Sarbanes-Oxley Act of 2002 as a five-member panel to be governed by the Securities and Exchange Commission (SEC, or the "commission"). The PCAOB was empowered to oversee accounting firms that audit public companies. It could inspect, investigate, and punish. The five members were appointed by the SEC and could be removed by the SEC only for cause and according to a carefully outlined procedure. The petitioners in this case argued that the PCAOB was unconstitutional because it exercised executive powers without the requisite presidential control. The president's removal power over the SEC commissioners is limited, they contended, and the SEC's removal power over the Board's members was also limited. Writing for the Court, Chief Justice John Roberts found the two layers of removal protection between the president and the PCAOB to be unprecedented and unconstitutional. He further wrote that the decision had no effect on prior precedents due to the "multilevel protection" involved with the SEC's commissioners and the Board's members.

The Chief Justice presented an orthodox version of what we call in this book the "executive power theory." Roberts argued that the Constitution divides the powers of government into three and then assigns them to distinct branches. All executive power is vested in the president, who counts on subordinate officers to assist him in the execution of federal law. The president's removal power is what keeps those officers accountable to him (and, thereby, to American citizens). Roberts relied upon *responsibility*, a principle first elaborated in 1789 by then–U.S. Representative James Madison and his allies in the First Congress. The principle of responsibility has been central to executive power theorists ever since. As we will see in Chapter 1: "The Decision of 1789," executive power theorists made the argument that a single, visible chain of responsibility between the president and his officers is essential to making the president accountable to the people. On these grounds of responsibility and accountability the Court found the president's relation to the PCAOB wanting.

The Supreme Court, in its previous jurisprudence, had legitimized some tenure protections separating the president from certain officers. But in the 2010 *PCAOB* case, according to the Court, the situation was different: The multilayer structure protected members of the Board by requiring removal by the SEC to be exercised only for cause. If that were the extent of the protection, then no constitutional problem would be present. But according to Roberts, Sarbanes-Oxley went further and "withdraws from the President any decision on whether that good cause exists."[2] The removal power is vested solely with the SEC, the Court determined, and the SEC is insulated from presidential control. Accordingly, that multilayer protection is unconstitutional precisely because it destroys the central and vital constitutional principle of responsibility — in both of its aspects. It upsets the chain of responsibility: The result of the double layer is "a Board that is not accountable to the President, and a President who is not responsible for the Board."[3] Equally important, the severing of these bonds destroys the external link between the president and the people. As Roberts put it (quoting *The Federalist*): "Without a clear and effective chain of command, the public cannot 'determine on whom the blame or the punishment of a pernicious measure, or series of pernicious measures ought really to fall.'"[4] Under the Sarbanes-Oxley Act of 2002, the Court determined, the president cannot superintend the actions of his subordinates and, thus, the people cannot adequately judge the president's efforts in this regard.

Whereas Roberts begins from the premise that executive power theory is the correct way to construe the removal clause, Associate Justice Stephen Breyer, who authored the dissent (joined by Justices Stevens, Ginsburg, and Sotomayor), begins from a very different place. Breyer's view fits within what we will call in this book "congressional delegation theory." Like Edward Corwin, one of the congressional delegation's prominent proponents, Breyer thought that the removal power must be construed at the intersection of a structural principle — the separation of powers — and the broad power of Congress under the necessary and proper clause. According to Breyer, neither principle is absolute. As he put it: "Depending on, say, the nature of the office, its function, or its subject matter, Congress sometimes may, consistent with the Constitution, limit the President's authority to remove an officer from his post."[5] Breyer pointed out that Congress delegated many different kinds of administrative authority to a range of agencies; the nature of the power exercised, as well as the location of the agency, have dictated limitations on the removal power. Breyer saw nothing in the statute at issue that departs from Court precedent: "The functional approach required by our precedents recognizes this administrative complexity and, more importantly, recognizes the various ways presidential power operates within this context — and the various ways in which a removal provision might affect that power."[6]

In his dissent, Breyer defended the statute on three grounds. First: Even though the SEC's removal power over the Board is limited it has extensive authority over the functioning of the Board. If it cannot exert control over personnel, it can exert control over policy. Second: The removal limitations are appropriate because the Board exercises adjudicatory functions and its members are "technical experts." These are exactly the type of functions and tasks that Congress has seen fit to shield from unlimited executive removal in the past, and they demand a kind of independence more akin to Article III judges than to normal executive officers. Third — and most important for the purposes of this introduction to the removal power: Even if one grants that the multilayer protection is constitutionally suspect, the Court's solution does not address the underlying problem. As Roberts wrote for the majority, the removal power is crucial because it is more than a mere "parchment" barrier — it is a real means of exerting control and preventing encroachments. But once the *for-cause* removal limitation of the SEC over the Board is gone, is the Board any more accountable to the president than before? Breyer responds:

> So long as the President is legitimately foreclosed from removing the Commissioners except for cause (as the majority assumes), nullifying the Commission's power to remove Board members only for cause will not resolve the problem the Court has identified: The President will still be 'powerless to intervene' by removing the Board members if the Commission reasonably decides not to do so.[7]

In his majority opinion Roberts wrote that "without a second layer of protection, the Commission has no excuse for retaining an officer who is not faithfully executing the law."[8] The SEC commissioners may not have an excuse, but they also need not fear for their jobs.

Each opinion—the majority and the dissent—fails to satisfactorily answer the uncertainties of the removal question. The problem with the opinion of the Court is that its solution (i.e., precluding the second layer of removal protection) did not address the underlying problem: the president's insulation from the officers tenured in the bureaucracy. As for Breyer's dissent, even if one disagrees with its characterization that this solution accomplishes "virtually nothing," it does not help all that much. More important, the majority's underlying basis for its opinion—executive power theory—ought to have made this problem perfectly plain—that is, the logic of the opinion demands more for the president than the Court was willing to grant. Still, Breyer's dissent fails to supply *any* principle that might limit the extent to which Congress can shield officers from presidential control. As the majority points out, at oral argument the government was unwilling to concede that even *five* layers of protection between the president and the Board would be too many. As Roberts explained, such officers would be "safely encased within a Matryoshka doll of tenure protections . . . immune from Presidential oversight, even as they exercised power in the people's name."[9] Breyer also practices some sleight-of-hand at the outset to veil the logic of congressional delegation. He places the removal power between the "principle" of separation of powers and the "power" of Congress under the necessary and proper clause: "Neither of these two *principles* is absolute in its application to removal cases."[10] But of course we are not dealing with two principles but rather *one* principle and *one* power. And the principle of separation of powers depends on specific powers—otherwise it would be a dead letter. Without an analysis showing what countervailing power(s) from Article II might oppose the necessary and proper clause, Breyer cannot explain why Congress could not control if not appropriate executive power as it sees fit.

The case also reveals that the Court's jurisprudence as to removal power remains unsettled. All sides seemed to agree that two other important cases—*Humphrey's Executor v. United States* (1935)[11] and *Morrison v. Olson* (1988)[12]—were crucial, but *why* and *how* they might be relevant was the subject of disagreement. For instance, the petitioners assumed that the president's relation to the SEC was akin to the president's relation to other so-called independent regulatory commissions (IRCs). That is, the petitioners took for granted the independence of the SEC in that it was not subject to the plenary control of the president, whether through supervision of policy or through removal. But as Breyer pointed out during oral argument, there is no statutory provision limiting the president to for-cause removal of the commissioners. Michael Carvin, counsel for the petitioners, pointed out that the SEC had always been considered similar to the Federal Trade Commission (FTC)—despite the statutory anomaly—and thus both agencies were governed by the limits sanctioned by *Humphrey's*. But shocked by Breyer's willingness to distinguish the SEC from other IRCs, a surprised Carvin noted, "If this court wants to say that—that those people are subject to the President's plenary [authority]." At this point Associate Justice Antonin Scalia interjected, "I'd love to say that. That would be wonderful."[13] Later, Solicitor General Elena Kagan (the future Supreme Court associate justice) made the case that the logic of *Humphrey's* did not call into question the status of the PCAOB, which prompted this telling exchange between Kagan and Scalia:

> General Kagan: I understand the temptation to say something like, well, we don't really much like *Humphrey's Executor*, but we are stuck with it, but not an inch further.
>
> Chief Justice Roberts: I didn't say anything bad about *Humphrey's Executor*.
>
> (Laughter.)
>
> Justice Scalia: I did, I did.
>
> (Laughter.)
>
> General Kagan: But this in . . .
>
> Justice Scalia: We did overrule it, by the way, in—in *Morrison*, didn't we?[14]

Scalia, of course, authored the lone dissent in *Morrison*. As we explain in Chapter 6: "The New Unitarians," that dissent is a seminal document in the recent argument from the unitary executive—indeed, it marks the first time a modern Supreme Court Justice uses the term "unitary executive" in an opinion. Despite the Chief Justice's efforts in *PCAOB* to leave the major removal precedents undisturbed, what is important here is that the logic of the majority's opinion has much in common with Scalia's dissent in *Morrison*. So even if there is no evidence that the four conservative justices who joined the Court since Scalia intend to overrule *Humphrey's*, it is fair to say that there is some uncertainty about the grounds of agency independence and where *Humphrey's* might apply, as well as about the relation between *Humphrey's* and *Morrison*. As Breyer pointed out in an extraordinary appendix to his dissent, the Court's ruling in the *PCAOB* case could potentially affect hundreds or perhaps thousands of jobs across the federal bureaucracy.

The Removal Power and American Political Development

The *PCAOB* decision is important at an even more fundamental level: It reminds us of the uncertainty of Article II. The Constitution speaks of something called "the executive power" without defining it. The Constitution tells us the president has that "something" — it seems to exist outside of, and prior to, the Constitution — yet never spells it out with respect to specific powers. This problem has received much attention in foreign affairs, but it has remained understudied in the context of domestic affairs generally and the removal power in particular. But even if the removal power has not been a subject of political science scholarship, debates over the removal power have a rich tradition in American political and constitutional development.

The differences between the opinion of the Court in *PCAOB* and the dissent take us all the way back to the First Congress, when it first debated the removal power in the Decision of 1789. When creating the major departments of government after approval of the new Constitution, members of the House had to decide whether the executive officials would be removable by the president. This, in turn, led to a discussion about whether the Constitution granted this power to the Congress and whether it could delegate removal power as it saw fit. As we discuss in detail in Chapter 1, four positions emerged from that debate that echo to this day:

1. *Impeachment*: The Constitution provides the impeachment process as the only means to remove executive officials.
2. *Advise and Consent*: The Constitution requires that the Senate give its advice and consent to a removal.
3. *Congressional Delegation*: The Constitution provides Congress with the authority to delegate this power where Congress pleases.
4. *Executive Power-Theory*: The Constitution locates this power in the president.

As is well known, James Madison embraced the executive power theory (number 4 above), and this position won a narrow victory in the House and the Senate in 1789. Even though executive power theory won the day, it is important to note that Madison and his allies might easily have lost. Madison was just one among several members of the Congress who had helped write the Constitution, and, as was noted during the 1789 debate in the House, Alexander Hamilton had previously supported the advise and consent position in *The Federalist*. More important, just as each position disagreed on the details of separation of powers under the Constitution, so too each position implicated a competing normative claim about the respective roles of Congress and the presidency. According to executive power theory, conferring the power of removal by statute enhances the power of Congress but unduly weakens the executive and, thereby, undermines democratic accountability. According to advise and consent theory, giving the removal power to the president alone would make administration too political, or at least discourage worthy individuals from serving in executive office. Alternatively, why not split the difference in the name of flexibility and, following the argument for congressional delegation of power, allow Congress to limit the president's power in certain instances?

Given the good arguments for alternatives to executive power theory, it would be strange if the 1789 decision had actually settled the debate. As even the most cursory reading of American political history will reveal, debates about executive power are reoccurring. With each realigning or "great" president, constitutional lines of authority are tested and reconfigured. Or, as scholars of the presidency in American political development have shown, presidents aspire to "order shattering" in the sense that new presidents seek new sources for governing authority. They aim to transform the constitutional order by transforming the presidency itself. The development of the two-party system, for example, changed constitutional design with respect to the executive's veto power and Congress's impeachment power in the sense that presidents can expect veto overrides and impeachments to be rare. And, as Justice Robert Jackson noted in his famous *Youngstown* concurrence (1952), presidents in the twentieth century have more power than presidents in the nineteenth century in part because democratization of presidential selection has the made the presidency the center of public attention.[15] However, as Stephen Skowronek has argued, the problem for presidents is that each transformation becomes more and more difficult.[16] With each rejection of the old way, the resources for presidential accomplishment narrow. At the same time, other institutions increase their own ability to thwart and even direct the trajectory of presidential initiatives.

We should expect, then, to find that both the justification for and the exercise of executive removal power would meet resistance throughout American political and constitutional development. Moreover, given the tendency of debates concerning the role of the executive to be constitutional debates, we should expect periodic returns to the interpretative positions of the Decision of 1789. When members of Congress object to arguments made on behalf of presidential removals, they should find that advise and consent theory or congressional delegation offer convenient interpretative and normative arguments. But this is not all: We should also expect that the arguments do not always fit the circumstances under which they arise. The rise of party patronage, for example, complicated the formal arrangements of separation of powers. Likewise, the rise of the administrative state has reoriented the congressional argument away from control and toward independence, even if control is still the objective.

Status of the Scholarship

Scholars have not yet sufficiently considered the removal power in American political development, but it has received some attention in the field of constitutional law. The removal power is implicated in the now quite extensive scholarly debate over the so-called *unitary executive*. The question of the scope of executive power heated up in the law-review literature after President Ronald Reagan's efforts to gain a measure of control over the bureaucracy. A vigorous debate erupted over the constitutional and historical legitimacy of his efforts. This literature is now vast, so here we examine a few of the leaders of this debate.[17]

The unitarians argue that the president has constitutional authority to control all exercises of executive power. They differ on the forms this executive control should take: first, the president could control the statutorily authorized discretion of his subordinates — that is, he could supplant their discretionary action with his own; second, he could have a more limited power to nullify the discretionary actions of subordinates; and third, he could have the power to remove his principal subordinates with whom he disagrees.[18] Unitarians rest their case primarily on the text of the Constitution. They argue this document identifies a trinity of governmental powers and then vests these powers in particular governmental institutions. The vesting clause of Article II vests executive power in "a" president — indeed, there is no other recipient of executive power in the Constitution.[19] Other constitutional clauses relating to executive power, such as the take-care clause or the opinions in writing clause, must be read in light of this fundamental vesting of power.[20] Though the Framers clearly understood that the president could not exercise executive power by himself — the Constitution itself mentions "heads of departments" and "principal officers" — this does mean they sanctioned the exercise of executive power outside the supervision of the president. In choosing a single chief executive, the Framers sought to ensure such goods as unity, energy, and responsibility.

Nonunitarians, by contrast, argue that the Constitution gives the president no such plenary authority; rather, it leaves to Congress much power to structure *and* supervise the execution of federal law. They argue that the unitary executive is actually an invention of the twentieth century and has little in common with the executive embodied in the Constitution. The nonunitarians also rely on a construction of the relevant constitutional clauses. First, they suggest the vesting clause is a thin reed on which to place so much weight. They argue that the vesting clause begs the question as to what constitutes executive power. Perhaps more important, though, nonunitarians argue that there are simply too many other clauses that are inconsistent with the unitarian reading of the vesting clause.

Some opponents of the unitarians also argue that the practice of the Framers conflicts with unitarian theory. They argue that whereas unitarians see the substance of executive power to be a simple whole, the Framers understood it to be a compound that included political and administrative aspects. In this view, "The framers meant to constitutionalize just some of what we now think of as 'the executive power,' leaving the balance to Congress to structure as it thought proper."[21] Put simply, Congress has significant authority to structure and supervise this nonpolitical, administrative sphere.

There have been, at best, only two book-length examinations of the removal power. One is Edward S. Corwin's *The President's Removal Power Under the Constitution*, published in 1927, and the other is Steven G. Calabresi and Christopher S. Yoo's *The Unitary Executive: Presidential Power from Washington to Bush*, published in 2008.[22] Corwin's book remains one of the very best studies of the removal power, but it is very old, and it was intended to be a critique of Chief Justice William Howard Taft's opinion in *Myers v. United States* (1926). Calabresi and Yoo's book is more recent and more comprehensive. Because it attempts to provide an exhaustive account of the way that presidents from George Washington to George W. Bush have exercised removal powers, it is an invaluable reference. But Calabresi and Yoo are most interested in the accumulated weight of the precedents set by chief executives. Left out of their account are the causes and qualifications of the events they examine and the counterarguments made on behalf of Congress. As a result, their narrative is frequently too focused on the executive branch and too inattentive to the changes in the arguments made during debates over removals over the course of American political development. More broadly, these two books are alike in that each argues for a particular resolution of the removal-power puzzle: Corwin argues for the congressional delegation position, and Calabresi and Yoo argue for executive power theory. Although this kind of constitutional analysis is important, it tends to omit what is perhaps most interesting for political scientists and historians.[23]

Far from being put in place in 1789 and then simply utilized by subsequent presidents, the removal power has provided the occasion for many stirring and revealing political and constitutional debates throughout U.S. history. If we assume that the question has been settled, then we miss the opportunity to examine how the meaning of executive power altered and was altered by domestic political events. There is a rich tradition in opposing executive power theory — serious political thinkers and actors such as Noah Webster, Henry Clay, Daniel Webster, Joseph Story, James Kent, Louis Brandeis, and arguably Alexander Hamilton all opposed the Decision of 1789. And even among the presidents who defended an exclusive executive removal power, there are often some important discontinuities. Even though, for example, Thomas Jefferson, Andrew Jackson, Grover Cleveland, and Franklin D. Roosevelt all argued for presidential control over removals, each made different arguments to defend their position. Important discontinuities also emerged among the critics of executive power.

Plan of the Book

We believe that the frequency and depth of the debates about the removal power offer an important way to understand the development of the presidency and separation of powers. Our goal is not to endorse one position — indeed, we are suspicious of any single solution to the constitutional and political problems that removals present. Instead we show how the arguments resurface throughout American political development but take on somewhat new shapes each time they surface. We also show that the opponents of executive power theory often face a strategic problem: Because advise and consent favors Senate control (and later Senate control over patronage), the argument for congressional delegation is more attractive to more members of Congress. But the argument for congressional delegation lacks the emphasis on the stability and independence of executive officials and instead drifts toward congressional control.

In Chapter 1: "The Decision of 1789" we undertake a detailed examination of that seminal outcome from the First Congress. As we mentioned above, this debate was the occasion for the emergence of the four proposed solutions to the removal question that would provide the boundaries and terms for the continuing debate on this question throughout history. Our first goal is to provide readers a brief overview of the evolution of the debate as it unfolded over the course of six days. Our second goal is to illuminate the constitutional logic of the four removal positions. As will become apparent, the debate was marked by incredible depth and seriousness. The major participants argued for their positions with much rigor and nuance. Each position was grounded in a coherent constitutional and political rationale, providing future participants in the removal question with a wealth of knowledge to draw upon.

In Chapter 2: "From Responsibility to Rotation" we examine the initial assertions of executive power theory by presidents, particularly Thomas Jefferson (1801–1809) and Andrew Jackson (1829–1837). In

Skowronek's language, these two were the first "reconstructive" presidents in early American history—meaning they were the most free to shatter their political order and remake its contours. Yet both served during early eras when political parties had not yet been accepted as "legitimate" (to borrow Richard Hofstadter's famous term), and therefore both executives had to defend partisan decisions to remove the sitting officials. Jefferson defended the president's power to remove, and he returned to the argument that Madison and congressional allies made in 1789. In this understanding of executive power, Jefferson emphasized responsibility while omitting textual arguments based on Article II. Like Jefferson, Jackson beat an incumbent political coalition in the national vote and needed to replace the current officeholders with his own. Like Jefferson, Jackson returned to the argument of responsibility, but he changed it by adding the principle of *rotation in office*. And unlike Jefferson, Jackson also returned to the constitutional arguments made in 1789 and then expanded them. The debate over control over the National Bank presented the most significant separation of powers crisis up to that point in the nation's history, and it forced Jackson to articulate a new theory of presidential representation to defend the president's power to remove.

In Chapter 3: "Jackson to Johnson: The Rise of Congressional Delegation" we examine the rise of congressional delegation, beginning with the Whigs and ending with the impeachment (and ultimate acquittal) of Andrew Johnson (1865–1869), who became president following the assassination of President Abraham Lincoln. When presidents returned to the argument for executive power theory, their critics responded with alternatives based on the advise and consent position and the congressional delegation positions. The Whigs, in particular, connected the removal debate to their larger assault on executive power and offered the first serious and sustained arguments on behalf of congressional participation in—and even control over—removals. These arguments, however, were complicated by the patronage interests among members of Congress, a consequence of the Tenure of Office Act of 1820. Congressional delegation won out over advise and consent, in part because advise and consent would favor the Senate but not the House. This movement between the two positions can be seen first in the development of Daniel Webster's arguments against executive power theory; and second in the awkwardness of the efforts to impeach and remove Johnson.

In Chapter 4: "The Revenge of Executive Power: From the Tenure of Office Act to *Myers v. United States*" we chronicle the resurgence of executive power theory after the triumph of congressional delegation with the impeachment of Johnson. The new ascendance of this theory is visible in the efforts of four presidential administrations during Reconstruction (and echoed in the landmark Supreme Court case *Myers v. United States* of 1926). During Reconstruction Presidents Grant, Hayes, Garfield, and Cleveland all battled with Congress over removals and sought to reassert executive authority despite the Tenure of Office Act of 1867. Only Grover Cleveland, the first Democrat elected to the White House since James Buchanan in 1856, was successful and oversaw the full repeal of the Tenure Act during his first administration. Cleveland would also elaborate a full-throated defense of executive power theory much like his party's founder, Andrew Jackson. *Myers* represents the Supreme Court's first significant consideration of removal. Taft, writing for the Court, struck down a law that had required congressional participation in the removal of executive officials and affirmed broad authority for presidents to remove officeholders without limitations. The case also deserves attention for the importance it gave to the Decision of 1789: The Chief Justice as well as the two primary dissenters undertook extensive historical analyses to ascertain the meaning of the decision of the First Congress as well as the extent to which that was settled by subsequent presidents and Congresses. We follow these historical arguments with care. Then we examine the constitutional grounds for the two positions in *Myers*: executive power versus congressional delegation. We show why the confrontation of these two constitutional understandings could not produce a middle ground.

In Chapter 5: "The Progressive Era and Independent Regulatory Commissions" we show how the failure to find a middle ground resulted in a new institutional arrangement, beginning in the late nineteenth and early twentieth centuries with the creation of *independent regulatory commissions*. On the removal question, the IRCs, which included statutory restraints on executive removal, seem awkward in light of previous debates. Ostensibly being independent, they were designed to exist outside the political influences of Congress and the president. Some Progressive thinkers argued that this arrangement was actually superior to the traditional separation of powers scheme in that it finally provided a place for expertise and technical knowledge for the administration of law in a complex industrial age. In reality, however, the argument in favor of IRCs proved to be another manifestation of Congress's hostility toward the strong assertion of executive power by the White House. Beneath the veneer of their case for independent expertise, members of Congress in fact hoped to tame the increasing use of discretionary and unilateral power by presidents well into the twentieth century. Their arguments reflected portions of both the advise and consent position as well as the congressional delegation position.

Finally, in Chapter 6 we examine the rise of unitarians and the challenges that the unitarian school has posed to the modern administrative state. Although no one has prevailed in convincing the Supreme Court to declare IRCs unconstitutional, as demonstrated by *Free Enterprise Fund v. PCAOB*, unitarians have had some success in calling into question the underlying rationale in federal courts. Beginning with Richard Nixon, presidents in the last third of the twentieth century argued that IRCs constitute a "headless fourth branch" of government where accountability for the administration of the law had been severed from any link to the people. Nixon demonstrated the absence of any substantive difference between the powers wielded among those agencies labeled "independent" and those under the direct control of the president. Nixon, however, failed to capitalize, and Congress—angered by Nixon's bold assault on its prerogatives—claimed new roles for itself in the conduct of war, the budget, and even prosecution. Later, during the Reagan administration, the unitarian school abandoned the political arena and instead saw the legal profession as a vehicle to define executive power theory and consolidate its achievements thus far. In the absence of support from political parties, their strategy focused on a judicial vindication of executive power theory.

A Possible Objection

Before we turn to the debate of 1789, we should address a concern that inevitably arises in work of this kind. That concern is something like the following: Is it not the case that these debates are simply debates about power? Like most debates about executive power or the filibuster, is it not the case that the argument depends not a principle but rather on which party is in power? To be sure, this is a bigger question than this book, and in attempting an answer, we do not claim to settle once and for all the debate between those who believe that it is possible to disentangle ideas from politics and those who believe it is not.

We believe that the arguments about removals can tell us a great deal about executive power more substantially. At its highest level this debate forces everyone to articulate "the" foundation for executive power, especially in domestic affairs. To explain whether the president or the Congress should control removal power, or why a commission member should be independent, it is necessary to first explain which constitutional clauses are implicated, how they should be construed, and how they relate to one another. This, in turn, requires some explanation of the meaning of the term "executive." As a large literature has shown, how we define that word has enormous consequences for liberal constitutionalism.

But we need not take the high road; a lower road is of equal, if not greater, interest. If we concede that arguments about removals have little to do with abstract theories of the executive and more to do with control over governmental authority and offices, we would still say that the arguments about removals can tell us a great deal about the development of the presidency—and the development of executive power—over time.

This is because it is not enough for someone in the 1830s or the 1980s to reach for a standard argument that the Constitution requires a particular reading of the vesting clause. Rather, that person will have to persuade others that such a reading remains applicable to a particular set of political circumstances. As a result, that person will have to make choices about which arguments to emphasize and which to conveniently forget. If that person has a certain kind of ambition, they will want to put that argument in a way that is consistent with their own professional reputation or institutional loyalty. By looking at these choices, we can get a better view of the way the competing views of executive power have affected the presidency and separation of powers.

Students of American political development have long considered the interplay among ideas, institutions, and politics. And despite considerable disagreement about the extent to which any one affects the others, scholars have shown how ideas rise out of particular political contexts *and* that ideas can direct and/or affect politics. The removal power offers a good opportunity to continue this examination.

Chapter One

The Decision of 1789

Article II of the United States Constitution might be considered the architectural plan for the executive branch. But even given the substance of these plans and their significant departure from what had existed under the Articles of Confederation, the actual above-ground structure could have taken on enormously different aspects. As was quickly discovered in the First Congress, a machinery of government needed to be erected to carry out the business of the emerging American state. But what should the executive departments look like based on Article II? What should be the relationship between these departments and the president, on the one hand, and the Senate on the other? How truly independent and, pace Publius, "energetic," would the president be? As Charles Thach puts it, "Nothing is more vital than the relations of the executive head to the chief officers of the administrative departments, and the relations of the latter to the legislature. And yet the Constitution furnishes no final and authoritative decision on this question."[1]

The range of opinion on executive power at the Constitutional Convention of 1787 had been quite broad, to put it mildly. And though the First Congress took up its work after ratification, the broad range of opinion on executive power would again reveal itself in how Article II would be interpreted. For the most part, the lines of disagreement over executive power during the First Congress mirrored those lines that had been drawn at the Constitutional Convention. In fact, eighteen former members of the Convention were also members of this First Congress (eight in the House of Representatives and ten in the Senate).[2] If this gave the work of the Congress a distinctive authority, it did not make it any easier. No less a mind than James Madison expressed his trepidation to his friend Thomas Jefferson: "We are in a wilderness without a single foot-step to guide us. Our successors will have an easier task. And by degrees the way will become smooth short and certain."[3] Though Madison was addressing the work of the Congress generally, his comments are applicable to the removal question. As Article II provided no easy answers, a look to the state constitutions was also of limited use. "The manner in which the state constitutions had dealt with appointments, terms of office, and removal did not suggest a consensus of any kind. . . . On the whole, the state rules were so diverse as to defy any synthesis."[4] Also complicating matters was Alexander Hamilton's defense of executive energy in *The Federalist*. In No. 77, the great defender of executive power wrote matter-of-factly that the "consent" of the Senate "would be necessary to displace as well as to appoint."[5]

The debate that ensued on the removal power in the summer of 1789 has been widely praised for the depth and seriousness that its participants brought to the chamber. Part of this has to do with the participants in the debate, but another is that it happened before Hamilton's Assumption Plan (his controversial plan for the federal government to assume state debts, which was opposed by his fellow cabinet member Thomas Jefferson) and before the development of national parties. For Louis Fisher, the "debate represents one of the most thorough expositions on the nature of implied powers."[6] The debate and what it decided would become the battleground for one of the Supreme Court's major entries into the removal question in 1926 in *Myers v. United States.*[7] The participants themselves were struck by the quality of the deliberations. Fisher Ames of Massachusetts noted to a friend, "There is less party spirit, less the acrimony of pride when disappointed of success, less personality, less intrigue, less cabal, management, or cunning than I ever saw in a public assembly. The question of the president's power of removal seemed to kindle some sparks of faction, but they went out for want of tinder."[8] William Smith of South Carolina, who argued vigorously against the position which Ames favored, was even more effusive in his praise: "This has been the most important question and the most solemn debate we have had since the meeting of Congress: tho' the house was nearly divided on the subject and the arguments were generally warm and animated, yet I never saw a debate conducted with so much temper and good humour."[9]

Our analysis of the Decision of 1789 will proceed in two parts. First, we provide an overview and chronology of the debate as it unfolded. Second, we lay out the logic and implications of the four positions in detail.

Introduction and Synopsis

On May 19, 1789, Representative Elias Boudinot of New Jersey urged colleagues in the First Congress to "carry [the] intention [of the Constitution] into effect" and create executive departments in order to attend to the critical business facing the infant nation. Boudinot noted it was up to him and his colleagues to "carry [the] intention [of the Constitution] into effect" through the creation of the executive departments.[10] After Representative Egbert Benson of New York suggested the three new departments should be Treasury, War, and Foreign Affairs, Representative James Madison presented a motion that would prove to be the keystone for the discussion until another motion was put forward by Benson on June 22. Madison moved "that there shall be established an executive department, to be denominated the department of foreign affairs; at the head of which there shall be an officer, to be called, the secretary to the department of foreign affairs, who shall be appointed by the president, by and with the advice and consent of the senate; and to be removeable by the president. That there shall be a treasury department, &c. And there shall be a war department, &c."[11] Representative William Smith of South Carolina objected to two parts of Madison's motion. First, Smith argued the clause beginning "shall be appointed" was needless as it appeared to confer a power that the Constitution had given expressly.[12] Madison offered to remove the language on appointments, and the Committee of the Whole voted affirmatively on a motion to strike out this language. Smith also objected to the clause relating to removal as it gave this power to the president alone. So the Decision of 1789 was launched. And it moved along the two axes first introduced by Smith: the location of the removal power and whether or not the location was fixed by the Constitution or could be manipulated by Congress through statute.

Interestingly, the debate proceeded quickly in the sense that the various positions on the central questions were visible on this first day, May 19. For six days, the First Congress would undertake one of the nation's most sophisticated and informative constitutional debates over the organization of the president's administration in American history. The debate would provide what for our book constitutes the framework for subsequent political controversies over the removal power. The positions outlined—totaling four by the end of the debate—on the removal questions were: (1) *Impeachment*: impeachment is the only mode of removal recognized by the Constitution and Congress cannot confer any other mode; (2) *Advise and consent*: the Constitution vests the removal power jointly in the president and the Senate and Congress cannot confer any other mode; (3) *Congressional delegation*: the Constitution is silent or ambiguous about where it vests the removal power, so (a) Congress ought to vest it in the president, or (b) Congress has some latitude but ought not vest it in the president alone; and (4) *Executive power theory*: the Constitution vests the removal power in the president alone.[13]

On May 19 the representatives spent much time refuting the impeachment theory (number 1) put forth by Smith, but in so doing the full range of possibilities was put on the table as the chief spokesmen for each of the four positions emerged. Madison, George Clymer of Pennsylvania, and John Vining of Delaware all spoke on behalf of executive power theory. Madison, who spoke four times on this day, introduced a principle he would elaborate more fully as the debate evolved: *responsibility*. Elbridge Gerry of Massachusetts, Theodorick Bland of Virginia, and Alexander White of Virginia each spoke in favor of advise and consent (number 2). John Laurance of New York spoke in favor of congressional delegation (number 3).

The first day set the tone as well as the framework for the debate that ensued.

What was the textual basis for understanding the removal power under the Constitution? What bearing did the appointments clause have on the removal power? Did the vesting clause of Article II have any significance for the removal question? What about the good behavior clause for judges?

As the textual questions related to removal grew and grew, it must have been clear to the participants in the debate that the seemingly narrow question of removal would involve core judgments about the separation of powers system as a whole.

On May 20 the House discussed a distinct but related issue. Gerry introduced a motion to have the Treasury Department run not by a single secretary or department head but by a board of commissioners. This was not central to the removal debate, but the discussion did show the type of executive power favored by a partisan of the advise and consent theory and the differing conceptions of such key goods as executive responsibility and security. Madison, Benson, and Abraham Baldwin of Georgia all spoke against the idea of a Treasury board, and Gerry's motion was defeated.

The Committee of the Whole did not take up the executive departments and the removal question again until June 16. Though William Smith's constitutional reasoning for removal by means of impeachment alone never garnered more than two other adherents, his undeterred insistence on his position forced others to carefully think through the constitutional merits of their own positions.[14] He spoke twice on June 16 and made the key point that the proponents of the removal clause were divided because they had not thought through the constitutional grounds of the issue. Some thought the Constitution itself granted the removal authority to the president, and others thought the Constitution was silent so it was necessary for Congress to grant it. But Smith astutely observed that if the former were true the clause was unnecessary and if the latter were true the clause was unconstitutional (Congress was nowhere authorized to grant such a power). This point about the clause's proponents would also be made by others such as Gerry and would eventually prove to have an important effect on the outcome of the debate. June 16 was marked by an enlightening exchange between Madison and Alexander White, the latter of whom would prove to be the ablest expositor of advise and consent as well as one of the ablest critics of executive power theory. Madison made his case for the distinctiveness of Article II's vesting clause and the nature of executive power more broadly, and White would engage precisely these issues in his response. Another important participant, Fisher Ames, would make the first of his two speeches on behalf of executive power theory on this day as well.

By the following day, June 17, the outset of the debate was marked by a long, forceful statement by Laurance on congressional delegation and an equally long statement by Smith's key ally, James Jackson of Georgia. Jackson would make a claim that would find particular resonance with those sympathetic to impeachment and advise and consent. Even if one considered the removal power to be incident to the executive branch, it would not necessarily follow that this power belonged to the president alone. Under the Constitution, argued Jackson, the president does not possess all executive power. And shortly after Jackson's statement, John Page of Virginia issued this warning: "Everything which has been said in favor of energy in the executive may go to the destruction of freedom, and establish despotism. This very energy so much talked of, has led many patriots to the Bastille, to the block, to the halter."[15] Such charged remarks on behalf of congressional delegation theory were a reminder to some proponents of executive power theory that, if the latter had superior constitutional merit, one would still have to persuade those with reservations about a strong executive that Congress was not planting here seeds of tyranny.

In addition to the positions developed above, this day would also include an elaboration of the advise and consent position. In an exhaustive exchange with Gerry, Madison would claim that it was advise and consent that he considered most inconsistent with his own views. In one of the lengthiest speeches in the course of the entire debate, he would go on to discuss other relevant clauses, the checks on the president, and the dangers of Senate involvement. Gerry, never one to shy away from bold statements, responded this way: "It does appear to me that the clause is as inconsistent with the constitution as any set of words which could possibly be inserted into the bill."[16] Gerry restated Smith's point on the division between the proponents of the clause: The clause was either "useless" (if the president had the removal authority from the Constitution directly) or "nugatory" (if the Congress was conferring a power not held solely by the president). Gerry also confronted Madison on the crucial question of the nature of the Senate's involvement in appointment. At this point Benson stepped in and made an important concession to the power of the critique of Smith and Gerry. After a lengthy speech defending executive power theory, Benson sought to alter the language in the clause to remove the possibility that the bill could be construed as Congress conferring the removal power on the president. He wanted the House bill to be construed as a mere declaration of a constitutional grant of power. Here he seemed ahead of Madison in his thinking. The day before, Madison seemed to indicate it was possible for the clause as it stood to be construed as a mere legislative declaration of constitutional meaning—and thus be satisfactory to proponents of both congressional delegation and executive power theory. Yet in that same speech on June 16 Madison also indicated that he was now of the opinion that the legislature had much less latitude in conferring a removal power than he previously thought; Madison was thus becoming a firmer adherent of executive power theory. Benson's proposed amendment was a harbinger of things to come and an important moment in that a central proponent of the clause recognized that a change in tactics was in order.

On June 18 White opened the debate with a trenchant analysis of many central issues under consideration by the Committee of the Whole. What were the precedents for the understanding of Article II implied in executive power theory? And how did such an understanding relate to a government of enumerated powers? Other members, not persuaded by the constitutional merits of executive power theory, introduced objections based on their reading of other Article II clauses including the opinions in writing clause[17] and the necessary and proper clause.[18] Smith continued to push an effective button: Why would adherents of executive power theory want to keep the clause explicitly granting the removal power so badly if by their reasoning the Constitution already vested that power? Perhaps they did not really believe that the Constitution vested such a power. Sherman and Gerry pushed a similar line. Madison, not fully committed to Benson's solution to Smith's challenge, responded by claiming that there was nothing wrong with Congress including an explanatory clause in the bill. Perhaps the most significant speech of the day belonged to Ames, who explained why executive power theory would keep both the president and the Senate within their proper spheres of authority.

June 19 was noteworthy in that the most frequent participants in the removal debate seemed to take a break on this day. Madison, Benson, Smith, and White were all largely silent. But that is not to say the debate suffered due to their absence. Infrequent participants such as Abraham Baldwin of Georgia, Peter Silvester of New York, and Michael Stone of Maryland each made significant arguments—Baldwin and Silvester on behalf of executive power theory, and Stone on behalf of advise and consent. Further, Vining made an important argument about the new context in which the executive would operate in America—an energetic executive acting in a republican system ought not to be feared. He drew on historical examples from Sweden and Poland to suggest that not providing an executive with adequate powers carried significant dangers. Gerry stridently asserted the danger of Congress putting any sort of construction on the Constitution at all, and Sherman continued to press the point that the proponents of the clause ought not to need any congressional affirmation of a constitutionally held power.

On June 22 Representative Benson dramatically changed the dynamics of the debate with a carefully crafted proposal to amend the original language of the bill in a manner that would advance the case for executive power theory while avoiding alienating at least some of the congressional delegation proponents. His proposed solution involved two steps. First, he moved to amend the current language in the bill in such a way as to entirely revise the bill's implications for the removal power. The new language would be inserted into a clause related to a chief clerk appointed by the secretary of foreign affairs. This clerk would be responsible for the records and papers "whenever the said principal officer [the secretary] shall be removed from office by the president of the United States." If this were agreed to, Benson would then move that the old language — in particular the phrase "to be removeable by the president" — would be taken out.[19] In Thach's view, "This was excellent tactics. By moving the amendment while the original clause was in the bill, a way was left open for the proponents of the legislative grant idea [congressional delegation] to support the amendment without formal abandonment of their position."[20] For Benson, this double move would have the effect of removing the possibility that the legislation could be viewed as a legislative grant of power and would thus be interpreted as a mere "legislative construction" of the Constitution. In fact, both Benson and Madison made the meaning of this alteration of the original bill explicit when they explained to the members that the adoption of the new language and the deletion of the old would mean an affirmation of an executive removal power rooted directly in the Constitution. This is how the *Gazette of the United States* reported the change.[21] And the opponents of presidential removal authority — whether constitutionally rooted or legislatively granted — agreed that this would be the effect of Benson's two motions. As John Page of Virginia put it, "It was now left to be inferred from the constitution, that the president had the power of removal, without even a legislative declaration on that point, which they had heretofore so strongly insisted upon."[22]

Benson's first motion for the inclusion of the new language passed by a vote of 30 to 18. The second motion deleting the old language passed 31–19. And two days later, on June 24, the bill to establish the Department of Foreign Affairs (which included the removal language) passed by a vote of 29 to 22.[23] Benson's two motions put the opponents of presidential removal power in a difficult position. On the one hand, these opponents got what they had been asking for all along: the deletion of the language granting removal power to the president alone. On the other hand, the new language seemed to root the removal power directly in the Constitution. As the addition of the new language passed first, opponents faced a difficult decision about whether they ought to support the second motion. If they stayed their course and voted in favor (i.e., to delete the old language), then they would reject Congressional authority to vest the removal power; but they would also seem to be acceding to the idea that the Constitution vests the removal power in the president alone. If they voted against (i.e., to retain the old language), then they would seem to be changing their ground and endorsing presidential removal power. George Tucker of South Carolina, a congressional delegation proponent, gave voice to the dilemma that resulted from Benson's parliamentary tactics: "Now, I would rather a law should pass vesting the power in improper hands, than that the constitution should be wrongly construed. If we say the president may remove from office, it is a grant of power—and we can repeal the law, and prevent the abuse of it: but if we imply by law that it is a constitutional right vested in the president, there will be a privilege gained, which the legislature cannot affect."[24] Tucker voted against the first motion as well as the second.

The Senate then took up the Foreign Affairs bill on July 14.[25] Records for the debates in the Senate are dramatically sketchier than those of the House. The Senate twice rejected motions that would have struck the language referring to the president's removal power, Vice President John Adams casting the tie-breaking vote in each case.[26] So the bill passed containing the identical language as the House version. Senator Oliver Ellsworth defended executive power theory, arguing, "I buy a Square acre of land. I buy the Trees, Waters and everything belonging to it. The executive power belongs to the president. The removing of is therefore his, it is in him, it is nowhere else."[27] But Senator William Maclay warned against any diminishment of the Senate's power, suggesting that "by the Checks which are intrusted with them upon both the executive and the other branch of the legislature, the Stability of the Government is evidently placed in their hands." Later in the same speech Maclay argued that impeachment was the only mode of removal sanctioned by the Constitution.[28] Others, like Senator Pierce Butler, thought the executive power theory would upset the balance of power between the branches and allow for executive aggrandizement. Senator George Read, defending executive power theory and citing the take care clause, asked, "How can he [the president] do his duty or be responsible, if he cannot remove his instruments?"[29] From the available evidence, it looks as if proponents of executive power theory, impeachment theory, and advise and consent made their case in the Senate, with no obvious proponent of the congressional delegation position. We do agree with Thach that "there can, then, be no question that the matter of removal was voted upon by the Senate with the full knowledge of what it signified in all its aspects. . . . The significance of the vote is the greater when it is remembered that instances where a political body voluntarily deprives itself of power are very few in all the history of government."[30]

By the end of the summer, in addition to the Foreign Affairs department, Congress also passed bills creating the Departments of War and Treasury.[31] Each bill contained the identical language recommended by Benson on June 22: "whenever the said principal officer [the secretary] shall be removed from office by the president of the United States." With the Treasury bill, the Senate initially voted to delete the text related to the removal power and then sent its version back to the House. The House, however, refused to relent, and Vice President Adams again cast the tie-breaking vote in favor of the Senate bill *with* the removal language.[32]

The crux of the scholarly debate today over the meaning of the Decision of 1789 has to do with those final three votes in the House on the Foreign Affairs bill (the first two on June 22 and the last on June 24). Though Benson designed his amendment scheme so the votes would result in an endorsement of executive power theory, the record is not so easy to discern. We will defer an in-depth analysis of these three votes until we take up the *Myers* decision in Chapter 4, but the crux of the dispute has to do with what Saikrishna Prakash calls the "enigmatic faction."[33] This group voted for the inclusion of the new language (Benson's first amendment), but against the deletion of the old (Benson's second amendment). Scholars have questioned whether this group can be counted as endorsing executive power theory. We will revisit this ground and confront these questions later with Chief Justice William H. Taft and Justice Louis Brandeis. Now let us take a closer look at the logic and implications of each of the four positions in the removal debate.

The Logic of the Four Positions in the Decision of 1789

Impeachment

According to the adherents of this theory, impeachment is the only mode of removal recognized by the Constitution. Therefore, Congress may not confer any other mode. Though this position gained few adherents in the course of the debate, Smith and Jackson argued for it repeatedly and consistently.[34] Smith disagreed with the two predominant positions during the debate: that the removal power vested either with the president alone or with the president and the Senate. He argued the Constitution granted no such removal power to any branch. In his view, if the Constitution does not explicitly grant a power, it prohibits it. Because neither party could point to a clause where one found the word "removal," the Constitution vested no such power. For Smith, proponents of the clause argued on the basis of what they thought ought to be in the Constitution rather than what actually was in the Constitution.

Smith and Jackson were able critics of the other positions, as we discuss in a moment. But their position itself is important in thinking through what sort of administration the Congress foreclosed by rejecting the impeachment theory. As Thach argues:

> To have declared the magistracy permanent except for the right of removal by impeachment would necessarily have made the department heads the real executive. An incoming president would have found in office men whose position, so far as he was concerned, was assured. They would have ideas of their own and connections of their own. Because he could not control them, they would very naturally act in accordance with these ideas in carrying out their duties. On the other hand, Congress would have been forced to use the weapon of impeachment as a means of political control. It is extremely probable that very soon some more easily worked system of control would have evolved, with the result that responsibility would have been to the legislature. This, of course, would have meant some sort of ministerial government.[35]

Similarly, Prakash argues Smith's position "would have led to the splintering and distribution of executive power."[36] By rejecting impeachment theory, one thing was sure in the mind of Congress: The administration of executive power had to be immediately responsible to some political branch, whether it be Congress or the president.

Though Smith failed to attract many others to the impeachment position, his understanding of the Constitution more broadly would find echoes — especially with proponents of advise and consent. For Smith, the Constitution outlined a government of expressly defined powers. This was true of the powers given to all the branches; thus there was no difference between the vesting clauses in any of the articles.[37] One can find all powers given to any branch clearly enumerated.

As we mentioned above, Smith and Jackson were also able critics of the three other positions. Smith rejected an idea central to executive power theory: Removal was "by nature" an executive power. Smith argued that there was no precedent for this idea in any of the state constitutions.[38] Further, he claimed that something that was executive in a monarchy might not be executive in a republic, so it was difficult to say what was executive "by nature" at all.[39] Relatedly, Smith rejected Madison's claim that Article II was distinctive and that the vesting clause provided the president with more extensive powers than those specifically enumerated. Smith said such an argument "proves too much" in that it suggested that powers actually enumerated in Article II should have been given without the express grant.[40] But if Madison's argument were true, then why bother to enumerate them at all? Smith assumed anything not granted is prohibited. Thus there arose the necessity, for Smith, of remaining rooted in what was plain to all who would look at the Constitution: the clearly enumerated powers.

Jackson made a similar point in his case against the idea that all executives must have the power of dismissing subordinates. This simply was not true, he said, under a republic that was ordered by a Constitution that enumerates powers (though it *might* be true in monarchies where there are no restraints imposed by fundamental law). Further, even if one assumed that such a power was executive, it did not necessarily follow that it vested in the president alone, because the president did not possess all executive power. Senate involvement in powers that some might consider executive—treatymaking, for example—was clear.[41] Jackson even rejected the idea that the president was the head of all executive departments. If this was so, why would the Constitution require the advice and consent of the Senate in certain cases, and why add the opinions in writing clause?[42]

Despite their very narrow view of executive power, Smith and Jackson both attacked congressional delegation theory. Both were very consistent in their case for strict interpretation: It was not only wrong to suggest that the president could construe the Constitution beyond the specific words of the text; it was also wrong for Congress to do so as well. Any legislative construction of the Constitution was inappropriate. Smith thought such construction infringed on the powers of the judiciary and argued that state governments had suffered from their legislatures wading into constitutional questions.[43] Jackson argued that the sort of legislative construction being undertaken in Congress would undermine constitutional, popular government: "There is a great difference between organizing and modifying a department and modifying the principles of the constitution; there would be great danger in this. If we begin to construe and define the principles of the constitution, there is no end to our power; we may begin with the alpha and go to the omega, changing, reversing, and subverting every principle contained in it."[44] Both Smith and Jackson were deeply opposed to the idea that if the Constitution somehow omitted the case—that is, if it were simply silent about removal—then the legislature could step in to supply a remedy to a perceived defect. They argued that this would give the legislature an unlimited power to fashion the Constitution as it pleased. So Smith and Jackson said to their opponents: If you don't like the fact that impeachment is the sole mode of removal prescribed in the Constitution, the solution is not to interpret this fact away through fancy readings but rather to amend the document.

Of course, as many members pointed out, such a position would have entailed many inconveniences in the daily administration of national government. Smith and Jackson replied that the inexpediency of the impeachment mode of removal was no argument against it. There were lots of mechanisms in the Constitution and other charters of government, they observed, that were inexpedient—but that was just the point: Inexpediency was often the bulwark of liberty (e.g., trials in criminal cases). Though impeachment was the only mode of removal prescribed by the Constitution, Smith pointed out that there was nothing to prevent the legislature from declaring a limited term for executive officers—they need not occupy them during good behavior like judges.[45]

Finally, though the theory excluded the constitutionality of advise and consent, this latter option was certainly less objectionable to Smith and Jackson than either executive power or congressional delegation. Smith took pleasure in quoting from *The Federalist* where Publius made the case for advise and consent.[46] A close acquaintance and admirer of Hamilton, Smith would later introduce into Congress central elements of Hamilton's economic plan. Although there is no way of knowing whether or not Smith was working closely with Hamilton at this point in time, Smith's impeachment theory and Hamilton's advise and consent both had the effect of shielding administrators from politics and thereby yielding a stable administration free from political control.

Finally, both Smith and Jackson feared the concentration or expansion of executive power at the expense of the other branches. The president as commander-in-chief already had the power of the sword. Jackson noted, "If he has the power of removing and controlling the treasury department, he has the purse strings in his hand; and you only fill the string box, and collect the money of the empire, for his use. The purse and sword will enable him to lay prostrate the liberties of America."[47] Smith had no doubt that the power of removal would be abused in the future—there would not always be a George Washington in office.[48] And if the president had the sole power of removal, then good, worthy men might be removed without out cause. Further, would such men be willing to serve if they knew they served at pleasure? It was a mistake to deprive these officers of independence and firmness. Such important officers ought not to be mere creatures of the president.[49] Jackson argued that as these officers were mentioned in the Constitution, they were not "mere creatures of the law" and could not be "instruments of the president."[50]

The proponents of the impeachment position thus made an argument which echoed that made by advise and consent proponents and eventually also by those advocating for a congressionally delegated removal power: *The Constitution did not grant all executive power to the president.* Indeed, they argued, the Framers avoided precisely this due to their healthy fear of unitary executive power. And Jackson's argument that constitutional officers were neither creatures of the legislature nor instruments of the president—though rejected during the Decision of 1789—anticipated an argument made by some during the Progressive era to justify the creation of the independent regulatory commissions with their "for cause" removal statutes—prohibiting executive removal except in cases of neglect or malfeasance in office. The impeachment position would have granted these constitutional officers an independence similar to members of the IRCs (though it might also have occasioned a more frequent and robust use of the impeachment power as a tool of removal). Thus, we see very early in our history an argument that favors administrative independence and stability, goods that would be more highly prized with the development of the civil service and the increasing need for policy expertise.

Though not successful in convincing their colleagues of the soundness of impeachment theory, both proponents ultimately had important effects on the debate. Smith in particular may have had an impact in moving Benson toward his solution that eventually would win out. Smith never tired of repeating that the initial language proposed by Madison was either unnecessary or improper. Either the president already had the power of removal by virtue of the Constitution and it would be needless for Congress to declare it to be so, or he did not have such power and therefore Congress could not confer it upon him.[51] Smith was also correct in that the proponents of the proposed language were divided (at least initially), and therefore their arguments lacked consistency.

Advise and Consent

Proponents of this position held the following: *The Constitution vests removal power jointly in the president and the Senate.* The removal process follows the explicitly defined appointment process outlined in Article II. At first glance, this position seems to be quite simple—perhaps the simplest of the four. But those arguing for advise and consent actually made two distinct yet related arguments for their position.

The first argument is straightforward and was made most forcefully by two Virginians: Alexander White and Theodorick Bland. As Bland put it on the first day of the debate, "The constitution declares, that the president and the senate shall appoint, and it naturally follows, that the power which appoints shall remove also."[52] White considered the "power of appointing and dismissing to be united in their natures."[53] This line of argument was open to two lines of attack. First, their opponents challenged this reading of the appointments clause. Of course, they acknowledged, the Senate played a role in the appointment process, but its involvement was merely advisory—the president did the appointing in the precise sense. Second, by what logic must the appointing power also be the power to remove? As Abraham Baldwin of Georgia put it, "The constitution opposes this maxim more than it supports it," pointing to the counterexamples of the president and judges.[54]

The second argument was rooted not only in the appointments clause but also the overall structure of the Constitution. Elbridge Gerry of Massachusetts and White argued that although neither they nor Madison and his allies could point to any explicit removal language, theirs was nonetheless the more natural reading of the Constitution. Adherents of the advise and consent position such as Gerry argued that Senate agency in the removal power was justified by the Senate's other functions such as treatymaking. Their interpretation preserved the unity and logic of several clauses of the Constitution, whereas Madison's reading was so incongruous with the other parts that it would subvert the purpose of the other clauses.[55] According to Gerry, sole presidential removal power would render the Senate's participation in appointment vain. The president, for instance, could circumvent the Senate's advise and consent privilege in appointment by simply removing a duly appointed official and substituting a recess appointment to fill the vacancy.

Disagreement on the removal power was a microcosm of the larger and more fundamental disagreements about the nature of the legislative function and its relation to the executive. In a long speech on June 19 Gerry elaborated one such view — likely held by most partisans of the advise and consent position:

> We [Congress] have the power to establish offices by law; we can declare the duties of the officer; these duties are what the legislature directs, and not what the president; the officer is bound by law to perform these duties. But this clause militates against the institution itself; for the president is to have the power of preventing the execution; the office, and its duties, are suspended on the pleasure of the president. Suppose an officer discharges his duty as the law directs, yet the president will remove him; he will be guided by some other criterion; perhaps the officer is not good natured enough . . . because he is so unfortunate as not to be so good a dancer, as he is a worthy officer, he must be removed.[56]

For Gerry, the administration of the law cannot be neatly separated from the creation of the law. In his view, there is very little room for executive discretion because that kind of prerogative jeopardizes Congress's constitutional responsibility for prescribing the terms of laws' execution in its own legislation. If Congress were deprived of the right to check the president's authority over his subordinates because the removal power inhered in the president alone, then Congress could not guarantee that its own laws would be executed according to the terms originally embodied in the legislation. Executive power theory, in his view, would allow the president to evade his duties — more specifically, the duties prescribed to members of the administration by Congress. As we will see, partisans of congressional delegation and executive power theory had a much different view, one more sympathetic to a more independent executive.

Relatedly, a recurring theme in the removal debate recalled a contentious point from the Constitutional Convention and the ensuing ratification debates: How much "mixing" of powers did the Constitution admit? During the Convention debates, the Federalists had defended the mixing of powers, arguing that each branch had to have the means of defending itself. A pure separation of powers would not allow each branch to repel encroachments.[57] Anti-Federalists, for their part, argued that the Constitution allowed for too much mixing and had thus abandoned the separation of powers doctrine altogether.[58] During the removal debate in 1789, something of a reversal took place. It was Madison and his allies in the First Congress who found themselves defending strict separation, whereas Gerry and his allies favored the replication of the mixing already evident in the appointment clause. According to advise and consent supporters, joint removal did not create any more blending than was already admitted in the document.[59] Gerry's critics argued that joint removal created a "two-headed monster," but, responded Gerry, if so, it should be a consistent monster, two-headedness for both appointment and removal.[60] Gerry also cleverly pointed to a problem for all parties in the debate about separation of powers. How could one tell what was executive and what was legislative? Was the power defined by the actor or by the function being carried out? Gerry acknowledged the necessity of keeping the departments distinct. But then, he asked the following: "What department is the senate of, when it exercises its power of appointment or removal? If legislative, it shows that the power of appointment is not an executive power; but if it exercises the power as an executive branch of government, there is no mixing of the departments."[61]

The advise and consent partisans had a general fear of executive power. In a sense they had a very different conception of what Madison called "responsibility." Whereas Madison linked unity with responsibility, partisans of joint removal thought unity would make the president less responsible—he would be more inclined to aggrandize himself and disregard the concerns of the other branches (the legislature in particular). The executive branch would be particularly dangerous if indeed the heads of departments were servants of the president alone. Gerry was particularly worried about presidential control of Treasury officers. "If this is the case, you may as well give him at once the appropriation of the revenue; for what use is it to make laws on this head, when the president by looking at the officer can make it his interest to break them?"[62] So in Gerry's view a responsible executive was not a unitary executive but a fractured one. And, like Jackson, Gerry read the opinions in writing clause as suggesting these officers were not meant to be mere instruments of the president. Bland seemed to anticipate ministries that would not change automatically every time a presidential administration changed. He worried about the disorder that would be created if changes were indeed that frequent.[63]

Partisans of advise and consent, like those of impeachment, all argued that sole presidential removal was a fundamentally new doctrine — there was no precedent for it in America. If precedents were sought, they must come from across the Atlantic.[64] So partisans of these first two positions argued (sometimes expressly while at other times by implication) that Madison and his allies were importing an essentially monarchical principle into the Constitution. They thought it likely that such an importation would lead rather rapidly to despotic or arbitrary government.

Because of this fear, Gerry and White also responded vigorously to the doctrine that removal was by nature an executive power. Like Smith, White argued that all power under the Constitution was enumerated — a power is of a certain kind because it is expressly given to a particular office or institution. There was thus no difference between Articles I and II in this respect. So if Madison's doctrine about implied powers were true of the executive branch, according to White, it must also have been true of the legislative branch. This would mean that each branch could call upon powers not specifically enumerated but that nonetheless belonged to it by nature. White asserted that such a doctrine would surely result in arbitrary government — as "absolute and extensive" as any despotism.[65]

White argued that the distinctiveness of the American system rested on the ground of specifically enumerated powers granted to particular branches for particular purposes. White pointed out that the proponents of the Constitution gained the support of Anti-Federalists precisely on this ground — there was even a promise to pass something like the Tenth Amendment to make this more explicit. As White argued, "If this principle had not been successfully maintained by its advocates in the convention of the state from which I came, the constitution would never had been ratified."[66] Now, if it were decided that such enumerated powers were somehow insufficient, then Congress was in no position to remedy this situation.

Both Gerry and White were also as adamant as Smith about the danger of Congress acting to declare the meaning of the Constitution. They were in many ways as emphatic in their rebuke of congressional delegation as they were of executive power theory. Congress could not unilaterally remedy a perceived defect, for this would be tantamount to amending the Constitution. Again, acts declaring the sense of the Constitution could not be linked to a delegated power of Congress. The danger, as White saw it, was that the federal government would ascribe to itself more and more power and eventually "swallow up the state government, and with them the liberties of the people."[67] This was an argument that had been made by the opponents of the Constitution during the ratification debates.

White argued that each branch could construe its own powers, but that all were subject to review by judges. White's solution was for the House to say nothing on the matter of removal. He thought it made more sense to let the occasion for removal arise and then let the president act — the necessity provided by a real occasion for the exercise would be a better comment on the Constitution than one given by the House. White went even further and made a Jeffersonian argument about executive power: It would be better for the president to extend his powers on extraordinary occasions than that the legislature grant him improperly extensive powers. A partial evil would be better than a general one.[68]

Finally, the advise and consent partisans were as relentless as Smith in asserting that the removal language was either useless or nugatory: useless if the removal power was indeed the president's alone constitutionally, as he would decide upon his powers by looking at Article II and not at this bill; nugatory if the removal power was held jointly according the Constitution, as the Senate would never consent to a diminishment of its powers. However, the advise and consent view of the Constitution was different than Smith's in that the removal power was held jointly by necessary implication, for it was not explicitly mentioned in the clause on appointments. So neither Gerry and his allies nor Madison and his could point to a clause that expressly vested the removal power. But unlike Smith, each party had to make the case that the power nonetheless was recognized by the Constitution.

As we will see in Chapter 3: "Jackson to Johnson: The Rise of Congressional Delegation," the advise and consent position would find adherents fairly early in the nineteenth century following president Andrew Jackson's vigorous use and defense of the removal power. Gerry and his allies during the Decision of 1789 laid the groundwork for such figures as Daniel Webster and, later, Justice Louis Brandeis. For such men, the extent of executive discretion consonant with a purely executive removal power was simply incompatible with republican government. In this view, republican government needed to find its center in the legislature — the branch closest to the people. The executive was first and foremost an agent of Congress dedicated to carrying out the will of the people's representatives. Hence, congressional involvement in appointment and removal was a crucial device in ensuring that executive officers remained faithful to the will of Congress. President Jackson's opponents were particularly put off by Jackson's deepening of the Madisonian position in the Decision of 1789 — the idea that the president had a source of power outside of Congress or the Constitution, the people. Such an idea, as seen by the partisans of advise and consent, would lead to the weakening of Congress — the truly popular branch and the bulwark of republicanism.

Advise and Consent: The Hamiltonian View

As mentioned above, one partisan of advise and consent, Representative Bland, did make the argument for this position on behalf of stability. Bland feared executive power theory because he thought it might lead to too frequent changes in executive officers, creating a disorderly administration. But Bland's remark was somewhat of an aside, and neither he nor any of his fellow advise and consent partisans elaborated this concern during the debate. Madison, however, explicitly associated this position with stability, arguing it would provide *too much stability* to the executive branch.

This concern with stability had indeed been explored, but by someone with a much more expansive view of executive power than Gerry or White. As we have seen, Smith delighted in pointing out during the debate that none other than Alexander Hamilton — that oracle of a strong executive — had favored Senate participation in removal in *The Federalist*:

> It has been mentioned as one of the advantages to be expected from the cooperation of the Senate, in the business of appointments, that it would contribute to the stability of administration. The consent of that body would be necessary to displace as well as to appoint. A change of Chief Magistrate, therefore, would not occasion so violent or so general a revolution in the officers of the government as might be expected, if he were the sole disposer of offices.[69]

This passage has been puzzling to scholars for many years, leading some to argue that Hamilton was simply inconsistent or confused in his advocacy for energy in the executive — especially given his position in the Pacificus-Helvidius exchange,[70] the debate between Hamilton and Madison over the constitutionality of President Washington's Neutrality Proclamation of 1793 — although others have suggested his advocacy of Senate participation in removal was merely for the purpose of getting the Constitution ratified.[71] One recent explanation, offered by Seth Barrett Tillman, is that Hamilton did not mean "remove" when he said "displace." Rather, according to Tillman, Hamilton meant "replace," which meant only that the Senate would of course have to consent to the appointment of the new officer.[72] There are problems with this interpretation, especially because Hamilton uses "displace" to mean "remove" in other writings, but we call attention to Tillman's proposed solution because it points to a larger solution to the problem of the removal power, a solution later embraced by Daniel Webster. Yet another possibility is that Hamilton simply changed his mind on the question of removals and that the debate helped bring about that change. Smith himself pointed to this last possibility in a letter to Edward Rutledge in June. In that letter, Smith claimed that on the day following his speech in which he quoted Hamilton's support of the advise and consent position, Benson sent him a note on the floor of the House that Hamilton had informed Benson that he had in fact changed his mind and was now convinced that the president alone held the removal power.[73] This remains a matter of speculation, however, because there is no corroborating evidence, and Hamilton himself never offered any record about any such conversion experience.

Leaving aside the question of whether Hamilton's position changed over time, we maintain that Hamilton's position in *The Federalist* is worth a closer look and that his advocacy of Senate removal in the context of an argument for executive energy reveals another ground for advise and consent that is largely absent during the Decision of 1789. Specifically, Hamilton's presentation of energy in *The Federalist* offers reason to support Senate participation on the grounds of stability. As is well known, Hamilton argued that "unity" in the executive would be conducive to energy in the executive while at the same time making such energy safe in "the republican sense."[74] Hamilton's first argument about the relationship between unity and energy in the executive is straightforward. Unity was an ingredient of energy in that it, as opposed to plurality, would allow "decision, activity, secrecy, and despatch."[75] Though deliberation would be a virtue in the legislature, deliberation across the government would embarrass the nation by crippling it during wartime or even by encouraging factious division during routine administration. As he put it, both history and common sense confirmed that effective administration would be more likely from a singular rather than a plural executive.

But Hamilton's second argument, which he described as an especially weighty argument about safety in the republican sense, deserves more attention. In *The Federalist* Nos. 70–72, Hamilton showed how unity would provide the accountability required by republican principles. Although plurality would be a "clog" upon an executive's "good intentions" and "a cloak to his faults," unity allowed republicans to bestow praise and blame with relative ease. Alone, however, unity could not render energy safe for republican liberty, because praise and blame would be mere words, like barriers of parchment, without some way for praise and blame to be credited. Thus, Hamilton explained that unity would need to be accompanied by an institutional hitch. "Duration" would make energy safe in addition to being essential.

For Hamilton, *duration* consisted of two parts: term of office; and eligibility for reelection. Hamilton showed that eligibility for reelection could work with unity to use accountability to appeal to the ambition or interest of the sitting president, for "it is a general principle of human nature, that a man will be interested in whatever he possesses, in proportion to the firmness or precariousness of the tenure by which he holds it."[76] In addition to giving the president an adequate amount of time in office, it was essential to give the president an opportunity to serve additional terms. Like unity, eligibility for reelection was essential to republican safety because it would connect the interest of presidents, those strange and noble men whose minds were ruled by a passion for fame and the public good, to the office. By giving the president indefinite prospects for reelection, the president would be willing to take on extensive and arduous projects and the people would be able to reward successful presidents with another term in office, thus making long-term administration both possible and responsible.[77]

But Hamilton complicated this otherwise straightforward presentation. Before showing how eligibility for reelection was a part of duration, Hamilton signaled that he would back away from his argument for unity in the executive. In the first paragraphs of *The Federalist* No. 72, Hamilton wrote of the "intimate connection between the duration of the executive magistrate in office and the stability of the system of administration" to warn against the "ruinous mutability in the administration of the government" that would result from frequent rotation of the "men who fill the subordinate stations."[78] Specifically, Hamilton mentioned the likelihood of removals to prepare the way for his argument for perpetual eligibility as one of the two aspects of duration:

> To reverse and undo what has been done by a predecessor is often considered by a successor as the best proof he can give of his own capacity and desert; and, in addition to this propensity, where the alteration has been the result of public choice, the person substituted is warranted in supposing that the dismission of his predecessor has proceeded from a dislike to his measures, and that the less he resembles him the more he will recommend himself to the favor of his constituents.[79]

Remarkably, Hamilton here went out of his way to show that elections would add to ordinary human pride in encouraging new presidents to remove officers appointed by prior presidents. Put another way, responsibility—the very thing that makes unity safe for republican government—would itself need to be checked. Because a change of chief magistrate would increase the likelihood of removals, it was better to limit the frequency of the change of magistrate by allowing the president to serve unlimited terms. Fewer presidents, according to this logic, would beget fewer removals. *Unity and duration combined would bring the "advantage of permanency" to republican government.*[80]

Hamilton's later mention in *The Federalist* No. 77 of the shared removal powers was thus more than an offhand remark, for it completed his larger discussion about the dangers incident to presidential selection. As he explained in that essay, which would be his last on the executive power:

A change of the chief magistrate therefore would not occasion so violent or so general a revolution in the officers of the government, as might be expected if he were the sole disposers of offices. Where a man in any station had given satisfactory evidence of his fitness for it, a new president would be restrained from attempting a change in favor of a person more agreeable to him, by the apprehension that a discountenance of the Senate might frustrate the attempt, and bring some degree of discredit upon himself.[81]

Here, Hamilton thus continued the thread he had started in *The Federalist* No. 72, where he warned about the relation between stability in administration and the duration of the president. But now he explicitly revealed how the Senate's stability would be a check on executive unity: "Those who can best estimate the value of a steady administration will be most disposed to prize a provision which connects the official existence of public men with the approbation or disapprobation of that body which, from the greater permanency of its own composition, will in all probability be less subject to inconstancy than any other member of the government."[82]

Steady, energetic administration then would not be a simple product of executive unity and *presidential* duration. Executive officers — those high officials crucial to the smooth functioning of the executive branch — would need stability or duration in their own right. What better way to secure such duration than by linking them with the most permanent body in government, the Senate? Because the "official existence" or will of such officers was inseparable from the approval and disapproval of the Senate, executive officers would, in fact, be more stable than their presidents who, being free from Senate control, would be more subject to "inconstancy" than their executives. In this light, Hamilton's discussion in No. 72 of the first "ill effect" of a limit on the president's eligibility might have been written with one eye on these executive officials: Even the "love of fame" would be insufficient to persuade a qualified man to serve in an administration if he "foresaw that he must quit the scene" whenever the administration changed hands.[83]

To summarize: Hamilton's initial argument for energy in the executive suggested that unity could complement — and even perfect — republican liberty. But in his argument connecting unity to duration Hamilton went out of his way to warn against the republican tendencies of a president who would have a fixed term and be eligible for reelection: Because each president would wish to curry favor with "his constituents" by removing executive officials associated with the outgoing president, unity and republican principles would conspire against stability and thus steer the republican government toward traditional republican vices. In his notes from the debates of the Constitutional Convention, Hamilton recorded,

"At the period which terminates the duration of the Executive there will be always an awful crisis—in the National situation."[84] Senate participation in the removal power would be a way to prevent such a crisis.

Congressional Delegation (a)

Partisans of this position argued the following: The Constitution is silent or ambiguous in terms of its vesting of the removal power, so Congress may vest this power where it pleases, and vesting removal in the president alone is most expedient. Congressional delegation partisans were adamant that Madison's removal language did not violate any expressly given power. Yet due to the very nature of government, a removal power other than impeachment had to be vested somewhere. Further, Theodore Sedgwick of Massachusetts argued that the Constitution, to put it awkwardly but accurately, did *vest the power to vest the removal power* in Congress. He argued "that where a general authority is granted to one branch, every thing subordinate and necessary to effect the object follows of course. The power of creating offices is given to the legislature: Under this general grant, the legislature have it under their supreme decision to determine the whole organization, to affix the tenure, and declare the control."[85] So because the power of creating these offices was given to the legislature, those powers necessary to carry into effect the object of that department followed, too. In Sedgwick's view, if Congress could create offices, then it could also affix tenure, vest removal power, declare causes for removal, and so on. Thomas Hartley of Pennsylvania pointed to the necessary and proper clause as the ground for precisely this understanding.[86] John Laurance of New York stated the argument for congressional delegation in the boldest terms—if the Constitution omitted something, he explained, the legislature was the proper body to supply the defect.[87]

Both Sedgwick and Laurance argued that the proponents of advise and consent were incorrect in deducing a joint removal power from the appointment clause. A proper reading of the appointment clause revealed that the president alone was the one who appoints; the Senate merely advises. Laurance also argued that if one looked at the inferior appointments clause (Article II, Section 2) the Constitution seemed to point to vesting the power solely in the president, not jointly. For if Congress were to vest the appointment of an inferior officer in the president alone, but say nothing of removal, would not the president also have the removal power? In Laurance's view, yes.[88]

Laurance and Sedgwick were equally convinced that Congress ought to vest the power in the president alone. On grounds of expediency, they agreed with proponents of executive power theory. Because the officers in these departments were subordinates of the president, the president must be the judge of talents and abilities and thus hold the power of removal.

If such a power would mean a turnover of officials when a new president was elected, so be it. The president was still checked by facing election and the looming power of impeachment. The president was certainly no more likely to abuse the removal power than the Senate would be. It would be unwise to place the Senate between the president and his subordinate. They would then be in the position of hearing testimony and having to decide what evidence might be sufficient to remove.[89]

Both Laurance and Sedgwick voted in favor of Benson's amendment of June 22, which sought to imply that the Constitution gave the president the removal power, but they also voted against striking out Madison's initial language that might be read as Congress conferring the power of removal. They considered Benson's new language problematic if indeed Congress conferred the power, so they argued for keeping the old language in addition to the new, thus enabling partisans of congressional delegation and executive power theory to vote for the establishment of the Department of Foreign Affairs. Though the House did vote to strike out Madison's language, Sedgwick and Laurance voted for the establishment of the department.

Their final votes on the matter appear consistent with some statements made during the debate. Both indicated that they thought the Constitution was certainly more supportive of executive power theory than it was of advise and consent. As Laurance argued on June 17, "If then we collect the power by inference from the constitution, we shall find it pointed strongly in favor of the president, much more so than in favor of the senate combined with him."[90] And shortly after Benson proposed his two amendments on June 22, Sedgwick rose to argue that Madison's original language was favorable to both partisans of congressional delegation and executive power, although Benson's new language might split the majority in favor of presidential removal power. But here is how Sedgwick described members of his own coalition: "Others think it a matter of legislative determination; and that they *must give it to the president on the principles of the constitution.*"[91] So even though Sedgwick thought Congress could confer the power, the Constitution suggested they had to confer it upon the president. Yet if one read the Constitution as requiring Congress to confer removal power upon the president, then the Constitution might also be read as itself conferring the removal power on the president. The distance between these two positions seemed slight indeed. So in some sense Laurance and Sedgwick were not pure congressional delegation partisans in that they did not argue Congress could confer the power upon any institution that it wished. In making their case that Congress ought to confer the removal power on the president, they made claims about the Constitution, thereby somewhat undermining their case for a congressionally held power to confer removal.

Congressional Delegation (b)

The only member to affirmatively make the case for congressional delegation, *without* also arguing that the power ought to be vested in the president, was Roger Sherman. Madison attributed the congressional delegation
position to Sherman on June 17 shortly after Sherman spoke, and Madison
also reported this position as one of the four in a letter dated June 21 — that
is, "that the power of removal may be disposed of by the Legislative
discretion."[92]

Sherman, however, like future critics of executive power theory, at
times had difficulty choosing between advise and consent and congressional delegation.[93] He based many of his objections to Madison's language on
the fact that the appointment power is held jointly with the Senate. He suggested, like Gerry, that a removal power held solely by the president rendered Senate participation in the appointment process moot. And Sherman
also considered it "an established principle" that the power that appoints
also removes, unless an exception is made expressly. Thus far, Sherman
would appear to fit well with the likes of Gerry and White.

But Sherman also considered whether the legislature had the power to
vest the power in the president alone, and if so, whether it makes sense on
grounds of expediency. Here is an especially crucial statement:

> As the officer is the mere creature of the legislature, we may form it
> under such regulations as we please, with such powers and duration as
> we think good policy require; we may say he shall hold his office dur-
> ing good behavior, or that he shall be annually elected; we may say he
> shall be displaced for neglect of duty, and point out how he should be
> convicted of it — without calling upon the president or senate.[94]

This seems to be perhaps the clearest statement of the congressional delegation position in the entire debate. But it is unclear from the context of
this passage whether Sherman was here talking only about inferior officers. Later in this same speech Sherman again called the officer "the mere
creature of the law" to rebut Smith's claim that impeachment is the only
constitutionally recognized mode of removal. He then suggested that if
the House said nothing on the subject of removal, then removal would take
place jointly (president and Senate), and that it would be "most expedient" for the House to say nothing. In his second longish speech Sherman
again reiterated that he thought the House ought to say nothing and let the
president sort out his duties and powers on his own. And he appeared to
undercut his congressional power argument. He remarked, "Some gentlemen suppose, if the president has not the power by the constitution, we
ought to vest it in him by law. For my part I very much doubt if we have
the power to do this."[95]

Sherman faced the same problem as Laurance and Sedgwick. On the one hand, they seem inclined toward the view that the Congress had the power to vest the removal power where it pleased, in part because the Constitution did not expressly vest it anywhere, and in part because Congress was the body that created the offices. On the other hand, the Constitution did provide some clues on this subject, and these clues seemed to suggest that Congress had better and worse options. But to the extent that the Constitution provided some clues, this suggested that the Constitution did not leave the matter unresolved for Congress to decide.

Somewhat surprisingly, then, there were no pure congressional delegation partisans during the Decision of 1789. Though Sedgwick offered a crucial rationale on June 18—that the congressional power to create offices must include the power to vest removal where it pleases—he seemed to back away from this on June 22. But this rationale would find important advocates such as Henry Clay and John Calhoun in the nineteenth century and Justice James McReynolds, Justice Louis Brandeis, and Edward Corwin in the twentieth century. Perhaps it would take the actual experience of an executive like President Andrew Jackson, who used the removal power quite vigorously to inspire congressional delegation partisans to assert themselves. For these later congressional delegation partisans seemed to hold a similarly narrow view of executive power as the view held by the adherents of advise and consent like Gerry and White. They recoiled against the notion that Article II granted the executive more power than the Constitution explicitly granted. And further, the most defining and confining source of executive power was Congress itself, which made the laws that the president and other officers must execute. If the United States were to be truly a nation of laws and not of men, then executive discretion must be circumscribed as narrowly as possible by congressional statutes. And it is precisely these statutes that confer the removal power, either expressly or by implication. Thus, according to this view, the president has *no* constitutionally rooted removal power to which he may appeal.[96]

There is also a precedent for another, more limited understanding of congressional delegation theory that arose during the summer of 1789. As we pointed out, the debate concerned officers from three different departments: Foreign Affairs, War, and Treasury. Most participants in the debate seemed to acknowledge that the discussion of the removal power in the specific context of the foreign affairs bill had direct application to the other two departments. And identical removal language was included in the acts for the establishment of these three departments.[97]

Yet as many observers have also pointed out, Congress treated the Treasury Department differently from the other two. First, Treasury was not denominated an "executive department" like War and Foreign Affairs.

Second, much more detail was given regarding the functions of the department as a whole, and particular duties were established for the secretary. Third, the Act created other subordinate officers (like the Comptroller) and prescribed duties for them. It is the status of these officers that has particular relevance for the removal debate. As Gerhard Casper put it, "The legislation was silent on the subject of presidential direction, yet did not vest the appointment of inferior officers in the Secretary. An elaborate set of officers and their responsibilities were spelled out in detail. The officers . . . were subjected to a detailed system of controls. For instance, disbursement could be made only by the Treasurer, upon warrants signed by the Secretary, countersigned by the Comptroller, and recorded by the Register."[98]

During the debate Madison had raised a concern about the Comptroller's tenure of office. He argued that the Comptroller's duties were not "purely of an executive nature" and partook "strongly of the judicial character." Therefore, Madison suggested, "there may be strong reasons why an officer of this kind should not hold his office at the pleasure of the executive branch of government."[99]

For some later participants in this ongoing removal debate, these facts surrounding the origins of the Treasury Department revealed that not all "executive departments" were created equal, in the sense that some such departments and officers ought to be insulated from presidential control. Madison himself seemed to have contemplated this possibility:

> Whatever . . . may be my opinion with respect to the tenure by which an executive officer may hold his office according to the meaning of the constitution, I am very well satisfied, that a modification by the legislature may take place in such as partake of judicial qualities, and that the legislative power is sufficient to establish this office on such a footing, as to answer the purposes for which it is prescribed.[100]

The congressional delegation partisans who would take up this line of argument suggested that the executive power theory of removal simply could not account for the varied duties and tasks that fell upon the executive branch of government. Perhaps it is Edward Corwin who stated this version of the congressional delegation position most clearly: "It is . . . the essential nature of the office under consideration, as shown by its characteristic duties, [which] determines the scope of the removal power in relation to the power of congress, in creating an office, to fix its tenure."[101] In contrast to the more radical congressional delegation position outlined above, this version suggested that the Constitution did place some limits on where precisely Congress could limit executive removal. The problem would be how to sort out exactly what those limits were and to what executive offices such limits pertained.

Executive Power Theory

The partisans of this last theory argued that the Constitution vested the removal power in the president alone. The case for the president's sole possession of the removal power was argued cogently and repeatedly by a number of House members, perhaps most significantly by Madison. Madison did not change his mind during the debate so much as he went into the debate with a reasonably open mind and became more and more convinced of the truth of executive power theory. Madison and others invoked an important principle in defense of their position: responsibility. As Madison argued on June 16, "I believe no principle is more clearly laid down in the Constitution than that of responsibility."[102] Madison and his allies made a three-pronged constitutional argument about the proper functioning and nature of the executive branch to buttress their normative claim about this guiding principle. Responsibility was invoked by such figures as Madison, Vining, Clymer, and Ames, in three senses: *the president as responsible for executive officers; the executive officers as responsible to the president;* and *the president as responsible to the people.* A president responsible for the conduct of his officers who in turn felt accountable to their chief would then be a president responsible to the electorate. An executive branch defined by a single, visible chain of command would allow the people to sit in judgment and in turn allow the president to effectuate a popular mandate. As Madison put it, "If the president should possess alone the power of removal from office, those who are employed in the execution of the law will be in their proper situation, and the chain of dependence be preserved; the lowest officers, the middle grade, and the highest, will depend, as they ought, on the president, and the president on the community. The chain of dependence therefore terminates in the supreme body, namely, in the people."[103] Responsibility could be achieved, for the executive power theorists, only by an executive branch defined by unity in its internal makeup and independent from Congress. Let us look in more detail at the three elements in this compound.

First, partisans of executive power theory suggested that presidential removal power would make the president responsible for the conduct of officers serving in the executive branch. The president could not fulfill all of the duties of his office on his own. He therefore needed officers to aid him in executing the laws.[104] But without the removal power, he would not be able to exercise responsibility over his own instruments. Benjamin Goodhue of Massachusetts put it this way: "It was the peculiar duty of the president, to watch over the executive officers, but of what avail, would be his inspection, unless he had a power to correct the abuses he might discover."[105] In other words, if one desired the president to really be the chief executive, he must be made responsible for the conduct of his officers. Responsibility in this sense was closely related to another important principle invoked, which was unity (a single, visible chain of responsibility).

Second, these executive officers must feel their responsibility to the president—and to him alone. Madison argued that good administration would be impossible without responsibility in this sense. He therefore argued vociferously against impeachment theory and advise and consent. As he stated against the former understanding:

> If it is said that an officer once appointed shall not be displaced without the formality required by impeachment, I shall be glad to know what security we have for the faithful administration of the government. Every individual in the long chain which extends from the highest to the lowest link of the executive magistracy, would find a security in his situation which would relax his fidelity and promptitude in the discharge of his duty.[106]

Just as threatening to good administration, according to Madison, was Senate involvement in removal. He asked, "Is there no danger that an officer when he is appointed by the concurrence of the senate, and has friends in that body, may chuse rather to risk his establishment on the favor of that branch, than rest it upon the discharge of his duties to the satisfaction of the executive branch, which is constitutionally authorized to inspect and controul his conduct?"[107] Executive officers, in Madison's view, could end up in a cabal with a portion of the Senate and even reduce presidential power to "a mere vapor."

Third, the president's responsibility *for* his officers is said to be necessary if the president is to be responsible *to* his country. Madison stated this principle in negative terms: "Therefore as we do not make the officers who are to aid him in the duties of that department responsible to him, he is not responsible to his country."[108] Clymer spoke of this principle as security, but it was explained more elaborately by Ames. If the president is responsible for the conduct of his officers, the people can see *who* is executing the laws. Further, the people would have recourse if they did not like what they saw—the president must be reelected every four years, and there was a mechanism for impeachment. Ames made an interesting comparison between officers removable by the president and judges: "The removability of one class, or immovability of the other, are founded on the same principle, the security of the people against the abuse of power."[109] So in this view, the clear executive chain of command was tied to security. If responsibility was clouded by Senate involvement in removal, the people would be less able to see and act on abuses of power. Partisans of advise and consent made precisely the opposite case. Senate involvement, for Gerry and White, was crucial on grounds of security. For them, it was sole presidential removal that would invite abuse.

Like their advise and consent antagonists, adherents of executive power theory based the legitimacy of their arguments on the ground of the central principle of the Constitution: separation of powers. During the debate in 1787 over the new Constitution and the subsequent ratifying conventions, defenders and critics alike used this principle to make their case for or against the new system. Some critics of the Constitution argued that the new document admitted too much mixing of powers—that it was not strict enough in upholding separation.[110] Baldwin, who had been a member of the Constitutional Convention, recalled that such critics called the link between the Senate and the president (with regard to appointments and treatymaking) "a monstrous and unnatural connection" and made it the "principle ground" of their refusal of their signature. But now, these critics, like Gerry, argued for involving the Senate in removal, thus extending this "unchaste connection."[111]

For proponents of executive power theory, all the devices that authorized mixing of powers were exceptions that ought to be taken strictly. Yes, the Senate joined the president in his power of appointment, but in no way did such a device suggest the Senate was further authorized to join in executive functions. Madison noted that the Constitution outlined a judicial role for the Senate in impeachment. Yet nobody would argue, according to Madison, that the judicial power could be blended further with the Senate.[112] Most important, these devices were for the purpose of maintaining separation—they enabled the several departments to defend themselves from encroachments from the other branches.[113] Senate involvement in removal would not preserve the independence of the branches but would enable the legislature to aggrandize itself at the expense of the executive. Senate involvement in appointment was a sufficient defensive mechanism, but extending it to removal would upset the delicate balance and separation. As Madison saw it, the legislative branch created the office, defined the powers, limited the duration, and annexed compensation—then its power ceased. Then the executive stepped in to designate the officer (with the Senate's approval) to superintend the officer's conduct and to remove if necessary.

A related point to this dispute about separation of powers has to do with Article II of the Constitution. Recall that proponents of advise and consent had argued that Madison's reading (and that of his allies) of the removal power would do violence to other clauses in Article II. Gerry and White had suggested that the Senate's role in the appointment process would be rendered moot with removal power being held solely by the president. Adherents of executive power theory also argued that their opponents abstracted from important clauses that must be taken into account when trying to understand the Constitution's stance on removal. Madison, Vining, Clymer, and Ames all pointed to the vesting clause of Article II.[114] According to them, the vesting clause granted all executive power to the president. Any involvement of another branch in executive functioning must be understood as an exception to this general rule. Though the Constitution does not specifically mention the power to remove, one must ask whether such a power would fall within the general grant made by the vesting clause. In other words, Madison asked whether the removal power was executive by nature. Madison argued, "I conceive that if any power whatsoever is in its nature executive it is the power of appointing, overseeing, and controlling those who execute the laws. If the Constitution had not qualified the power of the president in appointing to office, by associating the senate with him in that business, would it not be clear that he would have the right by virtue of his executive power to make such an appointment?"[115]

Adherents of executive power theory did not rely only on the vesting clause as the source for presidential removal power. Madison and Ames pointed to two other sources. For them, "Removal authority was implicit in the enumerated powers of the president, because he could exercise none of them without subordinates subject to his supervision and control."[116] Madison and Ames also pointed to the take care clause as granting removal authority to the president, arguing that such a duty would be impossible to carry out without the power to dismiss subordinates.[117]

The partisans of executive power theory also confronted their antagonists on the expediency question: Was it wise for the president to have this removal power? Might he not abuse it? Madison and others pointed out that the president operated under checks—the prospects of reelection and impeachment, to name two. But adherents of both impeachment theory and advise and consent worried that abuse might take the form of removing a good man from office. Madison thought it unlikely that a president would do this—public opinion would militate against it, as would the prospect of impeachment. The more likely danger, according to Madison and his allies, was the problem of bad officers being maintained in office. If, according to Madison, an "unworthy man be continued in office by an unworthy president," that could be remedied by the impeachment of the president.[118] By contrast, a joint removal power might prevent the removal of such a person, as he would always be able to find some allies (likely political opponents of the president) in the Senate. And as Vining would argue, there was a crucial difference in the kind of information essential to the tasks of appointment and removal: "A man's ability may be known to many persons, they may entertain even a good opinion of his integrity; but no man, without a superintending power, can bring this fidelity to the test. The president will have every opportunity to discover the real talents and honesty of the officer, the senate will have none but from common fame."[119]

As we have seen in looking at the proponents of impeachment and advise and consent, figures like Smith and White could find no relevant precedent for the type of executive power that the proponents of congressional delegation and executive power theory seemed to be proposing. On the one hand, partisans of the latter two positions must have acknowledged some truth to their opponents' claim here, because they did not counter with one single example drawn from state constitutions. On the other hand, they did try to meet this challenge in an interesting way. They argued that the American executive was operating within a new republican system — a popularly elected president did not pose the same dangers as a hereditary monarch. Such severe limits as denying the president the power to remove his own subordinates did not make sense under a republican form of government where the chief executive officer represented the entire nation. The removal power was an essential ingredient for securing executive energy and independence — precisely what was lacking under the Articles of Confederation. Goodhue argued that the people and their representatives had changed their outlook: "It has long been an opinion entertained of the people of America, that they would not trust the government with the power of doing good, lest it should be abused; but contrary to the expectation of its enemies, a constitution is formed providing those powers which we suffered so much for want of under the old confederation."[120] Opponents of presidential removal, for Goodhue, were stuck in the old mind-set of fearing the granting of any power lest it might be abused. But he argued that potential abuse was not only to be feared from the president; associating removal with the Senate had its own problems. Vining was perhaps the most eloquent on this point. In his noteworthy speech on June 19, he remarked, "There have been few governments overthrown by the independence of the executive. What are the consequences of clipping its wings? Anarchy and confusion, and a struggle between the legislative and executive, in which the latter is generally sacrificed on the altar of despotism."[121] So it was executive weakness and dependence that ought to be feared, not executive independence and energy. In Vining's view, to deny the executive adequate constitutional authority was to invite unconstitutional aggrandizement. He illustrated his argument here with Sweden and Poland. According to Vining, in Sweden the aristocracy had so weakened the king that the monarch, "for the security of his nation, assumed all the powers of despotism." Similarly in Poland, by depriving the executive of due authority, the nation swung between anarchy and absolute government.

Executive power theorists argued that executive independence was crucial to the functioning of the new system of separated powers under the Constitution. There must be room for executive discretion. The rocky history of the United States under the Articles of Confederation and the turbulent state governments revealed that systems dominated by legislative power would be plagued by inefficiency, weakness, and administrative neglect.

The removal power was a necessary part of the executive's ability to superintend his own administrative system. And like the veto power, it would be crucial in defending itself from legislative encroachment. Executive power theorists, then and now, saw presidential superintendence as the key to a consistent, visible, and vigorous administration of the laws.

As we have seen, the spectrum of opinion during the Decision of 1789 was quite broad. And this spectrum covered not only the specific question of the removal power but also the very nature of executive power and the system of separated powers in which the executive would operate. What did the Decision of 1789 truly decide? As we will see, this ground continued to be contested throughout the coming two centuries.

Chapter Two

From Responsibility to Rotation

Scholars often write that the Decision of 1789 settled the question of who holds the power to remove. But as scholars of American political development have long argued, serious constitutional questions are rarely closed in the way this statement suggests. Because they often arise out of irresolvable problems of constitutionalism, they instead tend to resurface, especially during moments of reconstructive or realigning politics. When they do resurface, the prior understanding gives shape to the new arguments, but it does not determine the outcome. As we argued in the Introduction, this is especially true with executive power in general and the removal power in particular.

Thomas Jefferson was the first president who had to create a removal policy. To do so, Jefferson returned to executive power theory, but he changed the path of development with regard to removals and pointed the way for later changes. Although he was a reluctant partisan, Jefferson looked to political opinion and loyalty as a measure of ability and integrity. Future presidents also had to offer a removal policy, but Andrew Jackson's defense of presidential removals as rotation in office marks the next major stage in the development of the removal power. Like Jefferson, Jackson not only replaced a governing coalition but also was the figurehead of the movement that repudiated it. Like Jefferson, he founded a new political party, and this party found its reason for being in a close presidential election marred by disputes over rules. Unlike Jefferson, however, Jackson led a party that had become comfortable with partisanship. Central to that party's emergence were changes in presidential nomination practices and the theory, suggested by Jefferson himself, that the president represents or at least should represent the people. Jackson thus took Jefferson's revised argument from responsibility to its logical extension and thereby revealed its excesses to those in Congress who held a different understanding of executive administration.

Jefferson and the Argument from Responsibility

Thomas Jefferson expanded the removal power after winning the presidency. This did not have to happen the way it did. After all, Jefferson, in his First Inaugural Address, famously called for conciliation between the parties, then promised that he would not remove officers based on their political views. And why would he? There was no precedent for partisan removals, and Jefferson believed that his election would usher in a "union of sentiment," freed from party. Instead, Jefferson soon set the precedent for partisan use of removal power.

Jefferson's use of removals was part of his larger transformation of presidential power. This transformation was in many ways the logical consequence of a decade in which public opinion emerged as a credible source of sovereignty. Consider the election of 1800. Bruce Ackerman has argued that the botched election forced Republicans to make an argument from what the people intended, but Federalists responded that there was no way under the Constitution to discern whether the people intended to elect Aaron Burr or Jefferson.[1] That is, Republicans argued from the will of the people, and Federalists argued from the letter of the law. In Ackerman's words, the Republican argument pointed to a "plebiscitary" presidency, which then culminated in an "institutional dance" between the president and the judiciary. Ackerman's account suggests that Republicans reached for their argument in order to win the presidency, but this was not the first time Republicans had turned to public opinion. As Colleen Sheehan has shown, James Madison's defense of Republican opposition required a theory that opposition, even if designed to be a temporary corrective, was legitimate.[2] Accordingly, Madison wrote a series of essays in the *National Gazette* arguing that public opinion was "sovereign." Scholars still debate whether this argument marked a departure from his writings in *The Federalist*, which are more concerned with the ways in which the Constitution would contain and limit the majority and, more generally, whether there are "two Madisons."[3] Pushing this question aside, it is important to note how this turn to public opinion helped transform American politics. Todd Estes, for example, has shown how the debate over ratification of the Jay Treaty provoked a contest over public opinion, forcing Federalists to organize public opinion and then appeal to it — thus embracing the very methods they had denounced.[4]

Recent scholarship has described the ways in which Jefferson was ready to fit the presidency to this argument about the will of the people. In addition to the well known symbolic changes in his dress and social arrangements, there were substantive changes brought about by Jefferson. One such change was an amendment to the Constitution, the Twelfth

Amendment, which was much more than an example of early Americans fixing presidential selection to avoid the Aaron Burr problem. Rather, the amendment came about after Republicans won an argument about making the presidency more popular, that is, more clearly aligned with the will of the majority. This transformation can be seen even in Jefferson's First Inaugural. Whereas Washington had used the occasion to primarily mark the oath of office as the formal beginning of power, Jefferson used it to declare the principles by which he would govern. This change helps clarify yet another change, namely, Jefferson's decision to retire after two terms. Jefferson did this for institutional rather than merely personal reasons. The idea was to institutionalize revolution, to have a new president, with a new declaration of principles, every eight years.[5]

Another change was more subtle but just as important. Jefferson famously embraced a strong executive even though he had criticized it throughout the 1790s. But Jefferson's version of executive power theory rested on the idea of the president being responsible to the people, yet it did not include arguments anchored in Article II. For example, Jefferson never defended the constitutionality of the Louisiana Purchase, even though most Federalists and many Republicans believed that the power was implied by the treaty power. Instead, Jefferson argued for a constitutional amendment, then chose silence about the authority for the purchase when he realized he could not get the amendment approved in the Senate. This reluctance grew out of his doctrine of prerogative, which he believed should be "extraconstitutional." That is, unlike Hamilton, who wanted the Constitution to be adequate for everything that governments must do, Jefferson believed that prerogative was necessary, but it was best tamed by being left outside the Constitution.[6]

Jefferson worked to fit his appointment and removal policies to this doctrine of executive power while at the same time meeting his immediate political interests. As the first reconstructive president, Jefferson faced a new leadership dilemma. He needed to reward those who made his electoral revolution possible, yet he also needed to do so without alienating moderate supporters of the party that had just lost power. On top of that, he had to decide whether his revolution would make good on its promise to scale back the powers of the executive. With respect to the appointment power, Jefferson resisted congressional attempts to require the president to lay before the Senate the president's reasons for an appointment. The occasion was a request from Connecticut Federalist Uriah Tracy on behalf of a Senate committee to provide information regarding the qualifications of two State Department officials. To be sure, these were likely nominees to the State Department, and, as secretary of state under George Washington, Jefferson had advised against Senate interference in the president's negotiations with other countries.[7] Here, however, he argued that senators themselves had recognized "the Constitution has made it my duty to nominate; and has not made it my duty to lay before them the evidences or reasons whereupon my nominations are founded: & of the correctness of this opinion the established usage in the intercourse between the Senate and the President is proof."[8] In a different context, he went even further, arguing that appointments provided an important way for the president to move closer to the people and embody public opinion:

> In a government like ours, it is the duty of the Chief Magistrate, in order to enable himself to do all the good which his station requires, to endeavor, by all honorable means, to unite himself in the confidence of the whole people. This alone, in any case where the energy of a nation is required, can produce a union of the powers of the whole, and point them in a single direction, as if all constituted but one body and one mind, and this alone can render a weaker nation unconquerable by a stronger one.[9]

Jefferson's situation was especially difficult with removals. There is no better illustration of the delicacy of this task than Jefferson's First Inaugural. There, Jefferson famously pointed to a fundamental unity in principles ("We are all Republicans, we are all Federalists") but also argued that even those who wish to change the republican form ought to be left "undisturbed as monuments of the safety with which error of opinion may be tolerated where reason is left free to combat it."[10] By this logic, both Federalists and Republicans might have reason to think, as Henry Adams remarked, that there had been no revolution at all.[11]

Jefferson at first seemed to embrace such a policy. To the New Englander Elbridge Gerry, Jefferson explained that he would do what his "predecessor ought in justice to have done" by removing "officers who have been guilty of gross abuses of office, such as marshalls packing juries, &c." But he would not remove officers who simply disagreed with his political principles: "The instances will be few, and governed by strict rule, & not party passion. The right of opinion shall suffer no invasion from me. Those who have acted well have nothing to fear, however they may have differed from me in opinion: those who have done ill, however, have nothing to hope; nor shall I fail to do justice lest it should be ascribed to that difference of opinion."[12] Jefferson went on to explain that this generous policy did not include John Adams's so-called midnight appointees. Those appointments would be considered as "nullities," because they were offered after Adams knew that he would not be president. But, excepting those few officers, Jefferson would not remove Federalist officeholders on the grounds that they disagreed with the Republican winner of the presidential election.

As scholars have long noted, Jefferson departed from this rule and quickly changed his policy. On top of removing corrupt officeholders and midnight appointees whom he believed had no rightful claim on the office, Jefferson removed Federalist officeholders in states where he believed Federalists held too large a proportion of the offices. As Jefferson put it in a letter to New York Governor and future running mate George Clinton, his policy and inclination was "to restore harmony by avoiding everything harsh, and to remove only for malconduct." But the "circumstances in your state, and still more in the neighboring states on both sides, require something more."[13] His primary target was Connecticut, the center of the Federalist Party. From his perspective, Federalists in the Connecticut legislature had removed "every republican" from the state offices. As a result, "In Connecticut alone a general sweep seems to be called for on principles of justice and policy."[14] Or as he put to Attorney General Levi Lincoln, "We must meet them with equal intolerance."[15]

It is important to concede that the details of Jefferson's removals are difficult to mark with precision. Scholars have long noted Jefferson's aggressive use of the removal power, and others have emphasized Jefferson's moderation. In an 1899 article, Carl Russell Fish wrote that Jefferson removed 109 presidential officers out of 433 during his eight years as president.[16] A century later, Stephen Skowronek used similar numbers to conclude that Jefferson "outpaced Andrew Jackson, the so-called father of the spoils-system, in removals and replacements."[17] More recently, and drawing on these accounts, Calabresi and Yoo note that that Jefferson "initiated removals in one-third to one-half of all presidentially appointed offices."[18] Leonard White, however, preserved the distinction between Jefferson and the later spoils system under Jackson. For White, the key point is that the power was used modestly: Jefferson was the only president to use removals for "party reasons between 1801 and 1829," and these removals were mostly limited to fixing the problem caused by John Adams's midnight appointments.[19] Jefferson, too, offered conflicting accounts concerning the number of removals. In an 1803 letter to allied newspaper publisher (and later Treasury Secretary) William Duane, Jefferson indicated that his policy had transformed the partisan makeup of the executive branch: "Of 316 offices in all the US subject to appointment and removal by me, 130 only are held by federalists."[20] But in an 1807 letter to his protégé William Short, Jefferson claimed that he had only removed fifteen Federalists because of their political opinions:

> Out of about six hundred offices named by the President there were six Republicans only when I came into office, and these were chiefly half-breeds. Out of upwards of three hundred holding during pleasure, I removed about fifteen of those who had signalized themselves by their own intolerance in office, because the public voice call for it imperiously, and it was just that the Republicans should at length

have some participation in the government. There never was another removal but for such delinquencies as removed the Republicans equally.[21]

It is possible that Jefferson misrepresented his numbers in one or both of the letters, but there is also the possibility that the two letters are not in tension with one another if we assume that Jefferson removed Federalists for reasons other than political ones. As Carl Fish documented, Jefferson used a broad definition of misconduct in office to purge young Federalist officeholders from the executive branch.[22]

What is more important than the number of removals themselves is the defense Jefferson offered of his removal policy. When he removed Elizur Goodrich, collector at the port in New Haven, a group of New Haven merchants sent Jefferson a letter of protest, and Jefferson responded with his own public letter. Jefferson's letter marks a critical step in the development of the removal power. He might have defended the removal on the narrow grounds that Goodrich's office was a "nullity," like other midnight appointments, but instead he defended his removal policy in sweeping language:[23]

> When it is considered, that during the late administration, those not of a particular sect of politics were excluded from all office; when, by a steady pursuit of this measure, nearly the whole offices of the US were monopolized by that sect; when the public sentiment at length declared itself, and burst open the doors of honor and confidence to those whose opinions they more approved, was it to be imagined that this monopoly of office was still to be continued in the hands of the minority? Does it violate their equal rights, to assert some rights in the majority also? Is it political intolerance to claim a proportionate share in the direction of the public affairs?[24]

According to Jefferson, then, the victorious party has "an equal right" to a proportionate share of offices, and the recent elections were a fair way to determine what was proportionate. Because Federalists had for so long refused to share Connecticut offices with Republicans, removals would have to be especially remedial. Jefferson added to this argument from proportionality:

> If the will of the nation, manifested by their various elections, calls for an administration of government according to those elected; if, for the fulfillment of that will, displacements are necessary, with whom can they so justly begin as with administration, not for its own aid, but to begin a career at the same time with their successors, by whom they had never been approved, and who could scarcely expect from them a cordial cooperation.

Jefferson was responding to the specific circumstances of Goodrich's office, but he did so with a larger principle: Because the administration must have the confidence of the people to be successful, it should reflect "the will of the nation." That is, because replacing Federalists with Republicans would invigorate the administration by connecting it to the public will, partisan removals could be justified without appealing to proportionality. Importantly, proportionality in federal offices in the states would be calculated more toward the nation rather than the states: "In the general government each state is to be administered not on it's local principals, but on the principles of all the states formed into a general result."[25]

Jefferson's defense of removals clearly drew from executive power theory, but there are two important differences. First, Jefferson never pointed to the president's vesting clause as a source of power. This was typical Jefferson: Strained textual arguments were to be avoided because they opened the door for even more strained textual arguments in the future. With each elaboration going further beyond the text, the people lose a measure of control over their representatives, jeopardizing the principle of consent. Accordingly, it was better to ground some acts of executive power in public opinion rather than in the law.

The second important development concerns the way Jefferson justified this partisan approach to removals. Specifically, Jefferson transformed Madison's argument for executive power theory by emphasizing public opinion and deemphasizing the take care clause and the vesting clause. As he put it in 1807, "Faithful service in either our first or second revolution" would give "preference of claim." Further, "that principle would gratify the public, and strengthen the confidence so necessary to enable the executive to direct the whole public force to the best advantage of the nation."[26] Jefferson's emphasis on party affiliation as a way to identify and sort public opinion was clearly a change from Madison's more abstract defense of responsibility over stability.

It is difficult to know whether Madison agreed with Jefferson's assertion and transformation of presidential removal powers.[27] Given Madison's importance as an adviser to Jefferson, it is likely that Madison was involved in crafting Jefferson's policy. He probably had a hand as well in drafting Jefferson's reply to the New Haven Federalists. Jefferson's open letter was written on July 12, 1801. Only two days earlier Madison had written Wilson Cary Nicholas, an important ally in the Senate, on the subject of removals.[28] Madison explained that the "task of removing, and appointing officers, continues to embarrass the Ex[ecutive] and agitate particular parts of the Union." Because there is "discord of information & counsel" even among those "whose principles & views are the same," coming up with a correct policy was especially "perplexing." Importantly, Madison pointed to the Connecticut remonstrance, noting that Jefferson's response would require a "peculiar mixture of energy and delicacy."

But Madison would have had good reason to be concerned about Jefferson's defense of removals. Parties had entered the picture, and Jefferson was the leader of the first transition from one party to another. To be sure, the party system had not yet become a system in this sense that parties were not yet, as Richard Hofstadter put it, "legitimate."[29] But even if Jefferson would not say that he believed in parties as such, he did make it clear that he looked to party, not simply merit and integrity, when making appointments. To make the administration more Republican, he had to remove Federalists. Even if Jefferson did not have in mind the spoils system, then, his argument from proportion made a connection between administrative jobs and partisan loyalty and thus politicized what had not yet become partisan.

The Response to Jefferson

Jefferson's critics did not concede Jefferson's argument. As we will see, Federalists objected to what they saw to be a step toward partisanship and a dangerous step toward a more democratic foundation for the presidency. In what follows, we present the reactions of Noah Webster and Alexander Hamilton.

A few days after Jefferson published his response to the New Haven merchants, Noah Webster wrote Madison with an extended critique of Jefferson's policy.[30] To his long case against making removals on the basis of partisanship rather than merit, Webster added a postscript addressing Jefferson's response to the New Haven Federalists. According to Webster, the recent Federalist monopoly on offices was justified in Connecticut because there had been "but *one party* in the State," and even after Jefferson's victory, "still the friends of the present administration form a small party in numbers—still smaller in respectability." More deeply, the argument for proportionality was especially flawed in that it failed to account for the quality of the men being counted. "The merchants in this city [New Haven] are a respectable body of men, not actuated by passion or moved by slight causes. That every man of that character should remonstrate [against] an appointment, is a proof that something is wrong." Because Jefferson placed "his confidence in men who are undeserving of it," that is, more "in a few hungry office seekers, or disgusted men, than in the collective voice of nearly all the respectable inhabitants of this city, the responsibility rests with him." For Webster, there was insufficient place for merit in the partisan argument.

Because Madison's response to Webster has not been discovered in the historical record, we cannot know how Madison defended Jefferson's removal policy, but we can piece together an impression of the response from two sources.[31] First, we know that Madison forwarded Webster's reply to Jefferson, and Jefferson responded with instructions for Madison on how to proceed. Madison pointed out to Jefferson that Webster's argument from merit did not "directly combat the principle of distribution laid down in your reply to the Remonstrance."[32] Jefferson responded by requesting that Madison make the case to Webster: "Tho' I view Webster as a mere pedagogue of very limited understanding and very strong prejudices & party passions, yet as a editor of a paper & as of the Newhaven association, he may be worth stroking."[33] Not only did Jefferson urge Madison to stroke Webster; he also listed "two very fair points whereupon to answer him." The first point was "the justice of making vacancies in order to introduce a participation of office." The second point was "the propriety of preventing men indecently appointed & not yet warm in the seat of office from continuing, rather than to remove those fairly appointed & long in possession." Even though convincing the "immovably biased" Webster on the particular removal "would be like talking to the deaf," there was a chance that Webster could be educated regarding the principle.

The second source is Webster's reply to Madison's reply.[34] Webster's reply consisted of two claims. First, the argument from proportionality tends to give too much room to the divisiveness of partisanship. In Connecticut, there had been one party until Jefferson's followers "seceded from their fellow citizens, mostly within two years." Such secession undercuts its own claim to office because it necessarily encourages future claims. Once merit, then, is replaced with loyalty, the government risks instability: "On this principle, where is the stability of govt, or its consistency? . . . I can not be tranquil under the operation of a principle, which postpones every important object of govt to private views. The principle is destructive of govt — & the precedent may be fatal to the administration which has established it."

This is to say that by defending a policy on the grounds of partisanship, Jefferson had improperly given partisanship a good name. This elevation of partisanship would undermine stability and perhaps even lead to revolution. Even though the Federalists were themselves partisan, "it appears to me that the principles avowed & pursued by the present ruling party, tend to relax law, weaken the national compact, bring government into contempt — & by diffusing a spirit of insubordination, & corruption or morals, to prepare the mass of our people for a revolution, or at least, a convulsion."

Because parties institutionalize opposition, or what Webster called "secession," they forever frustrate the argument from merit by politicizing it. Without the argument from merit as a moderating force, the distribution of offices is subject only to the worst passions and interests. By undermining merit, and unleashing the worst passions and interests, the architects of the Revolution of 1800 were institutionalizing revolution.

Madison's response did not deter Webster from publishing an extended critique of Jefferson's message to the New Haven Federalists. In 1802, Webster published a book-length collection of essays including a 76-page rebuttal of Jefferson's letter.[35] There, Webster charged Jefferson with having forgotten his inaugural address. The inaugural address promised mildness, but the answer to the New England Remonstrance "avows the existence of parties, of long duration" in order to justify removals.[36] Moreover, Webster claimed that Jefferson had "throw[n] off the veil" to announce himself as "head of party."[37] More than hypocritical, this turn was pernicious in Webster's view because it rested on private assessments of political opinion and opened the government to instability caused by the "scramble" for offices.[38] In a strange turn that does not get picked up again in American political development, Webster went on to dispute Jefferson's premise that a minority could have a right to office and, instead, argued if there were a right to office it would be because the majority alone can create rights.[39] More broadly, Webster argued that the "pleasure of the President" was directed by law.[40]

In addition to Webster, Alexander Hamilton signaled that he might obstruct Jefferson's removal policy. As we explained in Chapter 1 ("The Decision of 1789"), Hamilton's position on removal powers remains a puzzle. Before we turn to Hamilton's response to Jefferson, we consider Hamilton's postratification thoughts on the removal power. In *The Federalist*, Hamilton wrote that the president would share the removal power with the Senate, yet, in 1793 as Pacificus, he cited the Decision of 1789 as evidence supporting the argument to limit the exceptions to the broad grant of authority in Article II's vesting clause. Later, in 1802, George F. Hopkin's edition of *The Federalist* added a footnote to *The Federalist* No. 77 stating that the presidential position had been "settled in practice," and, in 1847, Hopkins told Hamilton's son, John Church Hamilton, that Hamilton approved the edition. Scholars have used the statement by Pacificus, and to some extent this footnote in the 1802 edition of *The Federalist*, as evidence that Hamilton came to his senses and was a defender of presidential removal powers.

It is not clear, however, that this conclusion is warranted. As Seth Barrett Tillman argues, the evidence that Hamilton approved the wording of that footnote is weak at best.[41] Moreover, even if Hamilton did approve the footnote, the footnote does not say that the settled construction is a good one. This last point applies to Hamilton's 1793 statement as Pacificus. There, and in the context of his claim that the treaty power was executive by nature, Hamilton wrote: "With these exceptions the EXECUTIVE POWER of the Union is completely lodged in the President. This mode of construing the Constitution has indeed been recognized by Congress in formal acts, upon full consideration and debate. The power of removal from office is an important instance."[42] Here Hamilton was using the Decision of 1789 to make a point about a larger interpretative principle—the vesting clause should be read broadly—but he did not say that that principle applies to the removal power. He did write that Congress decided it does. Just where Hamilton might have chosen broad strokes, he instead chose the narrow and precise.

The evidence from Hamilton's actions is confusing as well. Hamilton's first opportunity to defend strong presidential removal powers came in 1800, when John Adams fired Secretary of State Timothy Pickering and Secretary of War James McHenry. Instead, Hamilton wrote a pamphlet criticizing Adams for disregarding the advice of his cabinet regarding foreign affairs and endorsing Charles Cotesworth Pinckney over Adams for the presidency.[43] The occasion for Hamilton's pamphlet was Adams's appointment of William Vans Murray as minister to France—a reversal of policy that brought about an intracabinet conflict and resulted in a purge of cabinet members loyal to Hamilton. Hamilton entered the fray, and his goal was surely political, ending Adams's chances for reelection. But it is also important to see that Hamilton made a broad argument about the proper relationship between the president and cabinet officials. At first glance, Hamilton seemed to concede that President Adams could remove executive officers at his pleasure: "As the President nominates his Ministers, and may *displace* them when he pleases, it must be his own fault if he be not surrounded by men, who for ability and integrity deserve his confidence."[44] But, again, Hamilton left open the possibility that he was acknowledging that a particular legislative construction of the Constitution was victorious, even while questioning the prudence of actually removing officers. In fact, Hamilton devoted most of his argument to explaining why presidents should not fire executive officials.[45] He declared that one "fact" was "understood to be admitted": "Neither of the dismissed had given any new or recent cause for their dismission." As he put it, Adams's "measure was wrong, both as to mode and to substance." Regarding the mode, Hamilton wrote, "A President is not bound to conform to the advice of his Ministers. He is even under no positive injunction to ask or require it. But the Constitution presumes that he will consult them; and the genius of our government and the public good recommend the practice." What is worth noting here is that Hamilton's argument focused on the quality of advice that presidents would get by taking the perspective of the executive official.[46] Adams's refusal to consult his cabinet was dangerous because even the "greatest genius," or even a George Washington, knows that a single individual "will occasionally overlook obstacles which ordinary and more phlegmatic men will discover." But more than indicative of a character flaw, Adams's *method* would lessen the prospects for future effective administration, because "the stately system of not consulting Ministers . . . will tend to exclude from places of primary trust, the few men most fit to occupy them."

This move enabled Hamilton to elevate a critique of Adams's leadership style into a larger argument about administration. Just as Hamilton in *The Federalist* had characterized the combination of presidential removals and presidential elections as a "revolution," Hamilton here invoked revolution in his *Letter* on Adams to link Adams's "ungovernable temper" with the frequent change of government in France. The "primary cause" of the reversal of foreign policy toward the risky engagement with France was that Adams was beset with sudden "gusts of passion" and was liable to "paroxysms of anger." Like Adams, whose personal character flaws were exaggerated by his "dangerous and degrading system of not consulting Ministers," France too went through fits of passion: "Another Revolution: Another Constitution Overthrown." In this discussion of revolution, Hamilton added that Adams's 1800 pardon of the insurrectionist John Fries went "against the advice of all his ministers" and had rendered the national government incapable of putting down rebellion. Long after his alleged turnaround as Pacificus, Hamilton criticized the first high-profile presidential use of the removal power by emphasizing the need for expert judgment by the department heads and by associating Adams's use of the power with the revolutionary passions of France.[47]

Jefferson's election and his removal of Federalists brought about another public discussion of presidential removal powers and another chance for Hamilton. As we have seen, Jefferson responded to criticism of his removal of a customs collector in New Haven with an open letter to defend the removal power on grounds that administration should reflect the majority will, which itself could be determined by the presidential election. Hamilton was no supporter of Jefferson, so it is no surprise that he did not rush to Jefferson's defense. But if he did want to record his support of presidential removal powers, he could have easily criticized Jefferson's choices while also affirming the president's right to remove. Further, he might have compared Jefferson's removal of Goodrich to Adams's removal of Pickering, showing why both were poor uses of the removal power. But, like the Decision of 1789, Hamilton seems to have been silent, in public at least. It is possible, however, that Hamilton did enter the public debate, at least in a supporting role.

To answer Jefferson's open letter, "Lucius Junius Brutus" published a pamphlet. But more than simply disputing the facts of the case, Brutus continued Hamilton's principled argument in *The Federalist* against presidential removals: Presidential removals would undermine effective administration by making the office less attractive for capable men. Importantly, Brutus associated the quality of officers with the stability of the government by connecting the "stability" of the "tenure" of the officer, the "inducement to enter into public service," and effective administration:

> An intelligent and active man grows daily more useful in the employments to which he devotes his attention; he acquires a knowledge of business, and a promptness, which are of the highest service. But if every change of a chief Magistrate is to produce an entire change of subordinate officers, what is to be the consequence? Their places are to be supplied by a new set of men who have everything to learn, and who, by the time they have acquired the proper information, and have fitted themselves for their stations, must, in consequence of a new election, which changes the state of affairs, be swept off in their turn to make room for others equally ignorant, and unskillful with themselves at the time of their appointment.[48]

Hamilton told others that William Coleman was the author, but there are reasons to speculate that Hamilton had a hand in the work.[49] First, as seen in the text above, there is remarkable similarity in the words above and Hamilton's language in *The Federalist* No. 77.[50] Second, as in the case of William Loughton Smith in the First Congress, there is evidence of other collaboration between Coleman and Hamilton: In a matter of months, Coleman became the editor of Hamilton's *New-York Evening Post*. Third, there is the choice of the pseudonym: the Roman historian Livy describes Lucius Junius Brutus as the accomplice of Publius in the founding and early rule of Rome, and prior scholarship has shown that Hamilton chose his pseudonyms with care.[51] Even though Hamilton was silent, it is possible that he commissioned a surrogate to criticize presidential removals on the grounds that they would weaken administration by making administrative office less attractive to qualified men.

Even if we cannot conclude that Hamilton commissioned Brutus, or at least provided arguments for him, it is nevertheless significant that, for yet another time, Hamilton chose silence on the question of removals. Hamilton might have done so out of partisan calculation: Why offer the other side support in the form of constitutional argument? Or he might have discerned in Jefferson's expansion a form of executive energy that was too democratic and too unstable for his liking. When Jefferson sought to liberate presidential removal powers, Hamilton did not applaud but instead allowed Brutus to try to hobble it.

Hamilton was circumspect again in his 1802 arguments against the repeal of the Judiciary Act of 1801. This time, Hamilton entered the fray by writing a series of essays called *The Examination* and left evidence that his views on removals were complicated. On the one hand, Hamilton appeared to do what he had not yet done: criticize the policy but unequivocally concede the power. In No. 13, he explained, "There are two modes known to the Constitution, in which the tenure of office may be affected — one the abolition of the office; the other the removal of the officer. The first is a legislative act, and operates by removing the office from the person — the last is an Executive act and operates by removing the person from the office. Both equally cause the tenure, enjoyment, or *holding* of the office to cease."[52] So it would seem that Hamilton here and for the first time recognized removals as a presidential power, but Hamilton continued and complicated this discussion a few essays later in No. 17.[53] In the latter essay, which was meant to reject the theory that "all offices are holden of the president," Hamilton suggested again that the Senate would participate in removals just as it did in appointments: "The appointment is indeed confined to a particular organ, and in instances in which it is not otherwise provided by the Constitution or the Laws, the removal of the officer is left to the pleasure or discretion of that organ."[54] Having come close to the principle that the power to remove was incident to the power to appoint, he then explained how removals were both a "prerogative" of the president and could be directed under "the general competency of the legislative power to provide for the public welfare."[55] Rather than clarifying how he meant to reconcile the two points, Hamilton continued in prose that must have confused even his most attentive readers. His primary objective was to distinguish judges from executive officials in order to preserve the tenure of judges. With respect to executive officials, his main point was to find a way to balance the rights of the officeholder, the power of the executive, and the power of the legislature.[56] Again, Hamilton could have endorsed executive power theory in clear terms, but he chose against it.

The three events involve two different presidencies and plenty of room for alternative explanations. But the thread is clear. In each case, Hamilton chose either to remain on the sidelines in the debates on the removal power, perhaps for partisan or personal reasons, or to leave a confusing record of his own understanding of the removal power. Even though these events in the development of the removal power were complicated by partisan developments in which Hamilton was an active participant, each instance provided Hamilton with a chance to influence the frequency and character of presidential removal powers. In each case, Hamilton chose against endorsing the Madison position of 1789 and against clearly revising his stated position in *The Federalist* No. 77. It is possible that Hamilton did undergo a conversion, but it is also possible the most articulate defender of executive power in American history could not quite solve the puzzle of removals in his own mind.

Congress Includes Itself: The First Tenure of Office Act

Jefferson's reconstruction of the removal power opened the path for presidential dominance of executive patronage, but it also invited others to influence executive administration. Members of Congress and party leaders soon realized that a "responsible" administration was vulnerable to nonpresidential incursions. The 1820 Tenure of Office Act is a prime example of this unintended consequence of the Jeffersonian reconstruction. It revealed that patronage could benefit Congress just as much as it did the executive and suggested that Congress could control the removal power.

The 1820 Tenure of Office Act, also called the Four Years Act, provided for a fixed four-year term for many executive officials, adding that they would also be "removable from office by pleasure."[57] Specifically, it applied to officers who collected or disbursed money. This class included district attorneys, paymasters, and customs collectors, as well as those dealing with public lands. The bill was introduced by Democratic-Republican Senator Mahlon Dickerson of New Jersey, but, according to John Quincy Adams and scholars since, the person behind the bill was actually Treasury Secretary William Crawford.[58] Crawford's motives, and the design for the law, are less than clear. One explanation points to patronage. John Quincy Adams made this charge in his *Memoirs*, explaining that Crawford intended to use the windfall of vacated offices related to the Treasury to improve his chances for winning the presidency, presumably by being able to grant more favors to senators.

But intentions are difficult to prove, and the evidence for Adams's charge is hard to find. There is little in the *Annals of Congress*, and in hindsight James Monroe's victory in 1820 was a sure bet. In fact, according to Fish, Crawford wrote a letter in June 1820 indicating both that Crawford believed Monroe would be reelected and that Crawford believed the law would get rid of unfit men. Fish also points to correspondence between the Governor of Rhode Island and James A. Hamilton, another son of Alexander Hamilton, and concludes that Crawford did not use the opportunity to use removals to sway Rhode Island's votes from the Henry Clay column. He also notes it would have been hard to get patronage through the cabinet with others watching. Leonard White does not conclude one way or the other, but he does say that the need for reform was there, thus corroborating the explanation that Crawford was seeking genuine reform.[59]

If anything, the law proved to serve the advantage of individual members of the Senate. Notably, Jefferson and Madison criticized the law for this very reason. As Jefferson put it, the law would likely "sap the constitutional and salutary functions of the President," create a patronage system, and extend that patronage to the Senate: "It will keep in constant excitement all the hungry cormorants for office, render them, as well as those in place sycophants to their Senators, engage these in eternal intrigue to turn out one and put in another, in cabals to swap work; and make of them what all executive directories become, mere sinks of corruption and faction."[60] Madison agreed, and he pushed the criticism further in letters to Jefferson and Monroe, arguing that the law departed from the constitutional logic of the Decision of 1789. Under that logic, the Constitution permits the president alone to determine the tenure of the officer. Congress's role is confined to creating the office, discontinuing the office, or using its power to remove by way of the impeachment process. Once Congress creates the office, neither the House nor the Senate has "any power" over it.[61] One might ask why Madison in this instance thought that Congress lacked the power to limit the tenure of offices. The answer is that, in his view, the law implied that Congress could control removals by controlling the length of the officer's term: "If a law can displace an officer at every period of 4 years, it can do so at the end of every year, or at every session of the Senate, and the tenure will then be the pleasure of the Senate, as much of the President, & not of the P[resident] alone."[62] Madison continued this criticism later, when he argued to Monroe that the Senate does not even have the power to alter the date at which a nomination takes place, because that would be the power to "originate" the appointment and the president possesses that power.[63] This critique of the law by Jefferson and Madison later earned the praise of Leonard White, who characterized them as elder statesmen who understood that the law would tend toward spoils. According to White, the 1820 law marked a crucial step toward the spoils system under Jackson. "The shadow of things to come was visible in the Tenure of Office Act of 1820."[64] Likewise, Peter Zavodnyik writes that the law "greatly increased those occasions on which the Senate had before it a nomination for the civil service—thereby enhancing the ability of individual senators to find jobs for allies and supporters."[65]

Another key development in the removal power was the election of John Quincy Adams as president. The election of 1824 was the second time that the House had to select the president, but this was the first time that the winner who emerged could not claim a majority electoral coalition. A potential coalition was suggested in Adams's nomination of Henry Clay as secretary of state, but as Skowronek notes, Adams resisted Clay's entreaties to use removals and patronage for party-building.[66] Instead, he guided his appointments policy by his pledge in his First Inaugural Address to have an administration of "talent and virtue alone." Skowronek's analysis of this decision shows just how difficult Adams's leadership situation was. Adams's refusal to use patronage for party-building resulted in having an executive branch staffed with officials, like Postmaster General John Mc-Clean, who opposed Adams's administration. In the analysis of Mary W. M. Hargreaves, "The president was slow to recognize the role that McLean filled in supporting an opposition under the patronage dispensation within his charge." And when Adams did finally realize the extent of McLean's activity, "the chief executive retained in office an enemy whom he regarded as an able administrator."[67] But as Hargreaves's evidence confirms, political considerations are inevitable in the business of appointments: Even an Adams will sometimes choose a personal connection over talent and virtue. In this case, and as Skowronek emphasizes, the nomination of Clay gave the appearance of an appointment policy that was guided by electoral calculation; it thus emboldened the opposition. "While Adams was presenting himself as the very model of patrician rectitude, his opponents pointed to the coalition he had forged and imputed to it the motives most offensive to the patrician conscience."[68] Skowronek's analysis is confirmed by a letter from John C. Calhoun to Andrew Jackson. According to Calhoun, the Adams/Clay patronage regime threatened the very form of government because if the "Presidency be transmitted by the exercise of a corrupt patronage from hand to hand," then the people would consider the "form of electing by the people a mere farce."[69] For Calhoun, at least before he came to this theory of the concurrent majority, power by "voice of the people" was necessarily antithetical to power by "patronage of the executive."

This last point is also illustrated by a statement in the extraordinary pseudonymous exchange that took place in 1826 between Calhoun and, probably, John Quincy Adams. Under the names "Patrick Henry" and "Onslow," the president and vice president engaged in a series of public letters debating the parliamentary powers of the vice president in the Senate. In this little-known debate, the two writers looked to history and parsed Thomas Jefferson's *A Manual of Parliamentary Practice* to best the other on a rather technical question, but behind the debate was really the role of partisanship — and the legitimacy of an opposition party — within institutional design. For our purposes, what is most interesting is Calhoun's charge that even Adams's seemingly fair appointments were made for political reasons: "Do you not see in the distinction a confirmation of the charge that the appointment [by] the President of his bitter enemies to office was made for political purposes, with this very view of conversion, in imitation of European politics, and not from magnanimity on his part, as is pretended by his friends."[70]

Combined, the Tenure of Office Act of 1820 and John Quincy Adams's precarious leadership situation made the question of patronage all the more important as a political question. One example is Thomas H. Benton's 1826 Senate "Report on the Reduction of Executive Patronage."[71] One concern in Benton's report was that patronage would make the federal government overwhelm the states, but another was that it would increase the influence of the president relative to Congress. As White notes, Benton's solution was to ensure that Congress shared some of the powers of patronage. In addition to five other proposals giving Congress more control over public printing of newspapers, removal of Army and Navy officers, and appointment of postmasters, one recommendation anticipated future proposals coming from Congress. Specifically, and anticipating the Tenure of Office Act of 1867, Benton's report recommended that the president be required to state the reasons for every removal of delinquent collectors and disbursers of public revenue at the time the president nominated a replacement. To be sure, White went out of his way to argue that this was a Jacksonian attack on John Quincy Adams and that it was motivated by partisanship, not constitutional scruples.[72] But White also noted that "assumptions of Benton's Report on the role of patronage in the winning of elections are of profound importance." Specifically, the report was the "first systematic and public recognition of a new order of partisan warfare on the national scene which had the gravest consequences for the administrative system."[73]

This recognition of the new power of patronage is also captured in an exchange of letters between Edward Everett and John McLean in the summer of 1828.[74] McClean had served as postmaster general under James Monroe and John Quincy Adams and would later be appointed to the Supreme Court by Jackson. Everett had resigned his professorship at Harvard and as a U.S. representative from Massachusetts.[75] The exchange turned on the question of patronage, as Everett explained: "I differ with you, a little, as to the extent, to which the members of an Administration ought to carry their neutrality." In Everett's view, the "political condition" of the country had changed in the sense that parties were divided on "personal preferences" rather than on "principle."[76] As a result, patronage was necessary for political survival:

> What then binds the mass of the parties together, I say the mass, not the high-minded, few, patriotic individuals, but the mass? Indubitably the hope of office, and its honors and emoluments. The consequence is, that the moment any Administration is formed, every man out of office, and desirous of getting in, is arrayed against it. If the Administration then discard the principle of bestowing patronage on their political friends, they turn against themselves not only the expectants but the incumbents.[77]

In response, McLean wrote that he "differ[ed] essentially" on the subject of patronage. In place of patronage as the foundation, he would "found an Administration upon a totally different basis." In his view, administration "should rest on the virtue and intelligence of the people," and ambition should be excited from "high and noble principles, as far removed, as possible, from selfish considerations."[78]

These two very different positions turned on three key arguments.

The first concerned an empirical account of how to succeed in presidential politics. For Everett, patronage was simply better politics. His main piece of evidence here was that John Quincy Adams had failed: "I say has failed, for, whether he is reelected or not, it has, in my judgment, done him more injury than anything else, that, in making appointments to office, his friends have been neglected, for men no better qualified."[79] For McLean, the example of John Quincy Adams actually demonstrated the opposite point. Because of the appearance of corruption in Adams's appointment of Clay as secretary of state, all of Adams's appointments were tainted. So the injury to Adams's administration was not the stated policy of appointments by merit and virtue but rather the conviction in the public mind that the appointments had been made "with a reference to political effect."[80]

A second division concerned human nature. For Everett, it was clear that Adams had failed because the people could not support his high-minded policy. This was just as true at the national level as it was at the municipal level, where most men preferred a partisan over an opponent even for the position of "hog-reeve."[81] More fundamental, most people simply cannot separate partisanship from their estimation of merit. Because of the "astonishing facility" with which "men learn to think well of those who are acting with them," it is likely that any administration will "appoint its friends, in the honest belief, that they were the most worthy."[82] For McLean, however, human nature included the capacity for morality. When citizens see that merit and virtue are given priority, they will then see that patronage is used for the public rather than the private good: "The moral force arising from a deep conviction in the public mind, that patronage is used with a single eye to the public interest, will be overwhelming. It will enlist on the side of administration, the feelings of every good man."[83]

The third difference concerned the precedent set by Jefferson. Importantly, this difference was over the representative nature of the presidency. According to Everett, Jefferson's removal of Federalists provided a precedent for patronage. Just as Jefferson argued from the "declared will of the people in favor of republicanism" to direct his appointment policies, a future president might similarly look to the will of the people to direct patronage. "I cannot conceive, that any man can wish, for instance, to have Genl. Jackson president, rather than Mr. Adams, and not wish caeteris paribus, that a friend to the Genl. should hold an office, rather than a friend of Mr. Adams."[84] But according to McLean, Jefferson's policy demonstrated that Jefferson picked officials according to the republican *principle* and not according to political advantage. As he put it, Jefferson was part of a larger "cause," and appointments were directed by dedication to that cause: "Any personal advantage resulting to himself, was not direct, but consequential."[85] More broadly, McLean rejected the idea that the president alone could represent the people. Instead, he argued that an official was like a trustee of the national will rather than an appendage of the executive. "Like the chief magistrate, he is the representative of the people, and enjoys equal privileges beyond the sphere of his official duties."[86]

Jackson and the Argument from Rotation

Like Jefferson, Andrew Jackson was swept into office by a realigning election. Like Jefferson, Jackson offered a vigorous defense of presidential removal powers and turned to executive power theory and the argument that the president is uniquely responsible to the people. But, as Leonard White argued, Jackson went even further and broke away from what had been taken for granted. Before Jackson, as White put it, officeholders were gentlemen, vacancies most often came by death, and the "tradition of permanence and stability was as well established" as the two-term limit. Even though Jefferson removed officeholders because of their political views, he was reluctant to defend partisanship and unwilling to embrace broad readings of the Constitution. Moreover, as we have seen in the case of John Quincy Adams, later presidents were less than willing to embrace the removal power as a way to make room for political allies. Under Jackson, all this changed.

Jackson applied the theory of responsibility from the very first year of his presidency, but he took some time before he publicly explained it. Jackson alluded to the coming change in his First Inaugural Address, but he did not explicitly refer to his theory of rotation. Rather, Jackson spoke of "reform":

> The recent demonstration of public sentiment inscribes on the list of Executive duties, in characters too legible to be overlooked, the task of *reform,* which will require particularly the correction of those abuses that have brought the patronage of the Federal Government into conflict with the freedom of elections, and the counteraction of those causes which have disturbed the rightful course of appointment and have placed or continued power in unfaithful or incompetent hands.
>
> In the performance of a task thus generally delineated I shall endeavor to select men whose diligence and talents will insure in their respective stations able and faithful cooperation, depending for the advancement of the public service more on the integrity and zeal of the public officers than on their numbers.[87]

Like that of Jefferson, Jackson's First Inaugural left room for the notion that removals would be limited to those officers who had abused their office. But Jackson had something else in mind. This is clear from Jackson's

"Memorandum on Appointments." In this internal directive to his cabinet, submitted to the heads of departments before he was inaugurated, Jackson offered his first important statement on removals in an "outline of principles." Jackson directed his cabinet heads to remove officers who fall into one of four categories:

1. Those who were appointed against the will of the people.
2. Officers who used their position to interfere with elections.
3. Officers whose positions can be eliminated in the interest of saving money.
4. Officers who are dishonest.

Jackson did not refer here to the argument that the president is chief representative of the people. Rather, Jackson defended this policy on the larger grounds of "the rotative principle," which he described as a "fundamental" principle of his presidency.[88]

Jackson did not go to explain what the "rotative principle" was, but it could be inferred from its function as the "best check for the evils arising out of the growing propensity for office." More explicitly, Jackson explained that the last election had "exhibited the people acting against an improper use of patronage." Given the critique that his removal policy would provoke over the next decade, there is some irony in Jackson's explanation. But it is especially ironic given Jackson's elaboration of how this battle between patronage and the people was waged: "A patronage whose tendency was a corruption of the elective franchise, in as much as it sought to mould the public sentiment into an acquiescence with the exercise of power acquired without the sanction of that sentiment." As we will see, Jackson's charge that his opponents had used offices to corrupt elections would be more or less the very charge made by his critics. In addition to this historical irony, Jackson's claim was also circular. It blamed patronage for corrupting the people into favoring an administration that had "lost" an election. That is, Jackson alleged that had John Quincy Adams been reelected, it would have been because the people in 1828 were less pure than the people in 1824. At the same time, in not being corrupted, the people had in 1828 demanded that Jackson undo the source of corruption.[89]

Although Jackson did not recognize it, a large part of the difficulty in his strange argument grew out of the argument that the president should have the power to remove on grounds of responsibility to the people. The problem with the argument from responsibility is that it replaces a qualitative assessment of administration with a procedural one. It assumes that an administration close to the people will be a good one or effective one and thus defines merit in terms of political preference. At the same time, it understates the need for continuity and stability. But Jackson made this problem even more acute when he changed the argument from responsibility by bringing it to its logical conclusion. Responsible administration can be good administration only if turnover is valued as an end in itself. Because Jefferson and Madison could not bring themselves to accept the idea of a party system, they could not see the argument for rotation.

As we see in Chapter 3 ("Jackson to Johnson: The Rise of Congressional Delegation"), Jackson's policy soon met opposition. For now, a passage from the *Memoirs of John Quincy Adams* sufficiently shows how Jackson's removals changed the mood in the Washington community: "Every one is in breathless expectation, trembling at heart, and afraid to speak. Some of the dismissions are deserved: from age, from incapacity, from intemperance, from irregularities of private life; and these are made the pretext for justifying all the removals. The persons appointed are of equally various characters—some good, the greater part very indifferent, some notoriously bad—on the average, much less respectable than those dismissed."[90] To answer the concerns voiced by friends and opponents, Jackson used his first annual message to Congress to explain and defend his principle of rotation in office. Jackson's account of rotation in office has received much attention, but what is often underappreciated in Jackson's praise of rotation is its proximity to his recommendation of amending the Constitution to provide for direct election of the president. To preface this recommendation, Jackson cataloged the ways in which the "first principle of our system," namely, "that the majority is to govern," can be perverted: Members of the Electoral College can be faithless; in the contingency election in the House, representatives from a state with one representative were especially vulnerable to corruption; and, even under normal conditions, a minority may select the president. The Constitution needed to be amended, therefore, to remove the Electoral College and insert a requirement that the contingency election in the House be limited to the top two—instead of three—votegetters.

> In this as in all other matters of public concern policy requires that as few impediments as possible should exist to the free operation of the public will. Let us, then, endeavor so to amend our system that the office of Chief Magistrate may not be conferred upon any citizen but in pursuance of a fair expression of the will of the majority.
>
> I would therefore recommend such an amendment of the Constitution as may remove all intermediate agency in the election of the President and Vice-President. The mode may be so regulated as to preserve to each State its present relative weight in the election, and a failure in the first attempt may be provided for by confining the second to a choice between the two highest candidates.[91]

What is important to note about this proposal is that the concern with the number of options in the contingency election would not have solved his electoral problem in 1824: John Quincy Adams had finished second in that election. Indeed, by removing one more eligible candidate, it might escalate it. What Jackson's proposal would have done is that it would complete the logic of the Twelfth Amendment.[92] In those debates, Republicans wanted the number of eligible candidates in the contingency election limited to two, yet Federalists insisted on retaining five (the old way). Had Federalists won, the presidency would likely have moved more toward a parliamentary system, with Congress having maximum flexibility in choosing the president from among a slate of nominees. Three was a compromise. Like the first realigning president, then, the second realigning president was interested in amending the rules governing presidential selection.

It is no accident, then, that Jackson offered his praise of rotation in the context of recommending changes to presidential selection. Both passages stand out as the only statements about principles in a speech that is otherwise a laundry list of budgetary matters and diplomatic relations. But, by connecting the logic of the Twelfth Amendment with the principle of rotation, the reforms proposed by the second would go further. In his recommendation to amend the constitutional rules for presidential selection, Jackson presumed more than the debatable proposition that the first principle was majority rule: Jackson also presumed that electors and members of Congress were likely to be corrupted *and* that the majority was free from corruption. Jackson never defended or articulated this presumption with respect to presidential selection, but he did lay it out in the case of rotation:

> There are, perhaps, few men who can for any great length of time enjoy office and power without being more or less under the influence of feelings unfavorable to the faithful discharge of their public duties. Their integrity may be proof against improper considerations immediately addressed to themselves, but they are apt to acquire a habit of looking with indifference upon the public interests and of tolerating conduct from which an unpracticed man would revolt. Office is considered as a species of property, and government rather as a means of promoting individual interests than as an instrument created solely for the service of the people.

It is important to point out, as do Marc Landy and Sidney M. Milkis, that Jackson's emphasis on rotation was as much about what government should be doing as much as it was about who should be in government.[93] In short, the theory of rotation presumed that governmental business would be simple enough for ordinary people, or, as Jackson put it in the annual message, "The duties of all public officers are, or at least admit of being made, so plain and simple that men of intelligence may readily qualify themselves for their performance."[94] As we will see, the Progressives explicitly rejected this view on the grounds that some offices required expertise. But there is another problem in rotation, and this one has to do with the strategy of party-building. As Scott C. James has argued, the practice of rotation allows party leadership to "spread the benefits of party victory to more and more members" but it "weakened the incentive" for party members in government to remain loyal, as rotation presumed that no individual should stay in office forever. Even from the perspective of party organization, then, rotation in office is a good way to start a party, but it is a less than a rational way to maintain a party.[95]

From Responsibility to Rotation

Jackson's case for the presidential position helps clarify two questions raised in the Introduction. The first concerns the degree to which Jackson grounded his removal policy on a theory about separation of powers. The second is whether Jackson could have done any differently.

The assumption underlying the first question is that Jackson found a theory to dress up his practical policy objectives. Likewise, this argument would say that Jackson's opponents embraced the alternative because they hated Jackson. We discuss the critique of Jackson in Chapter 3 ("Jackson to Johnson: The Rise of Congressional Delegation") and conclude that members of the Whig Party were against removals not because they hated Jackson. Rather, they hated Jackson and his policies, in part, because of his removal policy. The methodological problem can be seen in Leonard White's administrative history of the period, which seems to make two different claims about Jackson. On the one hand, White argued that Jackson did not "have a theory" regarding administration and removals. As White put it, "Jackson took the administrative system as he found it, changed its leadership, made some improvements, and accepted the responsibility for operating it. He did not advance the art of administration or go beyond the precepts of morality and common sense. He wrote and thought in terms of individuals. His letters and writings betray only rarely a sense of administration as a process that could be described in general terms."[96]

White extended this argument to members of Jackson's cabinet, concluding, "Hardly one of them ever thought of administration in general terms or had a discernible body of administrative principles by which he was influenced."[97] But on the other hand, White also argued that historians have been wrong to think of Jackson's administration as one of spoils and confusion simply. Instead, White described it as a "huge experiment" in democratic officeholding based on the theory of responsibility to the people.[98] White also wrote that Jackson's defense of rotation was simply the principle of election applied to administration.[99] White thus seemingly had two positions: (1) that Jackson was not guided by a principled account of administration; and (2) that Jackson's removals were guided by the principle that administration should be connected to elections. So which is it? Perhaps White's first conclusion grows from the study of administrative politics and therefore sets a high bar for what would count as a "theory of administration." For us, the second part—that Jackson articulated a theory of rotation—is important because it shows how Jackson expanded the argument from executive power theory.[100]

Jackson's combination of reforming presidential selection with removals brings us to the second question. Did he have a choice? If we return to White, the new removal policy corresponded with the larger transformation of the political system, fueled in part by democratization as well as by increasing desire for jobs from members of both parties: "In short the voice of the people was loud, brazen, and insistent, and the words of its 'betters' were only a happy echo. Quite irrespective of the theoretical doctrine of rotation, it is doubtful whether such pressures could have been resisted. Doctrine nevertheless whetted appetites and combined with interest to launch a sequence of events of vast importance."[101] Under this view, there was something inevitable about patronage. That very well may be true, but it is no less important to recognize that Jackson had a choice about whether he would attach the removal power to the demand for patronage and about how he would defend executive control over removals.

But in some sense, Jackson did not have a choice because, as we have argued here, the original case for responsibility to the people was flawed in the sense that it never really explained why responsibility to the people was better than an administration grounded in, as John Quincy Adams put it, talent and virtue alone. Jackson meant to resolve this difficulty with the principle of rotation, but, as we see in Chapter 3, there was a different solution to the question of removals, and the Whig argument asserted itself precisely because of the way Jackson returned to executive power theory. Like Jefferson, and unlike Madison in 1789, Jackson articulated his defense of presidential control of removals in a partisan context. But unlike Jefferson, Jackson and his contemporaries saw that parties were likely to endure as critical institutional features of national politics. When Jackson thus appealed to the argument from responsibility to the people, he more clearly meant responsibility to the majority party. On top of that, he looked to a revised constitutional argument to enhance this political argument and became the first person in American history to combine the Madisonian and Jeffersonian arguments for executive power theory as well as the first to attach a neo-Hamiltonian reading of Article II to the removal power. And just as the argument for the presidential position was transformed by the new institutional arrangements, the alternative arguments for Congress were also changed.

Chapter Three

Jackson to Johnson: The Rise of Congressional Delegation

The Decision of 1789 did not settle the question of removals. As we have seen, presidential control of the removal power remained contested; opponents included those who were normally wary of executive power as well as those who normally wanted a vigorous executive. The first two "reconstructive" presidents (Thomas Jefferson and Andrew Jackson) expanded the grounds for executive removal power. Jefferson was the first president to assert and defend the removal power, and he did so on grounds of *responsibility* to public opinion. Jackson continued Jefferson's emphasis on public opinion, but he transformed it by attaching the principle of *rotation.*

Like Jefferson before, Jackson met opposition. But unlike Jefferson, Jackson's policy was criticized by allies and eventually formally repudiated by the United States Senate. Unlike those of Jefferson, Jackson's opponents made a frontal assault on the new governing coalition, offering a direct critique of executive power. That critique rejected Jackson's expansion of the veto (including the pocket veto), Jackson's use of informal advisers, the lack of a term limit for the president, and the theory that the president represents the people. On top of this, it rejected the argument that the president has the power under the Constitution to remove executive officers and even went so far as to include an attempt by the Senate to give the Senate a share of the removal power.

With each reconstruction, the opposition to removal powers increased. Like Alexander Hamilton and Noah Webster before them, subsequent politicians offered sustained arguments against presidential control over removals. These critics included Henry Clay, Daniel Webster, and Joseph Story. To be sure, these men were partisans and opponents of Andrew Jackson, but today they are often recognized as leading interpreters of the Constitution, particularly in the nationalist tradition. More important for this study, the critique amounted to what can be called the "ascent of Congress," an ascent that reached its peak in the post–Civil War Reconstruction Congress. Put differently, the new critics of executive power theory thought Congress was constitutionally bound to participate and even direct the removal power. Below we examine the turn to the argument for congressional delegation.

The Early Critique of Jackson

The critique of Jackson's removal policy blossomed during the controversy over the Second Bank of the United States leading to Jackson's removal of Treasury Secretary William Duane in 1833. As we will see, this was the controversy that resulted in an 1834 Senate bill requiring Senate participation in removals — a bill that passed 31–16 in the Senate but was never acted upon by the House of Representatives. This bill would have confined the removal power in several ways. First, it would have rejected the Decision of 1789 by stating clearly the interpretative position that the Constitution itself does not confer such power on the president. Second, like Thomas H. Benton's proposal described in Chapter 2 above, it would have taken a step toward *for-cause* stipulations by requiring that the president provide reasons to the Senate for removals. As Leonard White concluded, "This language, while not specifically asserting the prerogative of the Senate to judge the propriety of the reasons, left no doubt that such was the purpose and would be the consequence."[1] Third, it would ask the Senate's Judiciary Committee to consider the evidence for the advise and consent position. Again, White's analysis is worthy of quoting: "No President could have removed a district attorney, a collector of customs, a federal marshal, or any other officer appointed with the consent of the Senate without in effect securing Senate consent to the removal."[2] This reform effort failed, but it opened the path that would lead to the Tenure of Office Act of 1867, the impeachment of Andrew Johnson, and a full-blown constitutional crisis.

But the opposition to presidential control of the removal power developed before this controversy. As we will show, there were actually two stages to the opposition. The first is when Jackson met opposition from politicians inside and outside his party as soon as he announced and implemented his policy. The fact that there were two stages is important, because it suggests an error in prior scholarly accounts of the period. To the extent that scholars have noticed the debate, they have associated it with the Whig critique of Jackson made in response to the bank controversy. That is not quite right, for there was a critique that preceded the bank. Jackson's removal of officeholders and appointment of friendly partisans provoked criticism from friends and allies, so much so that Jackson defended his removals with an argument from the principle of rotation.

Jackson's removals provoked criticism from the very beginning. Much of it came from those who had lost jobs themselves or knew someone who had been removed.[3] Some of these critics, however, used the occasion to warn Jackson against overusing removals. Mary Chase Barney, daughter of Federalist Justice Samuel Chase, wrote Jackson to protest the removal of her husband and scolded Jackson for his rule of "punishment of your political opponents and rewards for your friends," warning him against staining the "robes of power" by this breaking of the precedents of his predecessors.[4] Jackson's predecessor (John Quincy Adams) was predictably unsupportive. According to Adams, some of the removals were deserved, but the problem was that these served as a pretext for removing the many that were not. Making matters worse, some of the new appointees were less qualified than those they replaced.[5]

Second, the realigning president also received criticism from among his supporters. Illinois Governor Ninian Edwards, for example, wrote Jackson that his removals were causing a division within the party and empowering rivals such as William Crawford.[6] As Jackson scholar Donald B. Cole has written, the opposition from within the party grew out of a principled intraparty debate about the desirability of patronage: the "regency junto types in the party" — such as the newspaper editors Amos Kendall (the *Argus* in Kentucky) and Duff Green (the *United States Telegraph* in Washington, D.C.), as well as loyalists to Van Buren's machine the Albany Regency — "believed that they must offer their followers the spoils of office." But "Old Republican idealists" (Thomas Ritchie, editor of the *Richmond Enquirer* and longtime Republican stalwart) "resolutely opposed patronage."[7]

The greatest criticism within the coalition came from Ritchie. In March 1929, Jackson's first month in office and after Jackson had removed only one person, Ritchie wrote Secretary of State Van Buren a letter intended to be passed along to Jackson. Ritchie's primary objection was Jackson's appointments, which he said "had thrown a cloud over our friends." He objected to what he saw as Jackson's tendency to elevate his friends and especially to Jackson's appointment of newspaper editors. From Ritchie's perspective: "It really looks as if there were a systematic Effort to reward Editorial Partizans." This appearance was especially objectionable for Ritchie, because it would undermine the freedom of the press by making the press appear too partisan. As he put it, the press had "fought manfully" against a "corrupt Coalition." But if they were rewarded with political appointments, it would bring the "vaunted Liberty of the Press into a sort of Contempt" and therefore undermine liberty generally. Ritchie went on to object to what seemed to him to be an overly partisan approach to removals:[8]

I go for reform—but what is reform? Is it to turn out of office all those, who voted against him, or who decently preferred Mr. [John Quincy] Adams? Or is it not rather those, who are incapable of discharging their duties; the drunken, the ignorant, the embezzler, the man who has abused his official facilities to keep Gen. Jackson out—or, who are so wedded to the corruptions of Office, as to set their faces against all reform. Is it not to abolish all unnecessary Offices, and to curtail all unnecessary Expenses. It surely is not to put out a good & experienced officer, because he was a decent friend of J. Q. Adams, in order to put in a heated partisan of the election of Gen. Jackson, which partisan choses [sic] to dub himself on that account the friend of Reform.[9]

To be sure, Ritchie was angling to limit the damage to old-guard officials from Virginia, as Ritchie knew that Virginia did not stand to gain from whatever Jackson had in mind. Instead of a partisan basis for removals, Ritchie recommended reform based on budgetary considerations as well as the ability and integrity of the officeholders.[10]

Van Buren sent Jackson Ritchie's letter, and Jackson in turn directed Van Buren to respond. Jackson's response pointed out, fairly, that Ritchie had probably received false or exaggerated information from one of Jackson's enemies. Further, as Jackson put it, his "illustrious predecessors" (Washington and Jefferson) had appointed their own "bosom friends" to their cabinet. But Ritchie's concern pointed to a problem in defining reform. As Jackson put it, "the people expect reform," but if Jackson meant to reform a system that interfered with elections, Jackson's argument from rotation also risked undermining what Ritchie called "popular liberty" by exchanging jobs for votes. Van Buren, however, chose not to pass along Jackson's extensive explanation—at least in writing. Instead, Van Buren explained that he did not know much about examples from previous administrations and assured Ritchie that Jackson's intentions were pure.[11]

The most serious of Jackson's opponents also criticized Jackson's removal policy during the early stage. These critics included Henry Clay and Daniel Webster. Clay was among the first to give a forceful critique of Jackson's removals during the first stage. The occasion was a public dinner at Fowler's Garden, in 1829, in honor of Clay's return to Lexington, Kentucky, where, according to Clay biographer Robert Remini, Clay delivered an address to 3,000 listeners.[12] Clay might have chosen to offer a few polite remarks about his time in Washington and extend best wishes to the new administration, but instead he chose to offer a long speech declaring his opposition to Jackson. For his subject, he chose removals, which constituted well over four-fifths of the speech. Clay's primary concern was the consequences of Jackson's policy for the political system, not the constitutional merits of the question. After describing the difference between a monarchy and a republic, and the danger of a republican executive tending toward monarchy, Clay charged Jackson with subverting the purpose of the removal power:

> The President is invested with the tremendous power of dismission, to be exercised for the public good, and not to gratify any private passions or purposes. It was conferred to prevent the public from suffering through faithless or incompetent officers. It was made summary because, if the slow process of trial before a judicial tribunal were resorted to, the public might be greatly injured during the progress and prior to the decision of the case. But it never was in the contemplation of Congress, that the power would or could be applied to the removal of competent, diligent and faithful officers. Such an application of it is an act of arbitrary power, and a great abuse.[13]

Clay went on to document the ways that Jackson had departed from this principle and from prior precedents, but there are several aspects of Clay's argument that are worth emphasis. First, Clay did not even consider the argument that the power might be vested in the president by the Constitution. Rather, he assumed from the very beginning that this was a matter of legislative direction. At this point, Clay seemed unaware or unimpressed with what others considered had been settled in 1789. Clay seemed to believe that Congress had granted the power in Tenure of Office Act of 1820 and could take it away.

Second, Clay's argument presumed that the only legitimate basis for removing an officer — even under the Tenure of Office Act — was when the officer had demonstrated that he was no longer fit for the office. "Men who accepted public employments entered on them with the implied understanding that they would be retained as long as they continued to discharge their duties to the public honestly, ably, and assiduously."[14] Clay did not even seem aware at this point of the argument that Jefferson borrowed from executive power theory, namely, that the president should have the power because he is responsible to the people. In fact, Clay associated responsibility with stability and merit under the old way: "One of the worst consequences of the introduction of this tenure of public office will be, should it be permanently adopted, to substitute for a system of responsibility, founded upon the ability and integrity with which public officers discharge their duties to the community, a system of universal rapacity."[15] Clay seemed unaware of the alternative understanding of responsibility. As to Jefferson, Clay spent several paragraphs arguing that Jefferson's example did not support Jackson. In his view, Jefferson followed an administration that did not include the other side in appointments, and Jefferson was moderate in his approach to the question of parties. Neither, according to Clay, was true of Jackson:

> The object of Mr. Jefferson was to break down a pre-existing monopoly in the hands of one party, and to establish an equilibrium between the two great parties. The object of President Jackson appears to be to destroy an existing equilibrium between the two parties to the late contest, and to establish a monarchy. The object of President Jefferson was the Republic, and not himself. That of President Jackson is himself, and not the State.[16]

Clay went on to associate Jackson with Napoleon, showing how the latter had transformed the French army by requiring loyalty to Napoleon himself. For Clay, Jackson's removal policy suggested that the American war hero, too, ascribed to the dictum "I am the state."[17]

Of all the opponents to the Decision of 1789, Daniel Webster provided what is arguably the most powerful and principled critique of executive power theory, and he did so before the second stage of the Whig critique. Unlike Clay, Webster was not an enemy of Jackson in 1830. According to Michael Holt, Webster "admired Jackson's strong nationalistic position" and saw Jackson not only as a potential ally against Calhoun and Southern efforts toward nullification but also against Clay's tendency to compromise away Northern interests. In Holt's analysis, Webster "fervently prayed" for an "alliance" with Jackson as a way to spur a realignment of the parties—"nationalists versus states-righters, Jackson and Webster versus Clay and Calhoun." It was not until the bank controversy that Webster publicly burned his bridges with Jackson. Nevertheless, while others were complaining about the particular men Jackson was hiring and firing, and about the partisan thrust of Jackson's policy, Webster considered the structure and text of the Constitution as well as the practical institutional consequences.[18]

Webster first put his thoughts on removals to paper in a memorandum he composed while sitting by the fire one evening in January 1830. In his analysis, the Decision of 1789 was wrong and dangerous: "By the Constitution of the U.S. the power of appointing to office is vested in the President & Senate." Furthermore, "no power of removal, as a separate & distinct power, exists anywhere" except in impeachment. Outside impeachment, "the power of removal exists only as consequential to the power of appointment." More than constitutional error, the Decision of 1789 would have serious consequences for administration. It "tends to a dangerous enlargement of influence by the patronage of office." And Webster concluded, borrowing on Hamilton's argument for stability, that presidential control of the removal power was "dangerous" to the "permanency of the Govt."[19]

Webster did not keep his fireside reflections private. He sent the memorandum to Federal District Court Judge Joseph Hopkinson, a member of the old Federalist judicial elite.[20] Webster's argument must have been passed around the community of older Federalist judges, because a few days later he received encouragement from James Kent, author of the famous four-volume *Commentaries on American Law* (1826–1830). To Webster, Kent confessed that he had once subscribed to the view that the president has the power under the Constitution but that he had been revisiting the position. Kent went on to say that he now understood why Hamilton had taken a different position in *The Federalist* than did Madison in the Decision of 1789. In fact, he thought Hamilton had the better view: "I begin to have a strong suspicion that Hamilton was right, as he always was on public questions."[21]

Joseph Story was another member of the legal establishment who questioned the Decision of 1789. In his 1833 *Commentaries on the Constitution of the United States*, Story went far in indicating his opinion that 1789 should not be the last word on removals. Indeed, he introduced his discussion of the removal power with a constitutional argument similar to that of Daniel Webster:

> The power to nominate does not naturally, or necessarily include the power to remove; and if the power to appoint does include it, then the latter belongs conjointly to the executive and the senate. In short, under such circumstances, the removal takes place in virtue of the new appointment, by mere operation of law. It results, and is not separable, from the appointment itself.[22]

To be fair, Story followed this statement in the next section by ascribing its argument to Hamilton, noting that this was the "doctrine maintained with great earnestness by the *Federalist*," and then later presenting the argument made on behalf of executive power theory in 1789. Likewise, he concluded his discussion by saying that the reader would have to decide which side had the better understanding of the Constitution.

But Story was not exactly evenhanded in his treatment of the two sides. For example, in explaining the position in *The Federalist* No. 78, Story enhanced the argument by emphasizing the practical merits of the advice and consent position, going beyond Hamilton's explicit argument in *The Federalist*. As Story put it, executive control of removals would undermine effective administration by rewarding "fawning sycophants" over "worthier and abler men," and encourage office seekers to "delude and deceive the people" thus "corrupt[ing]" elections "at their very source."[23] Moreover, it "would convert all the officers of the country into the mere tools and creatures of the president" and thus tend toward the prerogative of monarchy. And in his summary of executive power theory, Story did not mention Madison's emphasis on democratic accountability when cataloging the arguments for executive power theory.[24] Instead, Story seemed to associate democratic accountability with the opponents of executive power. He also argued that the result might have gone the other way had Washington not been president. Finally, he made the startling claim that the pro-executive arguments would have stood in the way of ratification, had they been made public at the time. Instead, in Story's view, Hamilton's assurance in *The Federalist* that the power would be shared with the Senate was crucial to quieting Anti-Federalist fears. As to the decision in 1789 itself, he stated:

> The doctrine was opposed, as well as supported, by the highest talents and patriotism of the country. The public, however, acquiesced in this decision; and it constitutes, perhaps, the most extraordinary case in the history of the government of a power, conferred by implication on the executive by the assent of a bare majority of congress, which has not been questioned on many other occasions. Even the most jealous advocates of state rights seem to have slumbered over this vast reach of authority; and have left it untouched, as the neutral ground of controversy, in which they desired to reap no harvest, and from which they retired without leaving any protestations of title or contest.[25]

It is worth pausing to note that Justice James McReynolds will later make this very point in his dissent *Myers v. United States* (1926): "If the Constitution or its proponents had plainly avowed what is now contended for, there can be little doubt that it would have been rejected."[26]

Taken in context, it is fair to say that Story went out of his way to undermine the precedential power of the Decision of 1789 in at least two ways. First, he reiterated that the losing side had able advocates. Second, he made the case that the public acquiesced in the decision for reasons that no longer held: The reason why the public had largely acquiesced to this increase in executive power was that it had been hitherto used in moderation. Now, Jackson had called attention to it, provoking opposition by the country's most "eminent statesmen."[27]

Removals and the Bank Controversy

When Daniel Webster first made his sustained case against presidential removals, he extended his campaign beyond the legal intelligentsia and to elected politicians. But he was surprised that the issue had not yet become more widely discussed. To Henry Clay and others, Webster predicted that the issue would one day gain traction: "Were it not for fear of the out of door popularity of Genl Jackson, the Senate would have negatived more than half his nominations. There is a burning fire of discontent, that must, I think some day, break out."[28] Webster's prediction was correct. In 1830 the Senate refused to confirm Lemuel Williams as customs collector in New Bedford, Massachusetts.[29] In time the controversy surrounding the bank brought opposition to removals to the surface. Jackson's veto of the bank was one among several high-profile vetoes that irked opponents and eventually provided a path to a critique of executive power theory. As Michael Holt has shown in his definitive study of the Whig Party, the Whigs found their organizing principle in opposition to executive power. In Holt's analysis, "Only a passionate devotion to the Revolutionary experiment in republican government and a common conviction that Jackson threatened it explain how men with such diverse views on other matters formed a united front against him."[30]

This debate about executive power is often associated with the meaning of the veto. As an example, when Jackson vetoed the recharter of the bank bill, he had already issued several controversial vetoes. Jackson certainly used the veto more frequently than his predecessors (twelve times versus the nine times of the six prior presidents combined), but his opponents also charged Jackson with wrongfully expanding the scope of the veto power. According to this argument, original constitutional design intended, and early practice confirmed, that the veto power would be used only in cases where a bill clearly violated the Constitution. The Whigs were not exactly correct in these claims; rather, one can argue that both original design and early precedent leave space for presidents to issue vetoes on policy grounds.[31] But the Whigs were right to notice the changes implicit in Jackson's expansive defense of the veto power. Because that defense has connections to the debate on removals, it should be considered here.

Jackson's veto message combined policy and constitutional arguments. As to policy, Jackson argued that economic policy sometimes adds "artificial distinctions" to the inequalities in nature. "It is to be regretted that the rich and powerful too often blend the acts of government to their selfish purposes." The Bank could set economic policy, favoring stockholders over the general public. As Marc Landy and Sidney M. Milkis put it, the Bank "combined the functions of a central bank and a commercial bank" by manipulating money and making loans to individuals. "This extraordinary combination of governmentally sanctioned privilege and vast economic resources put the bank in a very powerful political position."[32] For Jackson, this powerful leverage the Bank enjoyed was all the more dangerous because, according to Jackson, a large amount of stock was held by foreigners.[33]

Jackson also argued that the bank was unconstitutional. Alone, this might have been uncontroversial. His point was simply that the power did not fall under the necessary and proper clause because the Bank was in his opinion unnecessary. That is, the policy decision informed the constitutional decision. But Jackson did not stop there, for he appealed to the doctrine of *coordinate review* (or *departmentalism*) to argue that the president can interpret the Constitution for himself. In a well-known passage, Jackson parted with *McCulloch v. Maryland* and challenged the doctrine of judicial finality:

> It is maintained by the advocates of the bank that its constitutionality in all its features ought to be considered as settled by precedent and by the decision of the Supreme Court. To this conclusion I can not assent. Mere precedent is a dangerous source of authority, and should not be regarded as deciding questions of constitutional power except where the acquiescence of the people and the States can be considered as well settled.[34]

In place of judicial finality, Jackson argued that each department "for itself be guided by its own opinion of the Constitution." Perhaps emphasizing the president's unique oath, and certainly taking liberties of interpretation, Jackson said that each member of the three departments takes an oath to interpret the Constitution "as he understands it, and not as understood by others." As a result, "The opinion of the judges has no more authority over Congress than the opinion of Congress has over the judges, and on that point the President is independent of both."[35] Jackson carried the argument from Jefferson to Lincoln, an argument that has been especially attractive to realigning presidents as well as modern unitarians.[36] But Jackson's full-throated defense of coordinate review also marked the highwater mark of the doctrine. Jefferson was the founder of this doctrine, but it was not directed at the Supreme Court, and he was persuaded by his advisers to keep it private.[37] Later, in response to the 1857 decision in *Dred Scott v. Sandford*, Lincoln repeated Jackson's warning that precedent alone was dangerous for republican self-government, but Lincoln carefully qualified his doctrine by calling it a "political rule."[38] Neither Jefferson nor Lincoln attached the doctrine to a high-profile veto. In fact, during his first term as president Jefferson considered declaring the Alien and Sedition Acts "void" but chose instead to let them expire.

For Jackson's opponents, the veto message offered proof that Jackson meant to transform separation of powers with a new understanding of executive power. Clay echoed this point, making the disputable claim that the veto was "not expected by the [Constitutional Convention] to be used in ordinary cases" but was instead "designed for instances of precipitate legislation, in unguarded moments." For Webster, Jackson's argument was unprecedented in its boldness and its intended results. Pushing aside the question of the intended use of the veto, he was correct to say that "no President and no public man" had ever stated that a president may refuse to execute a law passed by Congress and approved by the Supreme Court. "Although Congress may have passed a law, and although the Supreme Court may have pronounced it constitutional, yet it is, nevertheless, no law at all, if he, in his good pleasure, sees fit to deny it effect; in other words, to repeal and annul it."

But Clay and Webster had identified another problem, this one associated with the rise of the two-party system. With a Jacksonian veto power in hand, and a two-party system now in place, the president would have little to fear from the threat of an override. In practice, this would result in a much more expansive version of the veto power: As Webster warned, presidents would have not only the power of "approval" but also "the primary power, the power of originating laws." Jackson himself had said that he should have been consulted on the recharter of the bank.[39]

But the bank veto was not just about the veto power. As Webster later reflected, the heart of the question was always about control of the Bank. That question came to the forefront when Jackson ordered Treasury Secretary William Duane to remove the deposits from the Bank and distribute them among friendly state banks (so-called pet banks). Duane refused, and Jackson fired him and then replaced him with Roger Taney. In response, the Senate passed a motion of censure, and the president responded with a formal protest.

Jackson's removal of Duane was the subject of months of debate, filling hundreds of pages in *Register of Debates*. The question of the removal power was central to the controversy, as Clay's proposal (outlined below) makes clear. But it was intertwined with other questions. Among those were the constitutionality of the Bank, the status of Treasury as an "executive" department, the scope of the impeachment power and the Senate's role in it, and the appropriateness of a resolution of censure. These questions were mingled with the question of control. Jackson believed that the president should able to control the Treasury, which meant that he could remove and relocate the deposits. Jackson's opponents believed otherwise.

On December 18, 1833, Clay proposed a resolution requiring the secretary of the Treasury to provide the Senate with materials related to transfer of deposits.[40] The next day, Clay explained that his motive was to counter the report by the Treasury secretary, which claimed that the Treasury secretary possessed the "exclusive power" concerning whether the deposits would be removed. As Clay saw it, this claim to exclusivity constituted a direct threat to congressional power.

Here is the assumption of a power analogous to the old exploded doctrine of the general welfare, in a most odious form. According to that doctrine, it was claimed by certain federalists of 1798–99 that the constitution vested in Congress power to legislate on all subjects for the general welfare. But, according to the new version of the heresy, a Secretary of the Treasury, a subordinate officer of the Government, the creature of Congress, arrogates to himself a power to administer the duties of his office, and to regulate the currency of the country, in conformity with his sense of the general interest and convenience of the people! And, at the very moment of setting up his enormous pretension, then denies any such power to Congress![41]

Given Clay's longstanding interest in internal improvements by way of the broad readings of the Constitution's general welfare and necessary and proper clauses, Clay's attempt to associate the removal of the deposits with an "exploded" doctrine seems disingenuous at best. But this was not the heart of Clay's argument. As he went on to explain, the real problem was that "this modern doctrine assumes for the Secretary not only a power equivalent to its ancient prototype, but it demands that it be respected as absolute and unconditional, and exclusive even of Congress."[42] The real problem, then, was that the doctrine embraced by Jackson and the Treasury secretary would narrow congressional power.

It is worth pausing to note that Supreme Court Justice Joseph Story agreed with this point. Like Clay, Story worried that Jackson's actions would undermine the authority of Congress. He recorded his concerns in a letter to Webster, written only a few days after Clay's proposal; given Webster's role in the debates, Story surely expected his letter to influence the outcome. According to Story, any authority the Treasury secretary has must derive from specific law. In this case, Section 16 of the Bank's charter required that the secretary give reasons to Congress before removing any deposits, but it also gave the broader discretion to the Treasury Secretary, *not the president*:

The only check upon his discretion is, that he must assign the reasons to Congress, who, of course, are thus placed in a situation to revise or review the decision if they please. But I think, (and in this I differ toto coelo from Mr. Taney) that it is a purely personal trust in the Secretary, and as much so, as if it had been confided to the Chief Justice of the United States. The power grows not out of any general authority, given by other laws, but it is, as between these parties, for this purpose, a special umpirage created by the Act, and binding as a part of contract. . . . I think, then, that the President has not the slightest right to interfere with the business. It is taken out of the sphere of Executive action. It belongs to the Secretary and to him alone, and any interference by the President to control or influence his judgment, much more to deter him from exercising his judgment, is, on the part of the President, a departure from his duty, and if the Secretary acts upon the opinion of the President, and not upon his own, I think he virtually violates the charter and abandons his trust.[43]

It is important to note how far Story's logic extends. Long before the debate over the impeachment of Andrew Johnson, Story argued that Congress may vest authority in the Treasury secretary beyond the supervision of the president. More broadly, it shows that Jackson's assertion of presidential control of removals and the Whig critique of Jackson had put Article I and Article II on a collision course. From the perspective of the Whigs, the main concern was that Jackson's broad reading of Article II's vesting clause would get in the way of Congress's use of its implied powers. If supervision of an executive officer necessarily falls under the vesting clause, then Congress would necessarily lose its rightful authority to delegate discretion to executive officers and then shield that discretion from the president.

Another key part of the debate concerned Jackson's defense of his bank veto. Jackson expanded the question beyond the scope of the veto by offering a theory of presidential representation. In a message delivered to his cabinet, Jackson explained that his reelection confirmed his veto of the bank. After pointing out the comprehensive nature of his bank veto, Jackson summarized what he saw to be the crux of the question: "On the ground the case was argued to the people; and now that the people have sustained the President, notwithstanding the array of influence and power which was brought to bear upon him, it is too late, he confidently thinks, to say that the question has not been decided. Whatever may be the opinion of others, the President considers his reelection as a decision of the people against the bank."[44] Jackson's argument made it into the public sphere, and Whigs considered this as a transformation of the presidency and a threat to separation of powers. Clay disputed the entire idea:

> I am surprised and alarmed at the new source of executive power which is found in the result of a presidential election. I had supposed that the constitution and the laws were the sole source of executive authority; that the constitution could only be amended in the mode which it has itself prescribed; that the issue of a presidential election was merely to place the Chief Magistrate in the post assigned to him; and that he had neither more nor less power, in consequence of the election, than the constitution defines and delegates. But it seems that if, prior to an election, certain opinions, no matter how ambiguously put forth by a candidate, are known to the people, those loose opinions, in virtue of the election, incorporate themselves with the

constitution, and afterwards are to be regarded and expounded as parts of the instrument![45]

Clay's concern was repeated and expanded by Senator Peleg Sprague of Maine. After listing the controversial expansions of executive authority claimed by Jackson, Sprague cut to what he saw as the most foundational principle of Jackson's argument. "We are told, and it is constantly reiterated in our ears, that in all these assumptions and claims of prerogative, the President is sustained by the people." As Sprague put it, this view misunderstood the premise of constitutionalism by replacing the rule of law with the rule of men:

> The people are the fountain of all power; they are politically omnipotent. They can make and unmake constitutions at pleasure. But they cannot have moral incompatibilities. Omnipotent as they are, they cannot have an elective monarchy and a constitutional republic at the same time. Let it be distinctly understood, that these two tremendous powers, the Executive and the People, cannot meet, and in their coming together, crush the legislature, the judiciary, and the Senate between them and still have a constitutional republic.[46]

Not only did Jackson misunderstand the doctrine of constitutionalism; he also misunderstood the people themselves. As Sprague put it, the people are not "infallible"; in fact, human history reveals that men have a "proneness to idolatry": "It is the nature of man to worship the work of his own hands, to bow down to idols which they have set up."[47]

These big questions about the sources of executive power were inextricably linked to the question of removals. On March 7, 1834, Clay attempted to clarify the debate by proposing four resolutions aimed at restricting presidential removal powers. Those resolutions are provided in Table 3.1 (below), but several features in Clay's introduction of the resolutions are worth mentioning here. He noted that the question had been deliberated in the First Congress, but for him the important point was that no Congress had yet "directly and deliberately" revisited the Decision of 1789.[48] Moreover, the Decision of 1789 was complicated and tenuous, but Jackson and his supporters had elevated it into a "doctrine," maintaining "that all persons employed in the Executive Department of the Government, throughout all its ramifications, were bound to conform to the will of the President, no matter how contrary to their own judgment that will may be." For Clay, this doctrine resulted in a new standing army of 40,000 executive officials, all ready to obey Jackson's command, and, as a consequence, undermined the "stability" of the government.[49] Like critics before him, Clay wanted a removal policy that would connect official duty with

Table 3.1. Clay's Resolutions on March 7, 1834

1. That the constitution of the United States does not vest in the President power to remove at his pleasure officers under the Government of the United States, whose offices have been established by law.

2. That, in all cases of offices created by law, the tenure of holding which is not prescribed by the Constitution, Congress is authorized by the Constitution to prescribe the tenure, terms, and condition on which they are to be holden.

3. That the Committee on the Judiciary be instructed to inquire into the expediency of providing by law that in all instances of appointment to office by the President, by and with the advice and consent of the Senate, other than diplomatic appointments, the power of removal shall be exercised only in concurrence with the Senate, and, when the Senate is not in session, that the President may suspend any such officer, communicating his reasons for the suspension to the Senate at its first succeeding session; and, if the Senate concur with him, the officer shall be removed, but if it do not concur with him, the officer shall be restored to office.

4. That the Committee on the Post Office and Post Roads be instructed to inquire into the expediency of making provision by law for the appointment, by and with the advice and consent of the Senate, of all deputy postmasters, whose annual emoluments exceed a prescribed amount.

Source: *Register of Debates*, Senate, 23rd Congress, 1st Session, March 7, 1834, 836.

the "ability, integrity, and fidelity" of the officeholder. His resolutions, then, were essential for the "purity and duration of the Government."[50]

In response, Jackson's defenders made the case that unity in the executive required that no executive officer be "independent" of the president. Like Madison and his allies in 1789, they looked to the argument from responsibility to the people, but also like modern-day unitarians, they looked to Hamilton's *The Federalist* No. 70 to make the case for presidential control of the Treasury. Democratic Senator from New York Nathaniel Tallmadge's criticism of Clay's resolution is one important example:

> Such energy and responsibility then, so essential to good government, are virtually destroyed whenever the unity of the Executive is interfered with or impaired. That may be done by conferring on any officer in either of the departments, a power, executive in its nature, to be exercised independent of the Chief Executive himself. Such an independence on the part of such officers, is destructive of the very principle on which the Executive department was founded. The intentions of the framers of the constitution are thereby defeated, and the benefits which were anticipated from the unity of the Executive are entirely lost.[51]

This debate culminated in the Senate's censure of Jackson on March 28, 1834, by a vote of 26 to 20. According to the text of the resolution, Jackson had "assumed upon himself authority and power not conferred by the constitution and laws, but in derogation of both."[52] As Michael Holt has argued, this result confirmed that for some senators the question of executive removals was about executive power and not only about bank policy: In 1832, only three of sixteen non–border state Southern senators voted to override Jackson's bank veto, yet in 1834 nine voted to censure Jackson.[53]

Jackson's Response

In April, Jackson responded to the censure with a formal protest, drafted in part by Roger Taney and Attorney General Benjamin F. Butler.[54] Although it was not delivered in person, the protest message marked a critical moment in the development of the presidency. Jackson was then, and is now, the only president to have been formally censured by the Senate. More than marking an important moment, his protest message stated in clear language the transformation that had been under way since 1800 and demonstrated the centrality of the removal power question to that transformation: "The President is the direct representative of the American people, but the Secretaries are not. If the Secretary of the Treasury be independent of the President in the execution of the laws, then is there no direct responsibility to the people in that important branch of this Government to which is committed the care of the national finances."[55]

It is important to notice that even as Jackson completed the logic of the first realignment, he changed it. In addition to responsibility, Jackson argued from expansive readings of the Constitution. Like the older Federalist defenders of George Washington, Jackson found a vast reservoir of authority in the vesting clause and the oath of office. Like the New Unitarians of today, Jackson wanted to have a strong executive, grounded in both of the older arguments about executive power — the argument from law and the argument from opinion. On top of all that, he added his own twist: the argument that there should be rotation in office.

Jackson's protest message only exacerbated Webster's worries about the expansion of executive power. As Webster put it in a speech responding to Jackson's protest message, the problem was that Jackson was undermining Congress's power to make laws. The logic of the protest was that Congress could not vest the powers of control over "public treasures" outside the president. This control flowed from the supposed power to remove. From Webster's perspective, this bold claim grew out of a bolder one, namely, that the president is the "peculiar protector of public liberty" by virtue of the president's oath of office. More than bold, the claim was also difficult in that it rested on a distinction between the wording regarding oaths: The President must "defend" the Constitution, but Congress swears to "support" the Constitution.[56]

For Webster, this claim was an argument for tyranny, because he may remove not for incompetence or mismanagement but merely because he is responsible. Webster noted that Jackson commonly called "the Secretaries" in office "his Secretaries." As Webster explained, the president defended this need to control the secretaries under the principle of responsibility. And this meant responsibility "to public opinion." For Webster, the logic of the argument for responsibility is that there is but "there is but ONE RESPONSIBILITY, ONE DISCRETION, ONE WILL!" (which is not far from Napoleon's claim: "I am the state"). For Webster, then, the real danger with Jackson's argument was that it multiplied executive power by the numerous expansive readings on which it drew. Jackson relied on an implicit argument from British history to define the meaning of "the executive power." It assumed, therefore, that the president had had the power "anterior" to the Constitution. At the same time, Jackson had added to the executive power two claims. First, the president's oath of office required that he interpret the vesting clause broadly. Second, the president claimed that the president was the sole representative of the people. As Webster put it, the problem with the people is that they had been corrupted by Jackson's one innovation of "rotation in office." Attracted by the prospect of office, and unwilling to see administration as a source of stability, the people had forsaken independent judgment and "throng and rush together on the altar of manworship."[57]

Senate Debate on the 1820 Law

On 9 February 1835, the Senate returned to the removal question when John Calhoun read the report of the Select Committee on Executive Patronage.[58] This was attached to other proposals regarding the deposits, and it returned the Senate to a full-blown debate on the sources of executive power. But the attempt to limit the president's removal power had now taken a more modest appearance. Specifically, the report recommended repeal of the first and second sections of the 1820 Tenure of Office Act, that is, those sections specifying the four-year term and the proviso at service by pleasure for many executive officials. Calhoun pointed out that this was "not the first time" for such as recommendation; eight years previously, the Democratic Party out of power then (but in power now) had made such a recommendation.[59] The reform of the 1820 law would provide a way for the critics of Jackson to dismantle Jackson's patronage system without having to win on the Bank question. As Clay was quick to point out, the

law would not take away the president's power to remove. All it would require is that the president state the reasons for removal.

Yet Clay left little doubt that he intended to thoroughly undo the Decision of 1789. Clay began his case for the law by trying to disentangle the
removal question from other political controversies. Given that the present
debate was about reforming the 1820 law, it had arisen without the "col-
lateral" questions. In the previous session, there was the removal of the
deposits and Jackson's protest against the Senate resolution. "The bank
mingled itself in all our discussions," but now that question had been settled in Jackson's favor. Somewhat optimistically, Clay claimed, "We can
now deliberately contemplate the vast expansion of executive power, under the present administration, free from embarrassment."[60]

For Clay, the source of the patronage problem was the confusion over
the power of "dismission." Under Jackson's use, the power rendered null the
Senate's share of the appointment power. The president was able to remove
in secret, and without providing reasons for removal the officer has no chance
to defend himself. Clay thus turned the argument of responsibility against
Jackson: "It is adverse to the genius of all free government, the foundation
of which is responsibility. Responsibility is the vital principle of civil liberty,
as irresponsibility is the vital principle of despotism. Free government can no
more exist without this principle than animal life can be sustained without the
presence of the atmosphere." Rather than making officers responsible to the
public, presidential control of removals would tend to undermine the judgment of the officeholder, who would have the incentive to embrace outright
partisanship. Pointing to the Post Office, where postal officials had been taking the lead in town-hall meetings to give the administration's view, Clay
predicted that the Army and Navy would also be made partisan.[61]

More than a problem of patronage, Jackson's defense of removals fit
within a larger effort to concentrate power in the president. In Clay's estimation, the loose collection of various attempts to change policy by way
of the executive branch fit together in a larger logic. For example, Clay
pointed out the connection between presidential control of removals and
presidential resistance to judicial review: "It has not, indeed, in terms, been
claimed, but it is as legitimate consequence from the doctrines asserted,
that all decisions of the judicial tribunals, not conformable with the President's opinion, must be inoperative, since the officers charged with their
execution are no more exempt from the pretended obligation to obey his
orders than any other officers of administration."[62]

Likewise, Clay went on to object to Jackson's use of Article II's oath
of office:

> Now, if the President, in virtue of his oath, may interpose and pre-
> vent any thing from being done contrary to the constitution as he

understands it; and may, in virtue of the injunction to take care the laws be faithfully executed, prevent the enforcement of any law contrary to the sense in which he understands it, I would ask what powers remain to any other branch of the Government? Are they not all substantially absorbed in the will of one man?[63]

This turn is important in that it shows how Clay sought to saddle the case for a strong executive with the case for nullification. In Clay's estimation, both Jackson and Calhoun had used a caricatured reading of one part of the Constitution to change the character of the Constitution. For Clay, the oath could not be a source of authority: "The President's oath obliges him to do no more than every member of Congress is also bound by official oath to do." Finally, Clay noted that the Constitution had already been changed by political development in a way that benefited executive power. Specifically, impeachment was now off the table. Clay did not elaborate whether the cause of this development was the rise of two parties, or whether it was the result of precedents such as the 1805 acquittal of Supreme Court Justice Samuel Chase, when Chase was impeached by Jeffersonians for making partisan statements from the bench. Neither could he anticipate that the next generation of critics of presidential removal powers would look to impeachment as a remedy. But he did see the irony in the fact that the argument from responsibility was now being offered in a context in which the president was less responsible: "Is not the President absolutely irresponsible in the exercise of this power? How can he be reached? By impeachment? It is a mockery."[64]

If, for Clay, the president lacked the power, then where did power reside? Like later opponents of executive power, Clay eliminated the argument from the vesting clause. According to Clay, the vesting clause does not vest power; rather it only tells who has the powers later enumerated in the article. Clay pointed to the impeachment power to argue that the Constitution presumed Senate participation in removals. Clay made this move by distinguishing the "mere act" of removal, which is executive, from the necessary judgment beforehand, which is judicial. The Senate came into play because impeachment is the only constitutional mention of removal, and that power was given to the Senate acting in its judicial capacity.[65]

Clay moved on, however, to the argument for legislative discretion and then expanded it. As we noted earlier (see Chapter 1: "The Decision of 1789"), Madison included congressional delegation in his summary of the four positions. But the argument for congressional delegation was complicated by the question of whether Congress could and should vest the power in the president, and, at least from the records we have of the debates, the argument for congressional delegation remained underdeveloped. Looking beyond those debates, perhaps, Clay provided the missing logic. As he put it, "We must look for it to a broader and higher source — the legislative department." Anticipating the dissenters in *Myers*, and expanding on an argument made by Sedgwick in the First Congress, Clay pointed to the simple fact that Congress has the power to create and destroy offices. "The office, coming into existence by the will of Congress, the same will may provide how, and in what manner, the office and the officer shall both cease to exist." On top of this narrow argument, Clay went on to use the necessary and proper clause to make a much grander claim on behalf of Congress. More than confirming the existence of implied powers in the national government, the clause revealed that "Congress is the sole depository of implied powers, and that no other department or officer of the Government possesses any." Because the necessary and proper clause made Congress supreme with respect to implied powers, Jackson's argument represented a broad attack on legislative power: Like Calhoun and the nullifiers, Jackson wanted to stand in the way of Congress's power to make the laws.[66]

In his closing argument, Clay attempted to undercut the precedential value of the Decision of 1789. In one deft move, Clay pointed to claims based on 1789 as evidence for the weakness of the argument. As there is no plausible constitutional argument for the presidential side (at least according to Clay), defenders of the presidential position had to appeal to precedent. And yet this was a very close vote: It was difficult to tell what the final vote was about, it included a powerful minority, and its outcome was likely shaped by the influence of George Washington. Moreover, Madison and his fellow executive power partisans in 1789 could not predict American political development: The demise of impeachment and the rise of parties had radically changed the implications of executive power theory. Given all these mitigating factors, why would this "solitary precedent" be more legitimate than other precedents, such as a protective tariff and the Bank, going back to 1789? More than that, Clay used a simple counterfactual to argue that the side that narrowly won the Decision of 1789 was simply wrong on the merits. Clay asked, if the Constitution had been silent altogether on appointments, would the president have the power to appoint? Staunch defenders of the presidential position would have to say that the president would indeed have the power to appoint, but they would have to rely on an overly muscular reading of the meaning of "the executive power." For Clay, it would be make more sense to say that if the Constitution were silent on appointments then Congress would then have to delegate the power to appoint by law. To make the point as clearly as possible, Clay said, "No one can carefully examine the debate in the House of Representatives in 1789, without being struck by the superiority of the argument on the side of the minority."[67]

On the other side, defenders of the presidential position responded with the argument from responsibility. Democratic Senator Silas Wright of New York, for example, disputed the idea that Jackson was creating an "army" of 100,000 officials. More than a numerical challenge, Wright argued that the exaggeration was best understood as an attack on normal people, which itself grew out of a reluctance to accept the Jacksonian premise that there was such a thing as a "popular will" and that the president was "elected by the people." For Wright, this was an attack on democracy itself: "How, then, does this assumption comport with the respect we owe to the popular will? To the judgment and intelligence of those we represent here?" In this sense, Jackson was no monarch and no revolutionary. In Wright's analysis, then, the 1820 law "was calculated to secure the cardinal principle of rotation in office." The proposed change, conversely, would undermine democratic government by giving officials tenure in office for life. Moreover, the proposed change would apply to inferior and noninferior officers and thereby undermine the vesting clause in Article II.[68]

An important advocate of the proposed change was Senator Hugh Lawson White of Tennessee. White was a Democrat but would eventually join the Whigs. He was originally a supporter of Jackson and had served on the Senate committee that considered the bill in 1826. According to White, the committee in 1826 had noted that the problem was that partisanship had resulted in unintended consequences of the 1820 law. Specifically, the goal of the 1820 law was to get rid of officials from the buildup in the War of 1812. In practice, the president would ask the department whether the officer had been dutiful. If so, the president would renominate him. But the committee in 1826 noticed that partisanship had changed the original question. In response to Wright's argument that the reform was grounded on antipathy to normal people, White said it was no insult to recognize that these officers are but men. That is, for White, most men would give up political independence in exchange for job security for themselves or their family members. This point was precisely the concern of the committee in 1826.[69] Like the Whigs, White disagreed with Jackson's argument from the vesting clause. In an important twist, White tried to show that Jacksonians should demur from executive power theory and instead embrace the argument for congressional delegation. Because all the officers treated by the bill were "inferior" offices, the tenure of each was subject to legislative direction:

> Ours is emphatically a Government of laws. We are a free people because it is so. Whenever the will of the people is expressed, either in the constitution or in a law passed in pursuance thereof, it must be complied with, because, according to the theory of our Government, the people are sovereign. No person doubts, or can doubt, the power of the President to remove in these cases; but the manner in which he acquires his power is a different question. Gentlemen who argue

against this section say he has it from the constitution, because it is an executive power. I deny this, and say it is an executive power because it is made so by statute; and he performs a constitutional duty when he removes, because he is as much bound by statute as he is to perform those specified in the constitution. It is an executive power, because it was the will of the people, through Congress, as their agent, to make it so; and the same power, through the same agent, could have made it a judicial duty, if it had been deemed wise to provide.[70]

White's argument is important because it shows how a one-time fellow partisan could be more interested in protecting Congress's powers than in supporting the president. In this, it anticipated the institutional showdown between Republicans and Andrew Johnson. More fundamentally, it also clearly revealed an alternative path for the argument from responsibility. Under White's view, responsibility and legislative flexibility were compatible and a desirable alternative to the corrupting influence of presidential control over patronage. Congressional control was the better match for democratic accountability.

But it was Daniel Webster who offered the most systematic rejection of Jackson's argument for presidential control of removals. As Holt has shown, Webster finally broke with Jackson during the controversy over the Bank. Specifically, Webster no longer saw Jackson as a tenable ally against Calhoun and the nullifiers. As with the other leading politicians of the day, the bank veto and the removal of Treasury Secretary Duane forced Webster to rethink the foundations of presidential power. But Webster had already began thinking about the questions involved, and he went further than the others. In the context of Senate debate about reforming the 1820 law to require the president to add reasons for a removal, Webster frequently returned to his constitutional analysis of a few years earlier.

He claimed that he did not wish to reduce the "constitutional and legal" part of the president's power. Rather, he was concerned with the increasing influence of the executive. This increasing influence amounted to a growing crisis: It constituted a serious threat to republican theory, because republican theory presupposes an electorate capable and willing to be independent. The underlying problem was that the officers are supposed to work for the good of all, yet the Jacksonian concept of office carried with it the incentive of self-interest: "Men in office have begun to think themselves mere agents and servants of the appointing power, and not agents of the government or the country." Because patronage had changed parties, and because parties with patronage would corrupt the electorate, some new check was necessary in order to protect the "stability of the government." The alternative was responsibility run amok: All forsake independent judgment and instead depend on one man for rule. In this sense, Webster was concerned that presidential controls of removals would contribute to the wrong kind of responsibility.[71]

To be sure, Webster tried to accommodate the proposed reform with existing precedent, and this required him to make peace with the Decision of 1789. He said that the new law would fix the unintended consequences of the Tenure Act of 1820. Under the 1820 law, the president had the benefit of patronage without having to undertake removals. This worked against even the principle of responsibility because it released presidents from being accountable. Before 1820, presidents had to be cautious about removals. Webster went on to say that even though he disagreed with the Decision of 1789, it had been settled by practice.

Scholars and jurists have been wrong to stop there, emphasizing Webster's willingness to acknowledge the power of precedent. In fact, Webster continued with a two-pronged attack on the Decision of 1789. First, he argued that "nothing in this bill" would "disturb that decision" (1789) and that the 1820 law was consistent with the 1789 result. But if Madison was right that the 1820 law was a step away from the logic of 1789, the requirement that the president report the reasons for removal to the Senate was even more clearly a step away from executive power theory and toward Senate participation in the removal power. The second prong of Webster's attack on 1789 was a constitutional analysis of the vesting clause. Like Clay, and anticipating twentieth-century critics of executive power, Webster denied that the vesting clause was a specific grant of power. Rather, when read properly, all of Article II provides the description of executive power. That is, like Alexander White in 1789, Webster believed that Article II should be read like Article I or, as Webster put it, "the executive power herein granted shall be vested in a President of the United States."[72] With respect to removals, then, there is no executive power of removal. Rather, *the power to remove is part of the power to appoint.* For Webster, this point is easily confirmed by the Constitution's treatment of the appointment power. Had the Constitution given the president the sole power of appointment, then everyone would agree that the president had the power to remove.[73] Given that the appointment power is shared, the "most plausible" argument for the Decision of 1789 is that executive power includes removal power, and exceptions to this general rule are to be taken strictly. The problem, however, is that this explanation needs to show why removals stay with the executive even when appointments do not. Like advocates of advise and consent, Webster concluded that it would be more sensible to say that appointing is shared and therefore removing must be shared.

Combined, these two prongs demonstrate that Webster did not intend to bind himself to the precedent of 1789. If anything, they push Webster close to what we call the advise and consent position. But following Clay, Webster went on to embrace congressional delegation, which relied on legislative flexibility and even legislative supremacy. As he put it, even if Congress in 1789 was correct to give the power to remove to the president as a matter of legislative discretion, Congress still retained the power to change it. Specifically, Congress would be well within its authority to change the tenure of the U.S. Attorney General to good behavior. This implies that the presidential position incorrectly limited the legislative direction. "While the power of nomination and appointment is left fairly where constitution has placed it, I think the whole field of regulation is open to legislative direction." Webster grounded his argument on a principle that clarified the question to a simple principle: The legislature simply decides the tenure of the officer.[74] More than that, Webster's call for stability had in mind an apolitical class of appointees. For example, he argued that the Post Office should be more like the Army or Navy. Rather than seeing their offices as a perquisite of power, postal officials should rather regard their offices as being connected to the national good.

Webster's critique provoked a response from Charles Francis Adams, son of John Quincy Adams. In 1835, Charles Francis published a 52-page defense of executive power theory in the pamphlet *An Appeal from the New to the Old Whigs*. He went back to the old Whig writers to argue that Webster's understanding of executive power and removals would transform the traditional meaning of separation of powers. As he put it, "The Senate is claiming for itself an undue share of power. It is endeavoring to reduce the President to a state of dependence upon it for his officers, which will, in the end, subvert the whole principle of balance of the three powers, so studiously introduced into the Constitution by its framers." Adams went on to rebuke Webster for joining with Calhoun, "standing as that gentleman already does on the outer border of the Constitution." To prove his own security as remaining inside the Constitution, Adams provided what is perhaps the first extended analysis of the Decision of 1789, showing how the House majority eventually came to side with the argument that the Constitution vests removal power in the president. Webster had provoked the son of the man who lost the presidency to Jackson to take up his pen to defend presidential power.[75]

Madison on Jackson

The new debate over removals also caught the eye of the winner of the first debate in 1789. Madison lived longer than any other signator of the Constitution. He was, as Drew McCoy puts it in his study of Madison's late career, the "last of the fathers."[76] Because he lived through Jackson's presidency, Madison had the unique experience of designing the government and then living through two reconstructions. McCoy reveals how Madison navigated the complex politics of the 1830s. On one side, Calhoun's argument for the concurrent majority explicitly appealed to the compact theory—the idea that the states are the parties to the contract laid out in the Constitution—underlying James Madison's and Thomas Jefferson's 1798 Virginia and Kentucky Resolutions even as it twisted that theory to suit Calhoun's more radical argument for nullification. On another side, Webster's response to Calhounite articulations of the compact theory came too close to Hamilton's argument from sovereignty. On yet another side, Jackson's democratic nationalism seemed to rest on the personality of Jackson himself and thus threatened to replace the Constitution of 1787 with the classic politics of demagoguery. Thus, for Madison, the Jacksonian realignment was more than a contest between two parties, or between an insurgent party and a party intent on conserving the old ways. It was instead a swirling contest among participants who changed not only the meaning of the Constitution of 1789 but also Jefferson's Revolution of 1800.

Madison was no fan of Jackson, and he was no supporter of the spoils system. But Madison did not associate Jackson with spoils. In response to Madison protégé Edward Cole's request for Madison's reflections on various controversies, including spoils, Madison explained that he was against spoils but had yet to see such a principle asserted by Jackson: "I have not seen any avowal of such a principle by the President, and suspect that few if any his friends would openly avow it." Interestingly, and in what seemed to be a critique of Clay, he added that the person who first "openly proclaimed" the principle was now "the most vehement" critic of the practice. Moreover, Madison seemed to understate the danger of spoils: If the principle and the practice were embraced, then presidential administration would be completely degraded, but the "odium" inevitably attached to it would serve as a "security" against its permanent embrace.[77]

But the controversy surrounding Jackson nevertheless caused Madison to revisit his understanding of the removal power. In letters written in 1834, Madison grouped the Whig position on removals with several dangerous "innovations" proposed by the Senate. Madison speculated on what would happen if the "controversy" on removals would "end in the establishment of a share in the power, as claimed in the Senate." Madison examined the consequences of either the advise and consent position or congressional delegation emerging victorious and found that either would "disturb the operation of checks & balances as now understood to exist." If the Senate were given a share of the power by the Constitution, it would enable the Senate "to force on the Executive Department a continuance in office, even of the Cabinet officers, notwithstanding a change from a personal & political harmony with the President, to a state of open hostility towards him." Similarly, if the Senate's participation depended on legislative discretion, cabinet officers might remain beyond the reach of the Senate, but the "new relation between the Senate directly, and the Legislature indirectly, with the Chief Magistrate, would be felt deeply in the general administration of the Government. The innovation, however modified, would more than double the danger of throwing the Executive machinery out of gear, and thus arresting the march of Govt altogether." The problem was that the Tenure of Office Act of 1820 established the principle of Senate participation in removals. If Congress could require that offices be vacated after four years, it could do the same for "3, 2, or 1" years. By shortening the tenure a year or two, Congress would in practice create a de facto system of "tenure at the pleasure of the Senate."[78] Madison repeated this concern a year and a half later, after receiving Charles Francis Adams's pamphlet criticizing the proposal to give the Senate a share of the removal power. On the merits, and if the large states were to agree with giving the Senate the power, a Senate "veto" on removals would be "worse than inconvenient in its operations, and in party times might, by throwing the Executive machinery out of gear, produce a calamitous interregnum." Madison acknowledged, however, that the "unforeseen multiplication of offices" had placed new "weight to the executive scale," adding that he supported an amendment to the Constitution to "guard against" disturbing the "equilibrium of government," provided that there would ever be a "lucid interval of party excitement."[79]

Madison's reference to times of party provides subtle evidence that Madison had changed his position in response to the new developments. To be sure, Madison still insisted that presidential control over removals was "fixed" by the Constitution and not subject to legislative direction—a point he goes out of his way to emphasize. Madison also retained his distrust of the Senate, calling it a "party" for small-state interests. But there were two subtle developments in his position. The first and most notable change is that Madison did not include the argument from responsibility. Rather, Madison used the gear-in-a machine metaphor to emphasize the efficiency of presidential control of the executive branch. Perhaps Jackson's transformation of the argument from responsibility gave Madison pause about the implications of that part of his argument. Second, Madison more directly confronted the congressional delegation argument for legislative flexibility. Specifically, Madison argued that the removal power, along with the appointing power, was like the "right of suffrage" and "the rule of apportioning representation": All were "fundamentals in a free Government; and ought to be fixed by the Constitution." If these fundamentals were subject to change by the legislative branch, then the Constitution itself would be a mere "creature" of the legislature. Madison alluded to political development and the doctrine of implied powers to support this broader point in his 1834 letter to Patton: "The Legislative power is of an elastic & Protean character, but too imperfectly susceptible of definitions & landmarks."[80]

The Tenure of Office Act and the Impeachment of Andrew Johnson

The Whig effort to change the removal power failed, but it was picked up and made more successful by Republican opponents of President Andrew Johnson. In 1867, Congress passed the Tenure of Office Act over Johnson's veto, going further than Clay and Webster could have hoped. Following Clay's 1834 proposal, it limited the president's power to remove officials during a recess of the Senate by requiring the president to submit the reasons for the removal and seek the consent of the Senate once the Senate returned. But it applied the principle of Senate consent to removals generally. Specifically, it provided that every officer appointed by the president and confirmed by the Senate would hold office until a successor was appointed by the president "by and with the advice and consent of the Senate."[81]

To be sure, we must be careful not to understate the political context of the Tenure of Office Act of 1867. Republicans passed that law primarily in order to impeach Andrew Johnson. Republicans wanted Johnson impeached and removed because he stood in the way of their plans for Reconstruction. In the House, Republicans had already failed in one attempt to impeach Johnson, because enough of them rejected the House Judiciary Committee's "Majority Report," which argued for a broad understanding of the impeachment power. Specifically, that report concluded that the president need not have committed a specific crime in order to be impeached and removed.[82] Instead, the report argued that Johnson had used executive power to undermine congressional prerogatives. That argument could not support a majority and lost by a vote of 57 to 106. Here a critical number of representatives accepted the argument, made by Johnson himself and accepted by several Republican senators in the later impeachment trial, that the Constitution required a law to be broken. In this, they employed the legal understanding of impeachment to cover what was really a political debate about policy.[83] To be sure, there were other considerations: One of Johnson's arguments was that he did comply with the 1867 Tenure of Office Act. According to this argument, the law specifically exempted officers appointed by Lincoln. Thus, Johnson could argue, "I have endeavored to proceed with the greatest circumspection, and have acted only in an extreme and exceptional case, carefully following the course which I have marked out for myself as a general rule, faithfully to execute all laws, though passed over my objections on the score of constitutionality." In this, Johnson was clearly keeping with his strategy to argue that he had consistently acted within the letter of the law.[84] Another complicating factor was Johnson's defense that he violated the Tenure Act only in order to get the federal courts to resolve the question, a defense that persuaded several Senators.[85] It is tempting, then, to conclude that the Tenure of Office Act was the means and removing Johnson was the end.

But it is also important that Johnson was effective in his obstruction, and the removal power was one of his tools. According to historian Michael Les Benedict, "The effect of these removals cannot be judged by their number alone. Johnson never intended to replace every federal officeholder; he meant to force them to endorse his policy of Reconstruction. As they saw their colleagues fall, they began grudgingly to do so."[86] As a result, "most Republicans believed that impeachment was necessary for the future success of the Republican party and therefore for the security of southern black and white loyalists."[87] It was necessary, in part, because "Johnson had removed every military commander in the South who was committed to carrying out the spirit of the Reconstruction Acts." The Tenure of Office Act, accordingly, allowed executive officials to "so speak out for their principles once more."[88]

Even if the question of removals were derivative of the effort to impeach Johnson, it is nonetheless true that Johnson sparked a crisis that was in part a crisis about executive power within separation of powers. Long before scholars spoke of a "modern" presidency, not to mention a "unilateral" presidency, Johnson found a vast reservoir of authority in Article II. As his opponents were quick to notice, he used "imperial proclamations" to extend amnesty to former Confederates and quadrupled Jackson's veto rate (twenty-nine in four years). His removals were no different. By controlling who ran the military and who held executive office, Johnson could obstruct Republicans' Reconstruction policy. According to one recent account, "Over a six-month period, Johnson had supplanted the commanders for four of the five military districts in the South."[89] Johnson's attempted removal of Secretary of War Edwin Stanton, as political as it was, was part and parcel of a larger debate about executive power—a debate that typically comes to the forefront during contests over control of public policy.

It would be a mistake, then, to reduce the debate over the 1867 Tenure of Office Act to Reconstruction. Rather, it is necessary to pause and note the larger development in the arguments concerning executive power. As Keith Whittington has shown in his study of constitutional construction, Johnson's use of removals had "sharpened executive patronage into a tangible threat to congressional power."[90] Specifically, Johnson removed and appointed without regard to party affiliation, thus undermining Republican patronage practices and enhancing his own resources for authority. This threatened Republicans not only because Johnson wanted to be the unitary head of the executive branch but because he combined "administrative responsibility" with "political influence."[91] According to Whittington, "The critical question for the Republicans was not whether the president was to have full authority over the executive branch, but whether the executive was to become a non-partisan administrative device. In either case, neither the removal power nor the executive power was to be allowed to become a political instrument for the consolidation of presidential power."[92]

But the argument with respect to removals had become more complicated in the time since 1789. As we have seen, the emergence of a party system and the emergence of patronage allowed Whigs to justify congressional control of administrative officers in terms of democratic accountability. Given the importance of such control, it is not surprising that contests for control arose within Congress itself. As Whittington states, the House argued that Congress held the power, but the Senate argued that the Constitution created a shared power between the president and Senate. That is, senators now returned to the advise and consent position, because they found that it was better to have the Constitution grant be a shared power. This tension can be seen in the initial arguments offered by impeachment manager Representative Benjamin Butler, Republican from Massachusetts. In a single speech, Butler argued that both the "theory of the Constitution" and constitutional practice supported advise and consent *and* that precedent established congressional delegation, but without noting the tension between the two positions: "Upon this point [a particular reading of the vesting clause] our proposition is, that the Senate being in session, and an office, not an inferior one, within the terms of the Constitution, being filled, the President has the implied power of inaugurating the removal only by nomination of a successor to the Senate, which, when consented to, works the full removal and supersede[nce] of the incumbent."[93]

This would seem to argue that the Constitution requires the Senate to consent to the replacement before the removal can take place. However, after listing the legislative attempts to limit presidential removals, Butler concluded that precedent had established that Congress has the power to place the removal power where it sees fit: "Thus it would seem that the ablest men of the day, of both parties, subscribed to the power of Congress to limit and control the President in his removal from office."[94] In addition to this tension between the explanations about the constitutional basis for the Tenure of Office Act, another source of division and confusion was the question concerning department heads. Democrats and moderate Republicans did not want the Tenure of Office Act to apply to department heads.[95] As a result, a conference committee had to resolve the differences between the House version (which included department heads) and the Senate bill (which did not). The final version was unclear about whether the current department heads were included or not. Another complicating factor is that it is possible that Republicans held a principled position on patronage. That is, it is possible that they believed Johnson was wrong to give the spoils to the losers rather than to the victors.[96]

By comparison, Johnson's position was clear. In his 1867 annual message to Congress, Johnson included the Tenure of Office Act in his list of unconstitutional laws passed by Congress. Like defenders of executive power theory, Johnson appealed to the principle of "accountability" and argued that the Constitution deliberately left the power to remove as "unrestricted" and instead restricted the power to appoint. In an important turn, Johnson argued that the new law would make the president into a "prosecutor" whose job would be "impracticable." If the president wanted to remove a man who no longer deserved his office, the president would have to show cause for removal. "The prosecution is to be conducted before a tribunal whose members are not, like him, responsible to the whole people, but to separate constituent bodies, and who may hear his accusation with great disfavor."[97] Like Jefferson and Jackson before him, and Woodrow Wilson and others after him, Johnson compared the president's responsibility to the whole ("the whole people") to Congress's responsibility to the part ("separate constituent bodies"). Like these presidents, he claimed presidential supremacy in removals based on the representative function of the president. As he put it a year later, in his fourth annual message, "an honest and efficient execution of the laws" presumes a "rigid accountability."[98] But Johnson gave this argument an important twist by repeating again and again that the Reconstruction Congress could not claim to represent the whole because representatives from "Virginia, Mississippi, and Texas are yet excluded from the two Houses [of Congress]."[99] To be sure, as Johnson noted, this applied to presidential elections as well, but by being the advocate of Confederate representation, Johnson could claim with some truth that he alone was responsible for the whole.

To this blended charge of sectionalism and institutional unresponsiveness, Johnson added the argument that the Senate's judgment would necessarily be flawed in questions of removals: "The Senate is absolutely without any known standard of decision applicable to such a case. Its judgment can not be anticipated, for it is not governed by any rule. The law does not define what shall be deemed good cause for removal."[100] Determining "cause" would be difficult enough, but Johnson went on to make the very good argument that the Senate would be an unfit jury for such a trial. Anticipating the problem in defining the scope of impeachment, Johnson noted that partisan calculations would cloud the discussion of removals.

It is impossible even to conjecture what may or may not be so considered by the Senate. The nature of the subject forbids clear proof.
If the charge be incapacity, what evidence will support it? Fidelity to
the Constitution may be understood or misunderstood in a thousand
different ways, and by violent party men, in violent party times, un-
faithfulness to the Constitution may even come to be considered meri-
torious. If the officer be accused of dishonesty, how shall it be made
out? Will it be inferred from acts unconnected with public duty, from
private history, or from general reputation, or must the President
await the commission of an actual misdemeanor in office?[101]

In noting the difficulty of stating the grounds for removal, Johnson
thus anticipated and flipped the arguments used by his opponents concerning his looming impeachment. If the Congress insisted on making itself
the judge of removals, then it would need to decide in advance whether
removals would be limited by a legal approach. If it chose a more flexible
policy, one that would allow removals for political reasons, then it would
necessarily be acknowledging that politics was inseparable from administration—the very claim that Johnson was making about the Republican
plan for Reconstruction. If members of Congress acknowledged this difficulty, they would also have been forced to be more forthright about their
motivations for impeaching and removing Johnson.

Continuities and Discontinuities

The former president Martin Van Buren spent very little time on removals
in his lengthy autobiography. In a dismissive paragraph, he mocked Clay's
1834 resolutions on the Tenure of Office Act of 1820 as one of the many
inconsequential attempts at "agitation" that are allowed to "lie on the table."[102] Van Buren could not see that the efforts to regulate presidential removal powers would gain new advocates and that the Whig critique might
one day return.

As Van Buren's dismissive comment suggests, it is very difficult to
extricate the arguments about removals from their contexts in the 1830s
and 1860s. And it would be very difficult for a politician to consider the
removal question apart from the question of who would be losing the office and who would be gaining it. But these debates reveal that it would
also be very difficult to disentangle the political context from the timeless
question about the role of the executive in republican politics. Moreover,
these debates confirm the conditional nature of executive power in American political development and the power of the opposition to presidential
control of removals. There was nothing settled in 1789 about presidential

removals, and the removal power did not have to develop the way it did. Rather, its path was altered by the presidents who asserted them and by the critics who resisted. Andrew Johnson's assertion of presidential supremacy in removals shows that the logic of the executive power theory tends to the unity of administrative and political control. James Madison defended executive power theory both on the grounds that the president would need the power to execute the laws and on the grounds that presidential control was better for democratic accountability. In this, the long chain of accountability was part and parcel of administrative control, and administrative control was part and parcel of democratic accountability. But Madison did not see the fullness of the doctrine because he did not foresee the transformation of the presidency that would happen—which he would help carry out—in the next fifteen years. In particular, Jefferson's defense of responsibility connected presidential control over removals to the principle of party organization—even if that connection was not well thought of or firmly embraced.

Andrew Jackson was the first president to embrace this connection, but he was also the first to glory in the expansion of executive power. Even though George Washington and Thomas Jefferson had each left the office stronger than they received it, neither made a public case for that expansion. Moreover, both Washington and Jefferson were most associated with expansions of executive power in matters of foreign policy. Jackson, by contrast, created controversy by his expansion of the domestic executive power, particularly his use of the veto power, the proclamation power, and the removal power. Washington and Jefferson both provoked opposition on grounds that they had used unwarranted executive powers, but both left the case for executive power to be made by others. Jackson, however, put himself directly into the argument. The Whigs, in turn, were the first opposition party to construct a platform that would limit their own power if they were to win the White House. Central to this contest over the role of the executive is the controversy over the removal power. In Jackson's hands, the argument from responsibility became explicitly attached to the argument for partisanship.

But the problem was not only that Jackson had added powers to the president's toolkit. Rather, it was that he had "multiplied" executive power by adding public opinion as a source of executive power. To be sure, Jefferson had made this argument possible by reconfiguring the cycle of presidential performance, and Federalists had resisted—especially with respect to Jefferson's transformation of the Inaugural Address and the ratification of the Twelfth Amendment. But Jackson brought the question to its clearest possible point by using his reelection in 1832 to justify his veto of the Bank bill and then his removal of Treasury Secretary William Duane. As the Whigs noticed, Jackson's logic pointed to a new kind of executive, one that would participate in and perhaps even control many of the implied powers granted by the Constitution. If the president alone has the power to remove, then the president has the power to control executive officials. Moreover, if the president also shares the power to interpret the Constitution, then it follows that executive officials too can disregard Supreme Court decisions if directed by the president. In serving at the pleasure of a president who also had the power to interpret law, executive officials would be liberated from congressional and judicial oversight.

The alternative argument wanted to separate administrative and political control, but that logic, too, was revealed by the Whigs and the Republicans. Whigs soon found that the argument for stability was less attractive than the possibility of control, so they found themselves favoring congressional delegation when they might have been better suited to use advise and consent to focus their attention on the unsettling implications of Jackson's principle of rotation. After the Civil War, Republicans found control to be so necessary that they looked to congressional delegation to support a larger posture of congressional supremacy. Neither Whigs nor Republicans could foresee an argument that would curb presidential dominance over removals without increasing the powers of Congress. That argument for independent executive officials would come, but it would take fifty years.

The Revenge of Executive Power: From the Tenure of Office Act to *Myers v. United States*

The Tenure of Office Act of 1867 represented the highwater mark of a congressionally centered removal power. As we have just explained in Chapter 3, this act was not solely rooted in the debate over Reconstruction. In its origins and implications, the passage of this act and President Andrew Johnson's reaction to it were linked to a long-standing debate about executive power and administrative control. Here we chronicle the ascendance of executive power theory after its repudiation by Congress in the 1867 Tenure of Office Act. First we examine the efforts of four presidential administrations to reassert executive authority in the area of removals. Presidents Ulysses Grant, Rutherford Hayes, James Garfield, and Grover Cleveland all battled with Congress over appointments and removals with varying degrees of success. Second we undertake an in-depth analysis of the landmark case of *Myers v. United States* (1926). For the first time the Supreme Court affirmed executive power theory. We argue that the case reveals the difficulty of finding a middle ground between a unilateral executive removal power and a wide-ranging congressional power to structure and manage the executive branch.

The Tenure of Office Act: Aftermath and Repeal

Johnson's successor, Ulysses Grant, pressed for the repeal of the act. As Grant put it in his first annual message on December 6, 1869:

> It may be well to mention here the embarrassment possible to arise from leaving on the statute books the so-called "tenure-of-office acts," and to earnestly recommend their total repeal. It could not have been the intention of the framers of the Constitution, when providing that appointments made by the president should receive the consent of the Senate, that the latter should have the power to retain in office persons placed there by Federal appointment against the will of the president.

The law is inconsistent with a faithful and efficient administration of the Government. What faith can an Executive put in officials forced upon him, and those, too, whom he has suspended for reason? How will such officials be likely to serve in an Administration which they know does not trust them?[1]

However, Grant did not wait until that December to press for repeal. Grant stated publicly he would continue to enforce the act as it stood and would leave Johnson's appointees in place, filling offices only that were vacant. By going along with this weakened executive removal power, Grant in effect denied to "Congress the spoils it was expecting. There would be no new postmasters, pension clerks, or customs collectors until the Senate acted."[2]

Shortly after Grant's inauguration in March 1869, Congress convened, and Representative Benjamin Butler of Massachusetts, a Grant ally, led an effort in the House to overturn the act. The Senate did not endorse the House bill. The Senate Judiciary Committee reported an amendment to the bill that would have suspended the Tenure of Office Act only for that particular session of Congress. Senator George F. Edmunds of Vermont, who favored this approach, remarked, "Owing to the peculiar circumstances that have attended the last administration, it is desirable that there should be an immediate and general removal of the office-holders of the country as a rule; and as an agency for that removal, . . . we are willing to trust this Executive with that discretion."[3] Grant's supporters in Congress were not inclined to accept this solution, and it looked as if there was a majority in favor of total repeal. The Republican leadership, however, favored the temporary suspension of the act, so they brought the House bill back to the Judiciary Committee. Eventually the Republican caucus came up with another attempt at a compromise: They favored an amendment that would have ended the requirement that the president provide the names of the officials he intended to suspend (removals initiated during a Senate recess) along with the rationale for the suspensions. The Republican leadership then, reportedly, met with Grant at the White House and forced him to accept the compromise.[4]

The day after the conference committee meeting, the meaning of the compromise was unclear — even to those intimately involved in the legislation. A member of the conference committee on the House side, Benjamin Butler, told his colleagues that the amendment had essentially the same effect as total repeal. His counterpart, Senator Lyman Trumbull of Illinois, came to a strikingly different conclusion. Trumbull argued that the new version of the act meant that a president's suspension would only be final if the Senate confirmed a successor. If no such confirmation was forthcoming, the suspended official would resume his position at the conclusion of the next session of Congress.[5] A look at the relevant sections of the

Tenure of Office Act of 1867 and the revised version of 1869 makes the confusion understandable.[6] The proposed revisions replaced the first two sections of the 1867 act. Section 1 of the 1867 act specified that removal of an officer would take place only upon Senate confirmation of a successor. With a few exceptions (including the secretary of war), removal could also take place jointly with the Senate. In the newly proposed version, removal could occur by either means (express joint removal or joint appointment of a successor) irrespective of the particular office. So far there was little substantive difference between the two. Section 2 of the 1867 act, however, dealt with recess suspensions and included three key provisions. First, the president could suspend an officer for a number of specified causes during a Senate recess. Second, the act required the president to report the reasons for the suspension to the Senate upon coming back into session. Third, if the Senate failed to ratify the suspension, the suspended officer would resume office. Section 2 of the revised act looked quite different in these three respects. The president could suspend "in his discretion"; the president was not required to provide reasons for the suspension to the Senate; and if the Senate failed to confirm the successor, the president was required to make another nomination — nothing was said about the suspended officer resuming his place.

So it should now be clear that even though some congressional intervention into the removal arena can be ascribed to opposition to Johnson in particular, by no means can all of it be so ascribed. Even though Republicans now held the White House, and Congress gave up some of its power in the revised bill, the legislature was not ready to surrender all of its gains. Thus, congressional delegation theory had sincere and persistent adherents in this period following the Civil War.

During his second term (1873–1877) Grant also signed into law the bill that would become the issue in *Myers v. United States* (1926), the most influential Supreme Court case dealing with removal power. The statute specified that three classes of postmasters "shall be appointed and may be removed by the president by and with the advice and consent of the Senate," thus reasserting the central role of Congress in removing executive officials. As Wilfred Binkley has written, "The Senate attained the pinnacle of its power by the end of Grant's administration. . . . They no doubt regarded the position of the upper house secure in its mastery over the Executive. Their conduct was soon to show that they believed the Senate's place in the government then to be the culmination of its constitutional development."[7] The amended Tenure of Office Act of 1869 did not settle matters. Though the Senate and perhaps Congress more generally appeared predominant, a series of challenges from the executive was to come. "When Grant retired from the presidency no one, in or out of the Senate, could have believed it possible that within the following decade the Executive would four times successfully challenge and decisively repulse the Senate in its pretension of control over the executive."[8] These challenges were all related to appointment and removal, and it is to these challenges we now turn.

President Rutherford B. Hayes (1877–1881), who had campaigned as a civil-service reformer, "was determined to emancipate the executive from congressional domination. During the Hayes administration, the powers of the presidency were defended persistently and effectively for the first time since the Civil War."[9] Hayes first clashed with fellow Republicans in the Senate by making cabinet-level appointments without consulting them. Particularly galling to the Senators was the appointment of Carl Schurz, the well-known civil service–reform advocate, as secretary of the Interior. They feared that party patronage would come under attack. As future president and Congressman James Garfield then wrote at the outset of the Hayes administration, "During the last twenty-five years, it has been understood, by the Congress and the people, that offices are to be obtained by the aid of senators and representatives, who become the dispensers, sometimes the brokers of patronage."[10] The Senate would delay confirming any of Hayes's cabinet-level appointments, but after losing the contest for public opinion, it backed down and confirmed the nominees.

Though the 1869 Tenure of Office Act "presented him with a formidable obstacle in his efforts to clean the Augean stables of corrupt patronage politics within his own party," Hayes was determined.[11] This determination was certainly on display when Hayes appointed a few independent commissions to investigate the conduct of federal customs houses in New York, New Orleans, and elsewhere. Most problematic were the findings in New York. The commission authored a number of reports detailing the nature of wrongdoing and corruption. One found that hiring practices were based solely on political party, that employees were woefully unqualified, and that a percentage of an employee's salary was expected to be given to the party. Another report detailed incompetence and corruption that cost the government between $3 million and $5 million. Hayes's initial response was to issue an executive order that prohibited federal officials from participating in partisan activity. One top official in the New York customs house, Alonzo Cornell, responded by presiding over a state Republican convention.[12] Hayes's next step was to ask for the resignations of the three top officials in the New York customs house: future president Chester Arthur, George Sharpe, and Alonzo Cornell. They refused to resign, so the president sent the names of three successors to the Senate for appointment. Senator Roscoe Conkling of New York, the chairman of the Committee on Commerce, prevented a floor vote by blocking them in committee. Hayes would resubmit the names of his preferred appointees at succeeding sessions of Congress and was continuously rebuffed. "The three incumbents were apparently secure in their offices. The Senate seemed virtually to have extinguished the president's power of dismissal."[13] The battle continued for nearly two years. Hayes discovered that the "amended Tenure of Office Act severely limited his power to remove undesirable officials. . . . The amended law was just as much a threat to independent executive power as the old law had been, and it was now clear that as long as it stayed on the books, the power of the president would be greatly reduced and his position badly compromised."[14]

Eventually Hayes suspended the officials during a recess and prepared for the coming fight when Congress came back in session. In January 1879 he sent a message to the Senate:

> Convinced that the people of New York and of the country generally wish the New York custom house to be administered solely with a view to the public interest, it is my purpose to do all in my power to introduce into this great office the reforms which the country desires. With my information of the facts in the case, and with a deep sense of the responsible obligation imposed upon me by the Constitutional duty "to take care that the laws be faithfully executed," I regard it as my plain duty to suspend the officers in question and to make the nominations now before the Senate, in order that this important office may be honestly and efficiently administered.[15]

Thus, President Hayes invoked his responsibility to the people and his constitutional duty to make his case. After Senator Conkling made an ill-advised and ill-tempered speech against Hayes that proved off-putting to many of his former allies, the Senate finally voted to confirm the president's nominees on February 3, 1879.[16] As Hayes would note in his diary one year after his victory: "The end I have chiefly aimed at has been to break down Congressional patronage and especially Senatorial patronage. . . . I have had great success. No member of either House now attempts even to dictate appointments. My sole right to make appointments is tacitly conceded."[17]

Hayes may have been premature in his understanding of what had been conceded. His successor, James A. Garfield (inaugurated in March 1881 but assassinated that September), discovered quickly that the Senators were not eager to relinquish their prerogatives with respect to appointments. Garfield's appointment of William Robertson as Collector of the Port of New York drew the ire of Senator Conkling. The president noted in a letter: "Summed up in a single sentence this is the question: shall the principal port of entry in which more than ninety per cent of all our customs duties are collected by under the control of the administration or under the local control of the factional senator?"[18] Here Garfield had recourse to a key tenet of executive power theory as elaborated at the First Congress and after: It was the president, as a representative of the whole people and not a particular district, who was most fit to superintend the administration of the law. Conkling and his allies decided to confirm all of Garfield's nominees except Robertson and then adjourn. At the urging of an ally in the Senate, James Blaine of Maine, the president promptly withdrew all of his nominations save Robertson. Thus, in a maneuver similar to Grant's, Garfield denied to Congress any appointments until it would yield on the central point in the controversy. The move buoyed the president's friends and steered public opinion in his favor. An editorial in the *Baltimore American* stated: "At last president Garfield has answered the question: 'Who is president?'"[19] Senators Conkling and Thomas Platt of New York resigned and sought to vindicate their cause by putting themselves up for reelection. They were defeated when the New York state legislature chose their opponents, and President Garfield was triumphant.

With the election of Grover Cleveland, the first Democrat to hold the office of the presidency in more than two decades, the conflict continued and reached its highest pitch. President Cleveland suspended 643 officials during his first ten months in office, and the Republicans who controlled the Senate countered by approving only fifteen of the nominees.[20] Like his predecessor, Rutherford Hayes (who also pressed for repeal of the Tenure of Office Act in his fourth annual message), Cleveland came into office claiming the mantle of civil-service reformer. As Calabresi and Yoo point out, "Although Cleveland was not afraid to clean house with respect to partisan jobs through vigorous exercise of his removal power, he did make major efforts to extend the merit system of classified appointees created by the Pendleton Act."[21] But it is also important to note that Cleveland had gone a step farther than advocating for the extension of civil-service protections to a wider range of offices. He argued that there were many offices outside the purview of the civil-service statute that were not related to the policies of a particular administration. As he put it, "These [offices], though beyond the protection of Civil Service legislation, should not be removed merely for the purpose of rewarding the party friends of the president."[22] He hoped to establish a precedent faithful to the "spirit" if not the "letter" of civil-service reform. Once in office, Cleveland defended his removals on precisely these grounds. Although some suspensions he justified as being necessary so officers would be in accord with the policies of the new administration, he noted that "by far the greater number of suspensions, however, were made on account of gross and indecent partisan conduct on the part of the incumbents."[23]

The test case was Cleveland's suspension of George M. Duskin, a U.S. attorney for the Southern District of Alabama. Cleveland nominated Democrat John D. Burnett to replace the Republican Duskin. Senator George Edmunds, chair of the Judiciary Committee, asked the U.S.

Attorney General to send over all documents related to both the removal of Duskin and the appointment of Burnett. The Attorney General granted the latter request, but not the former.[24] The Senate countered on January 25, 1886, by passing a resolution demanding that the Attorney General turn over all documents relating to Duskin's suspension. At President Cleveland's direction, the Attorney General refused to comply with the Senate's request. It is worth pointing out that he did not think he was doing anything contrary to the 1869 Tenure of Office Act, though he doubted that this law or its immediate predecessor would survive a judicial challenge. In particular, he noted that the Senate still insisted on its right to hear the reasons for suspensions by the president—though the revised act had repealed that provision of the law.[25] Cleveland then responded with a lengthy message to the Senate on March 1.

With recourse to many elements of executive power theory as elaborated in the Decision of 1789 and by chief executives since then, President Cleveland asserted sole removal authority for the president. He rooted such authority in both the vesting clause and take care clause, while also arguing that the Senate's role in appointment was an exception to the general plan of government and thus ought to be construed strictly. Interestingly, he also argued that the occasional attempts by Congress through legislation to limit this executive authority conceded the constitutional basis for a presidential removal power. As Cleveland said of the Tenure of Office Act, "This statute, passed in 1867, when Congress was overwhelmingly and bitterly opposed politically to the president, may be regarded as an indication that even then it was thought necessary by a Congress determined upon the subjugation of the Executive to legislative will to furnish itself a law for that purpose, instead of attempting to reach the object intended by an invocation of any pretended constitutional right."[26] Cleveland coupled his emphasis on the Constitution and its separation of powers with another echo of Madison from the Decision of 1789: the president's responsibility to the people. The demands placed on the Attorney General, Cleveland noted:

> Assume the right of the Senate to sit in judgment upon the exercise of my exclusive discretion and Executive function, for which I am solely responsible to the people from whom I have so lately received the sacred trust of office. My oath to support and defend the Constitution, my duty to the people who have chosen me to execute the powers of their great office and not to relinquish them, and my duty to the Chief Magistracy, which I must preserve unimpaired in all its dignity and vigor, compel me to refuse compliance with these demands.[27]

Cleveland also emphasized his past commitment to not make removals on purely partisan grounds. "The pledges I have made were made to the people, and to them I am responsible for the manner in which they have been redeemed."[28] He would not submit his conduct in this area to the Senate for judgment.

Cleveland was also at pains to highlight the authority he believed he held under Article II. Like Presidents Jackson and Johnson, Cleveland argued the oath of office conferred upon him a special duty to be a caretaker of the powers of the office itself. If the Constitution placed certain responsibilities upon the president, he argued, these ought not to be divided. Executive discretion ought to be preserved—even if propriety might be ensured by the Senate review of suspensions:

> I do not suppose that 'the public offices of the United States' are regulated or controlled in their relations to either House of Congress by the fact that they were 'created by laws enacted by themselves.' It must be that these instrumentalities were created for the benefit of the people and to answer the general purposes of government under the Constitution and the laws, and that they are unencumbered by any lien in favor of either branch of Congress growing out of their construction, and unembarrassed by any obligation to the Senate as the price of their creation.[29]

Thus did Cleveland couple a unitary vision of executive discretion in the separation of powers scheme with presidential authority rooted in democratic accountability.

Despite Cleveland's message, initially the Senate continued to press its case. It passed a resolution asserting that unless the documents relating to Duskin's suspension were handed over, it would not act on any of Cleveland's nominations. Soon, however, it was discovered that the controversy was effectually over, as Duskin's appointment had officially expired anyway. The Senate confirmed Duskin's nominated successor; also, Congress soon passed legislation repealing the Tenure of Office Act entirely. It was signed into law by President Cleveland on March 3, 1887. Reflecting on this whole episode later in life, Cleveland would write:

> Thus was an unpleasant controversy happily followed by an expurgation of the last pretense of statutory sanction to an encroachment upon constitutional Executive prerogatives, and thus was a time-honored interpretation of the Constitution restored to us. The president, freed from the Senate's claim of tutelage, became again the independent agent of the people, representing a coordinate branch of their Government, charged with responsibilities which, under his oath, he ought not to avoid or divide with others, and invested with powers, not to be surrendered, but to be used, under the guidance of patriotic intention and an unclouded conscience.[30]

Myers v. United States: An Introduction

Things were relatively calm on the removal-power front until the land-mark Supreme Court case *Myers v. United States* (1926). Prior to that there were three noteworthy court cases touching on the removal power: *United States v. Perkins* (1886), *Parsons v. United States* (1897), and *Shurtleff v. United States* (1903); we take these up in the course of our examination of *Myers*. The facts of the *Myers* case are as follows: Frank Myers was first appointed a postmaster of the first class on April 24, 1913, for a four-year term. He was reappointed for another four-year term on January 24, 1917. On January 22, 1920, the Postmaster General requested Myers's resigna-tion, but he refused. On February 2 Myers was removed by the Postmaster General, acting on the order of the president, while the Senate was in ses-sion. President Woodrow Wilson appointed John Jones to replace Myers in September while the Senate was in recess. At no time when the Senate was in session (until the expiration of Myers's second term) did the Senate either consent to Myers's removal or consent to the appointment of Jones.

Myers argued that his removal was illegal precisely because the Senate never consented to it. Wilson's unilateral removal violated the 1876 postal statute, which read: "Postmasters of the first, second, and third classes shall be appointed and may be removed by the president by and with the advice and consent of the Senate, and shall hold their offices for four years unless sooner removed or suspended according to law." Myers sued to recover the balance of his salary due to him from January 31, 1920, to July 21, 1921. Chief Justice William Howard Taft, writing for the Court, decided against Myers and thus held the 1876 statute covering the three classes of postmas-ters to be unconstitutional. Taft affirmed a wide-ranging removal power for the president alone. Taft was joined by five justices; Justices Louis Brandeis and James McReynolds wrote lengthy dissents and Justice Oliver Wendell Holmes a one-page dissent.

The *Myers* case takes up more than 200 pages in the Supreme Court reporter. It was before the Court for more than two years and twice ar-gued. Before the second argument, Taft invited Senator George Wharton Pepper of Pennsylvania to submit an amicus brief and speak on behalf of the appellant (Myers) at oral argument. All the opinions are marked by a striking depth of constitutional and historical analysis. And as noted by Edward Corwin, "The quality of the argument before the court, too, was extraordinarily high; the arguments of Mr. Pepper and Mr. [James] Beck, then solicitor general of the United States, fully sustained the best tradi-tions of the court."[31] Taft affirmed the original executive power theory; Justices McReynolds and Brandeis each offered slightly different versions of congressional delegation theory.

Taft's decision included an exhaustive discussion of the Decision of 1789, and his own arguments followed Madison's closely. For Taft, this legislation of the First Congress was a particularly authoritative expression of the meaning of the Constitution on the removal question, as it included many figures who had sat at the Constitutional Convention. The votes taken were on the precise question of the president's removal power and should thus guide the Court in its thinking about the statute at issue in the *Myers* case. Further, that decision of the First Congress was also taken as authoritative in subsequent debates on the question in the nineteenth century. According to Taft, executive power theory carried the day at this crucial moment, and this was the prevailing understanding of the Constitution on the removal question up until the passage of the Tenure of Office Act of 1867. As he noted,

> Some effort has been made to question whether the decision carries the result claimed for it, but there is not the slightest doubt, after an examination of the record, that the vote was, and was intended to be, a legislative declaration that the power to remove officers appointed by the president and the Senate vested in the president alone, and, until the Johnson impeachment trial in 1868, its meaning was not doubted even by those who questioned its soundness.[32]

He further argued that subsequent members of Congress not only agreed on the meaning of the decision; they also acquiesced in that meaning. Future Congresses passed legislation thoroughly consistent with the decision of the First Congress, and presidents subsequently acted according to that understanding.

All of this was challenged by the dissenters in the *Myers* case. We first turn to the debate over this two-part historical question: the very meaning of the Decision of 1789, and then the degree of acquiescence in that decision. Then we examine the constitutional logic of the two positions in *Myers:* executive power theory and congressional delegation theory.

The Meaning of the Decision of 1789

Taft's argument to the contrary, the meaning of the Decision of 1789 had been previously contested. As Senator Pepper noted in his amicus brief on Myers's behalf, this very issue had arisen in the course of the impeachment trial of Andrew Johnson. Johnson himself had argued the Tenure of Office Act was unconstitutional and departed clearly from the authoritative expression of the First Congress. Yet in his opinion on the matter of

Johnson's impeachment, Senator Edmunds argued that "the construction, then, claimed to be derived from [the Decision of 1789] ceases to have any foundation in point of fact."[33] By Edmunds's count, only nine of the fifty-four members of Congress could be identified for certain as adherents of executive power theory, whereas fifteen openly opposed it. These identical numbers were repeated in McReynolds's dissent in *Myers*. McReynolds argued that Taft had cleverly elided an important distinction: The final votes on the House bills creating the three original departments did not necessarily reflect an agreement on the logic behind the president's removal power. Taft argued that the final votes creating the departments carried the identical language on removal power and could thus be interpreted as an endorsement of the views of Representatives Benson and Madison, who had each pushed for this final settlement and had each explicitly endorsed executive removal power. But according to McReynolds, the final language was susceptible to various interpretations and "probably did not mean the same things to all."[34] In his own dissent, Brandeis also called into question Taft's interpretation, identifying only six House members who could be said to have affirmatively supported executive power theory. In an influential monograph published the year after the *Myers* decision, Edward S. Corwin also disputed Taft's interpretation of the Decision of 1789 along similar lines as the dissenting Justices McReynolds and Brandeis. Corwin also distinguished those who voted in favor of the final bill from those members who could be said to have endorsed Madison's executive power theory: "A mere fraction of a fraction, a minority of a minority, of the house, can be shown to have attributed the removal power to the president on the grounds of executive prerogative."[35] Brandeis offered a detailed analysis of these crucial votes in a lengthy footnote.

Before looking at Brandeis's analysis, let us recall (see Chapter 1: "The Decision of 1789") how the final votes in the establishment of the Department of Foreign Affairs played out. On July 22, Benson first proposed the adoption of new language: A clause would be inserted that related to a chief clerk appointed by the secretary of foreign affairs. This clerk would be responsible for the records and papers "whenever the said principal officer [the secretary] shall be removed from office by the president of the United States." If this were agreed to, then Benson would move that the old language—in particular the phrase "to be removeable by the president"—would be taken out. Then on July 24, a vote was taken on this final version of the bill. Benson's professed purpose was to revise the bill to ensure that the language reflected the idea that Congress was merely declaring a power already granted to the president by the Constitution, not itself granting the removal power to the president.

Here is Brandeis's analysis of those votes in his *Myers* dissent:

The individual votes on these two motions are given. An examination of the votes of those whose opinions are also on record shows that Benson's first motion succeeded only as a result of [a] coalition between those who accepted Madison's views and those who considered removal subject to Congressional control but deemed it advisable to vest the power in the president. The vote on Benson's second motion to strike out the words "to be removable by the president" brought forth a different alignment. The minority now comprised those who, though they believed the grant of power to be expedient, did not desire to imply the existence of a power in the president beyond legislative control.[36]

Brandeis's objection rests on a problematic fact for any side in this debate. A group of representatives voted in favor of Benson's first motion, that is, the inclusion of the new language that was thought more directly to imply a constitutionally existing removal authority for the president. These representatives then voted against the second motion, that is, the deletion of the old language that was thought to perhaps imply that Congress was delegating the power to the president. Then this group voted for the passage of the final bill. Saikrishna Prakash calls this group of representatives the "enigmatic faction."[37] Taft's antagonists argued that this enigmatic faction must not be understood to endorse executive power theory; rather they were adherents of congressional delegation theory. After all, they voted not to delete the language that aligns most clearly with congressional delegation. Thus, in the view of Brandeis and McReynolds, as well as Corwin, Taft's interpretation of this legislation passed by the First Congress rested on false assumptions about what the representatives thought they were voting for. See Tables 4.1–4.4 for the three votes and the voting patterns.

Though Taft curiously did not respond to his critics in his own opinion, his position is certainly defensible. The most obvious problem for the critics is the third and final vote. For at this point, after Benson's motion to strike the old language succeeded (despite the votes of the enigmatic faction), this group was voting for a bill whose purpose, as stated by its key proponents, was to imply a constitutionally rooted executive removal power. If this enigmatic faction were truly proponents of congressional delegation theory, why would they vote for such a bill?

Prakash argues that Taft's critics are wrong and that it is their assumptions about this enigmatic faction that are in fact faulty. In Prakash's view, the votes of this faction against striking the original language are not necessarily votes against executive power theory. First, he argues, some members of this faction, Elias Boudinot of New Jersey and John Laurance of New York, for example, thought the original language was

Removal Power Votes at the First Congress[1]

Table 4.1. Vote 1. June 22, 1789. On the first Benson motion: adding the new language "whenever said principal officer shall be removed from office by the president of the United States . . ."

Ayes (30)	Noes (18)
Fisher Ames	Lambert Cadwalader
Abraham Baldwin[*]	Isaac Coles
Egbert Benson	**Elbridge Gerry**
John Brown	Jonathan Grout
Aedanus Burke	John Hathorn
Daniel Carroll	Benjamin Huntington
George Clymer	Samuel Livermore
Benjamin Contee	George Matthews
Thomas Fitzsimons	John Page
Nicholas Gilman	Josiah Parker
Benjamin Goodhue	George Partridge
Samuel Griffin	Jeremiah Van Renssalaer
Thomas Hartley	**Roger Sherman**
Daniel Hiester	William Smith (SC)
John Laurance	Jonathan Sturges
Richard Bland Lee	Thomas Sumter
George Leonard	Thomas Tudor Tucker
James Madison	Alexander White
Andrew Moore	
Peter Muhlenberg	
Thomas Scott	
Theodore Sedgwick	
Joshua Seney	
Thomas Sinnickson	
William Smith (MD)	
Peter Silvester	
George Thatcher	
Jonathan Trumbull	
John Vining	
Jeremiah Wadsworth	

[1] Source for these votes: Linda Grant DePauw, Charlene Bangs Bickford, and LaVonne Siegel Hauptman, eds., *Documentary History of the First Federal Congress*, vol. 3, *House of Representatives Journal* (Baltimore: Johns Hopkins University Press, 1977), 92–93, 95.

[*] Members of the House of Representatives who also sat at the Constitutional Convention are in **bold**.

Table 4.2. Vote 2. June 22, 1789. On the second Benson motion: to strike out "to be removable by the president . . ."

Ayes (31)	Noes (19)
Ames	Elias Boudinot
Baldwin	Cadwalader
Benson	**Carroll**
Brown	Contee
Burke	**Fitzsimons**
Clymer	**Gilman**
Coles	Hartley
Gerry	Heister
Goodhue	Laurance
Griffin	Lee
Grout	James Schureman
Hathorn	Sedgwick
Huntington	Seney
Leonard	Smith (MD)
Livermore	Sylvester
Madison	Thatcher
Matthews	Trumbull
Moore	Tucker
Muhlenberg	Wadsworth
Page	
Parker	
Partridge	
Van Renssalaer	
Scott	
Sherman	
Sinnickson	
Smith (SC)	
Sturges	
Sumter	
Vining	
White	

a stronger, clearer declaration of the president's constitutional authority.[38] So they voted against striking out the old language, but they were also inclined to vote for the final bill, as they thought it consistent — if less forceful — with their understanding. Second, voting to strike language that they had fought for days to retain was distasteful to some. Conversely, striking the old language must also have felt like a victory for the opponents of executive power theory. As Prakash explains, "Having fought to alter the original removal text in May and delete it in June, opponents of executive power theory seized the opportunity to delete it, even if its removal was in the service of a subset of executive power partisans."[39] Third, not only

Table 4.3. Vote 3. June 24, 1789. On the bill to establish an executive department to be denominated the Department of Foreign Affairs

Ayes (29)	Noes (22)
Ames	Coles
Benson	**Gerry**
Boudinot	Grout
Brown	Hathorn
Burke	Huntington
Cadwalader	James Jackson
Carroll	Leonard
Clymer	Livermore
Contee	Matthews
Fitzsimmons	Page
Gilman	Parker
Goodhue	Partridge
Griffin	Van Renssalaer
Hartley	**Sherman**
Hiester	Smith (MD)
Daniel Huger	Smith (SC)
Laurance	Stone
Lee	Sturges
Madison	Sumter
Moore	Thatcher
Muhlenberg	Tucker
Schureman	White
Scott	
Sedgwick	
Seney	
Sinnickson	
Sylvester	
Trumbull	
Vining	

was this deletion distasteful; it also felt like a capitulation to the opponents. Representative William Smith of South Carolina, the main adherent of the impeachment theory, appeared to relish the moment and taunted those who were in favor of the change in language: "Will they pretend to carry their point by a side blow, when they are defeated by fair argument on due reflection?"[40] Fourth, some members might have voted against the second motion because they thought Benson's new approach was poor tactics. What if the majority in favor of executive removal power (whether constitutionally rooted or congressionally delegated) was split? Fifth and last, Prakash suggests perhaps some might have favored an approach that could

ambiguity in the meaning of "settled." Story, for his part, had argued that Congress still retained the power to regulate the removal of inferior offices, a line also taken by Brandeis in his *Myers* dissent. Thus, Story appeared to disagree with Taft's understanding of the Decision of 1789: Congress, according to Story, had some power to regulate certain removals. And Webster had argued that even though the decision was "settled" in the sense that there had been general acquiescence up to 1835 during the conflict with president Jackson, "it is our duty to act upon the case accordingly for the present, without admitting that Congress may not, hereafter, if necessity shall require it, reverse the decision of 1789."[46] Though he granted that executive power theory won the day back in 1789, he did not think that Congress must automatically acquiesce in that faulty decision for all time. As we argue above (see Chapter 3: "Jackson to Johnson: The Rise of Congressional Delegation"), Webster was not alone in his willingness and desire to revise what at the time was the prevailing understanding of the removal power. The crisis over President Andrew Jackson's use of the power provoked strong replies from figures like Henry Clay and John Calhoun. As we see below, Clay and Calhoun provided key arguments for Senator Pepper and the dissenters in *Myers*.

The battle over the degree of acquiescence in the Decision of 1789 was also fought over Congress's subsequent legislation. Did Congress itself pass laws that complied with Taft's understanding the Decision of 1789, or did future statutes reveal a different understanding of executive removal power?

McReynolds argued that the Judiciary Act of 1789 — a contemporaneous piece of legislation — already revealed Taft's understanding to be wrong. Section 27 of the act provided that marshals be appointed in each district, specified a four-year term, and stated that they be removable at pleasure. Section 35 created district attorneys and an Attorney General, but neither fixed a term or specified anything regarding removal. According to McReynolds, "The legislature must have understood that, if an officer be given a fixed term and nothing is said concerning removal, he acquires a vested right to the office for the full period; also that officers appointed without definite terms were subject to removal by the president at will, assent of Congress being implied."[47] In other words, McReynolds argued that by fixing terms and specifying the removal power, the Judiciary Act of 1789, far from endorsing executive power theory, actually accorded with congressional delegation theory. The crucial point is that in McReynolds's view there did not seem to be any underlying constitutional removal power for the president. Even in the case of the absence of removal language, the basis for executive removal power was the implied assent of Congress. Taft, for his part, explained Section 27 by arguing that Congress merely was making its understanding of executive removal power explicit:

This was a declaration of an underlying power and not a grant. Section 35 — where nothing was said with respect to term or removal — confirmed this for Taft. "The difference in the two cases," he argues, "was evidently to avoid any inference from the fixing of the term that a conflict with the legislative decision of 1789 was intended."[48]

Another important point of contention between the majority and the dissents in *Myers* concerned the first Tenure of Office Act (1820), which we discuss in Chapter 2 ("From Responsibility to Rotation"). Brandeis and McReynolds interpreted this legislation as more evidence that Congress never acquiesced in an unlimited executive removal power, whereas Taft claimed the act was in perfect accord with such an understanding. Recall that this act provided for a wide range of federal officers, from district attorneys to assistant apothecaries-general, to be appointed to four-year terms and also be removable at pleasure. So, again, the question was whether this specification of "removable at pleasure" meant that in the absence of such a provision the president would have *any* power of removal. McReynolds's answer was no. Taft argued that the *Parsons* case was directly on point. That case involved a district attorney who had been removed prior to the expiration of his four-year term. He sued for the balance of his salary. The revised statute was derived from the first Tenure of Office Act, but the relevant section omitted the provision "removable at pleasure." The appellant, Parsons, argued that this omission resulted in a vesting of the rights of the office for the full four-year term. The Court decided against Parsons, holding: "The provision for a removal from office at pleasure was not necessary for the exercise of that power by the president, because of the fact that he was then regarded at being clothed with such power in any event. . . . We must construe this act as providing absolutely for the expiration of the term of office at the end of four years, and not as giving at term that shall last, at all events, for that time."[49] So according to the Court in *Parsons*, McReynolds was wrong that the fixing of a term in the absence of an express removal provision meant the vesting of the rights of the office in the officeholder.

But McReynolds's line of argument was not the only sense in which the first Tenure of Office Act might be understood as a challenge to unlimited executive removal. Brandeis, who, as will we see, had a slightly different understanding of Congress's removal power than McReynolds, made a different case. He pointed out that the intent of this act was to *ensure* removals. That is, Congress did not intervene in the removal arena during these early years to limit removals (or to restrain the president from making removals) because executive removals were not numerous enough to generate concern. Indeed, the opposite was the case with the first Tenure of Office Act. As we saw in Chapter 2 ("From Responsibility to Rotation"), part of the impulse behind the act was to enable Congress to get its share of patronage. As Peter Zavodnyik put it, the act "greatly increased those occasions on which the Senate had before it a nomination for the civil service — thereby enhancing the ability of individual senators to find jobs for allies and supporters."[50] Brandeis identified two other acts prior to the Civil War that were more concerned to secure than prevent removals.[51]

Soon, however, the intent of congressional involvement with removals changed. It was during and after the Civil War — after the so-called spoils system had been in place for some decades — that Congress began to act to prevent removals. The roots of the controversy at issue in *Myers* were found, according to Brandeis, in the Currency Act of 1863. This legislation included the following provision for the Comptroller: He "shall hold his office for the term of five years unless sooner removed by the president, by and with the advice of the Senate."[52] This same provision was then incorporated into the controversial Tenure of Office Act of 1867, which applied to all "presidential offices." Three acts relating to the postal laws were passed in 1872, 1874, and 1876. In all three of these acts the first three classes of postmasters were all made subject to this same removal clause. Though the repeal of the Tenure of Office Act succeeded in 1887, no effort was made to repeal or revise the postal laws that included a similar removal clause.

Brandeis's understanding of the history of the nineteenth-century legislation stands in stark contrast to Taft. Whether inserting itself into the removal process to encourage removals or to prevent them, Congress inserted itself consistently. There was no acquiescence in the executive power theory. If any degree of acquiescence was to be found, it ran in the opposite direction from what Taft supposed to be the case. Brandeis argued that presidents acquiesced to Congress's interventions, not the other way around. Here he drew a distinction to which we return between the removal of "presidential" (or cabinet-level) and inferior officers. Thus, though President Johnson vetoed the Tenure of Office Act and argued that his removal of Secretary of War Edwin Stanton was perfectly constitutional, he "approved other acts containing the removal clause which related only to inferior officers."[53] Neither did President Cleveland make any effort to repeal the removal provisions relating to postmasters as his campaign against the Tenure of Office Act unfolded. Those presidents most assertive in bringing their constitutional rights to bear against Congress in the storm over the Tenure of Office Act thus appeared to regard congressional interventions in the removal of inferior offices as unobjectionable.

We are now in a position to see a telling difference in the historical arguments of the two principal dissenters in *Myers*. Though at first blush it seems that McReynolds and Brandeis were equally intent on attacking Taft's understanding of the Decision of 1789, it is significant that Brandeis consigned the real substance of his critique to a footnote. We suspect Brandeis knew his evidence on how to construe the meaning of the votes in the First Congress was, at best, as problematic as Taft's evidence. So

Brandeis focused his line of argument on the subsequent congressional interventions in the removal of inferior offices. Here his critique of Taft was more sustained and, in our judgment, more powerful. So ultimately Brandeis implied that the Decision of 1789 simply was not that relevant, as its conclusion applied only to cabinet officials. He did not go so far as to suggest, as did Will King in his brief on behalf of Myers, that the Decision of 1789 did not matter because the country had departed from it.[54] But he very clearly wanted to steer the dispute away from that ground and fight elsewhere.

The Constitutional Logic

Now that we have laid out the dispute over the history of the removal power as understood and employed by Congress and the president, we turn to the constitutional logic of the various positions in *Myers*. We should also note all of this was far from ancient history, and there was a lot more at stake in the *Myers* decision than the control of postal officers. Almost precisely five months after removing Frank Myers from office, President Wilson vetoed H.R. 9783, an act to reform the budget system of the federal government. Section 303 of that bill included the following provision:

> The Comptroller General and the Assistant Comptroller General shall hold office during good behavior, but may be removed at any time by concurrent resolution of Congress after notice and hearing, when, in their judgment, the Comptroller General or Assistant Comptroller General is incapacitated or inefficient, or has been guilty of neglect of duty, or of malfeasance in office, or of any felony or conduct involving moral turpitude, and for no other cause and in no other manner except by impeachment.[55]

This provision was significant for two primary reasons: First, it took the president out of the removal process and placed that process squarely in the hands of Congress; and second, it included a "for cause" provision, thus making the office more secure and independent from the political branches than had heretofore been the case. President Wilson argued there was no warrant in the Constitution for Congress ascribing the removal power to itself in such a manner and that Article II, Section 2 precluded such action.

All three briefs in the *Myers* case pointed to this legislation, which was eventually signed into law by President Harding. In addition, Senator Pepper, in an appendix to his amicus brief, pointed to twenty-nine active statutes that limited the president's removal power in some way.[56] Some denied to the president any role in the removal of an officer, some required Senate consent for removal (e.g., the statute at issue in *Myers*), some limited executive removal power by specifying certain causes as legitimate triggers, whereas others specified certain causes and required the granting of notice and an opportunity for defense. Thus, for the appellant Myers and Senator Pepper, the strategy was in part to show that this minor provision in a postal law was part of a very broad class of legislation that demonstrated Congress's significant and variegated role in the construction and supervision of executive administration. The dilemma for the government in the case was to decide how broadly to pitch its challenge.

Solicitor General James Beck argued that the removal statute at issue was unconstitutional because it impaired the president's constitutional duty to execute the laws. Like Madison and his fellow executive power theorists in 1789, Beck rooted the president's removal authority in both the vesting clause and the take care clause. What Congress had done in the removal statute was take a portion of the president's constitutionally based removal power and divide it with the Senate — in effect creating a plural executive in place of the unitary executive created by the Framers. So Beck asserted a broad, constitutionally based removal power for the president, but he also pointed to an equally great congressional power to create offices, limit terms, and abolish offices. These two powers, according to Beck, need not and do not conflict. The congressional power, however, and contrary to the case of the appellants, does not warrant congressional invasion of the president's removal power. Creation, term limitation, and abolition of offices are all legislative powers, and none of these justify the control of removal.

The other place where partisans of congressional removal looked to justify such authority was the inferior appointments clause. Beck granted that this clause allowed for Congress — when granting the appointment power to the president, or the heads of departments, or courts of law — to place conditions on the removal power in such cases. But this power, Beck argued, was rooted in statutory authority and thus cannot detract from the constitutional authority of the president. And further, as the Chief Justice would write for the Court, nothing in the clause suggested that Congress may involve *itself* in the removal power.

This last distinction would prove very important to the government's case. Beck, both in his brief and at oral argument, outlined two paths for the Court. It could strike down the law as an infringement upon executive power and affirm, in total, the president's authority to remove any member of the executive branch without limitations from Congress. But the court could also strike down the law on the much narrower ground noted above — that is, Congress might place some limits on executive removal power, but what it could *not* do was give that power to *itself*. Beck suggested that the Court might thus find a middle ground where Congress could place certain limitations on executive removal power. Congress could put in place a "legislative standard" that would merely guide the executive act of removal. Congress might name certain conditions under which re-moval would take place, without positively precluding other conditions. Or Congress might say removal must take place under these conditions and no other. Now, Beck declined to explicitly affirm the constitutionality of either of these scenarios (though he suggested that the latter was much more constitutionally suspect than the former). But he did suggest that the statute at issue was unlike either of his hypotheticals: "A very different question, however, is present in the instant case, where no legislative stan-dard is prescribed and no general policy laid down except that the president may not exercise his Executive function of removal except with the consent of the Senate. . . . Such a law does not regulate the power of removal. It asserts a right to exercise it."[57] So Beck opened the possibility for the Court to find principled distinctions amid the different classes of active statutes in the appendix to Senator Pepper's brief.

The Solicitor General's suggestion generated some interest among the justices during oral argument. The Chief Justice specifically asked for an elaboration of that possibility, and Beck complied with more hypotheticals similar to the ones outlined above. Justice George Sutherland then inter-jected with this: "Your contention as I understand it, is that Congress has authority to regulate or limit the power of removal but it has no power to appropriate it."[58] Beck took this as perfectly encapsulating his argument. And he again invited the Court to respond narrowly and explained why it ought to limit itself to this ground. It is worth quoting at length:

> You need not determine in this case whether Congress may not rea-sonably regulate or guide the discretion of the president as to the act of removal, so long as it does not impair his essential power of re-moval. You do not have to decide that. It would be, in my judgment, unwise to decide it, for this reason; that if Congress passes a law such as I instanced before, that a man shall be removed for inefficiency and for dishonesty, and for no other cause, it might well be that the presi-dent would have the fullest justification for removing that man and yet neither of the statutory causes existed in the case. And I do not want to question any part of the great prerogative of the president by conceding, or by inviting this court to say, that there is any power of control which would prevent the president, in a case properly within his discretion, from exercising the power of removal in the teeth of an act of Congress.[59]

Beck here tacitly conceded the instability of his proposed middle ground, and the justices knew it. As the Chief Justice interjected soon af-ter, "Mr. Solicitor General, how much of a concession do you make[?] If you say that Congress may provide reasons why a man shall be removed and the Executive may still retain the power to remove him absolutely, how much of a concession do you make?"[60] This elaboration by Beck and the response by Taft provide some clarity as to why the court did not decide the case more narrowly. For the justices inclined toward the appellant, this so-called middle ground would have provided no principled, constitutional basis for the preservation of some role for Congress in removals, however limited. Indeed, Beck indicated that a narrow decision striking down the statute in question but saying nothing about alternative congressional interventions would in fact tacitly preserve "the great prerogative of the president" in removals. For the justices inclined to strike down the statute, the constitutional grounds for doing so would have seemed to push them further in the direction of an unlimited executive removal power. In other words, despite the offer of the middle ground, the justices were in fact pushed into perhaps the most distant poles in the constellation of positions on the removal power: congressional delegation theory and executive power theory.

Executive Power Theory in *Myers*

Let us first look at the claim that was perhaps most troublesome for the three dissenters in *Myers:* the idea that the president's removal authority was unlimited under the Constitution. First, we have some familiar arguments. If all executive power is vested in the president, and the removal power is by nature executive, then the whole power of removal must belong to the president.[61] Second, we have the notion that if the president must take care that the laws be faithfully executed, then he can accomplish that goal only if he is fully equipped with the removal power. His constitutional duty can be accomplished only with agents, and those agents are truly his only if he has the power to remove them.[62] Brandeis intervened during oral argument with a question meant to challenge this position. He asked why, if the president has this "inherent prerogative" of removal, he would not also have a similar inherent power of appointment without the involvement of the Senate. Beck's reply was simple: Because the Constitution states otherwise—it specifies the involvement of the Senate. But then, countered Brandeis, if that exception is constitutionally meaningful, does not the inferior appointments clause also suggest that the removal authority can vary according to the office? Beck pointed back to the language of the Constitution. The president's appointment power is, he argued, over *all* officers. The appointments clause reads: "He shall appoint Ambassadors . . . and all other Officers of the United States, whose Appointments are not herein otherwise provided for, and which shall be established by law: but the Congress may by Law vest the Appointment of such inferior officers." Congress *may* vest the appointment elsewhere in certain exceptions, but it need not do so. In Beck's view, as far as the removal power is concerned, the nature of the office does not matter. It is surely the case, he said, that Congress could vest the appointment of an assistant postmaster to the Postmaster General and also place limits on the Postmaster General's power of removal. But then he made his crucial distinction, which drew a telling reply from McReynolds:

> Beck: . . . Congress has control over those upon whom it confers the mere *statutory* power of appointment. But it has no power as against the president; because the president's power is not statutory, it is *constitutional*. That is my point, for what it is worth.
>
> McReynolds: Do you mean that every officer appointed by every source in the United States is subject to removal by the president?
>
> Beck: Yes; every officer in the executive department of the Government.
>
> McReynolds: He is provided for by Congress, and paid by Congress, and the method of his appointment is provided by Congress. Can the president remove him?
>
> Beck: In my judgment, the president can remove anyone in the executive department of the Government.[63]

This was clearly a troubling argument for Brandeis and McReynolds. Brandeis, in particular, as we will see, thought the inferior appointments clause was an important basis for Congress to control removal as it saw fit. Beck, for his part, said that Brandeis's argument about the importance of the inferior appointments clause would be compelling only if it were true that the president's removal power flowed primarily from his appointment power. But Beck argued that "the power to remove is not a mere incident and is not solely attributable to the power to appoint. It has a much broader basis."[64] Now, by this he did not mean only the argument from the vesting clause. Beck also argued that "appointment" was one piece of a four-step process that included nomination, confirmation, appointment, and commission. Senate participation in appointment (only one part of this four-step process) was merely a recognition of the need for local knowledge. Further, nomination must be understood as selection. Selecting someone for office, according to Beck, must also imply making a judgment as to a person's fitness for office as compared to the incumbent. So the power to nominate someone must also include the power to remove an existing incumbent; otherwise nomination would be an empty power.[65]

But Taft did not wholly follow Beck down the path outlined above. The Chief Justice argued that the removal power was the president's alone by "the well approved principle of constitutional and statutory construction that the power of removal of executive officers was incident to the power of appointment."[66] Taft then rooted the removal power in the vesting clause of Article II or the general character of the office *and* specifically in the appointment power. Corwin thought this to be a real weakness in Taft's argument. In his critique of Taft he suggested that these two theories were "generally regarded as flatly opposed" and that those who argued most insistently that removal flowed from appointment were the partisans of advise and consent theory.[67] Taft openly admitted this latter point in his opinion, but he explained this by utilizing a reply made by the opponents of advise and consent at the First Congress: "The power of removal is incident to the power of appointment, not to the power of advising and consenting to the appointment."[68] Thus, it is the president who in reality appoints; the limited participation of the Senate in a merely advisory capacity in appointment does not make its participation in removal legitimate.[69] Taft further argued that appointment and removal are different in kind. They demand different forms of knowledge before their exercise. Even though the Senate might be in a good position to add the president's knowledge about suitable candidates, it would not be in position to add anything to the president's knowledge about an officer's performance.[70]

Although Corwin is incorrect that the above two theories were regarded at the First Congress as "flatly opposed," the arguments about the nature of the removal power on the one hand and executive power on the other seem to make the removal-as-incident-to-appointment claim superfluous if not problematic. As Abraham Baldwin of Georgia suggested during the debate in the First Congress, the Constitution opposes the principle of removal flowing from appointment more than it supports it (see, for example, the president and judges).[71] Prakash has aptly restated Baldwin's point here: "Numerous entities select various federal officials, with apparently few supposing that the selectors may remove the selected."[72] Taft was in error here on the extent to which the partisans of executive power theory at the First Congress relied on removal as incident to appointment. They were concerned to establish the different character of the powers and reveal other constitutional provisions as firmer ground for removal.

The Supreme Court, however, had made the removal-as-incident-to-appointment principle central to its limited removal power jurisprudence. In *United States v. Perkins,* the plaintiff was a naval cadet engineer who had graduated from the U.S. Naval Academy in 1881. In 1883 he was honorably discharged from service by the secretary of the Navy. He sued to recover salary and argued his discharge violated the following statute: "No officer in the military or naval service shall in time of peace be dismissed from service except upon and in pursuance of the sentence of a court-martial to that effect, or in commutation thereof."[73] The government argued the statute violated the executive's constitutionally based removal power. The Court affirmed the judgment of the Court of Claims in favor of the naval officer. Quoting the lower court, it argued:

Whether or not Congress can restrict the power of removal incident to the power of appointment of those officers who are appointed by the president by and with the advice and consent of the Senate, under the authority of the Constitution (Article II, Section 2) does not arise in this case, and need not be considered. We have no doubt that when Congress, by law, vests the appointment of inferior officers in the heads of departments, it may limit and restrict the power of removal as it deems best for the public interest. The constitutional authority in Congress to thus vest the appointment implies authority to limit, restrict, and regulate the removal by such laws as Congress may enact in relation to the officers so appointed.[74]

Taft discussed the *Perkins* case at two junctures in his opinion in *Myers*. The first came in a discussion designed to refute the idea that the enumerated powers of Congress in Article I, Section 8 authorize it to control removal. Taft argued, "By the specific constitutional provision for appointment of executive officers, with its necessary incident of removal, the power of appointment and removal is clearly provided for by the Constitution, and the legislative power with respect to both is excluded save by the specific exception as to the inferior offices."[75] Thus, for Taft, the principle that the removal power is incident to the appointment power was crucial in that it provided a specific and effective limit to congressional intervention in removal. The inferior appointments clause was the *only* place in the Constitution where Congress could look to find the authority to limit the removal power.

Later in the opinion Taft again brought up *Perkins* to show that the Court had, in the past, authorized regulations limiting the heads of departments in the exercise of their removal power. But what the Court had never authorized through the inferior appointments clause was for "Congress to draw to itself, or to either branch of it, the power to remove or the right to participate in the exercise of that power."[76] Taft's fundamental point here was to argue that *if* Congress chose to vest the appointment power in the head of a department (or presumably a court of law), *then* it could regulate removals. But if it did not vest the appointment power, and the appointment was made by the president with the advice and consent of the Senate, then removal remained with the president alone, not subject to regulation by Congress.

In the context of this second discussion of *Perkins* and the inferior appointments clause, the Chief Justice mentioned, almost as an aside, another problem that is particularly illustrative of tensions not only in Taft's argument but also in any attempt to ascertain the constitutional boundaries of the removal power. Congress could also, according to the clause, vest the appointment power in the president alone—in effect removing the necessity for the Senate to advise on and consent to the appointment. The problem, not addressed by the Court in *Perkins*, is whether this vesting of the appointment power in the president alone makes his removal power any more subject to congressional regulation than it would have been had Congress done nothing and left the appointment with the president and the Senate. Taft replied this way: "Under the reasoning upon which the legislative decision of 1789 was put, it might be difficult to avoid a negative answer, but it is not before us and we do not decide it."[77] Put more clearly: No, Congress's vesting of the appointment power in the president alone does not likely make the office in question more subject to congressional regulation than it would have been had the appointment been left to the president and the Senate. But why not? The opposite would seem to the case, if it is true that the removal power is incidental to the appointment power. The distinction that would make the removal of the inferior officer whose appointment rests with the president alone more subject to congressional regulation than before is this: The appointment power, in this instance, would flow from statutory authority; if appointments were left to the president and the Senate, in contrast, then that authority would flow from the Constitution. Congress, under its constitutional authority to vest inferior appointments, would have, in effect, moved the executive removal power from its constitutional basis to its statutory basis. Why, then, does Taft retreat from the logic of this line of argument? Notice he specifically mentions the reasoning of the Decision of 1789 as leading to the opposite conclusion. Why would this be so? Well, as Taft well knew, executive power theorists at the First Congress did not rest the executive removal power solely or even primarily on the principle that removal was incident to appointment. As Solicitor General Beck put it in his exchange at oral argument with Brandeis, "The power to remove is not a mere incident and is not solely attributable to the power to appoint. It has a much broader basis."[78] Thus, both Beck and Taft thought that the inferior appointments clause alone was an insufficient ground for executive removal power. Though this clause, properly construed, might seem to narrow congressional regulation of the removal power, it could also invite Congress to take the appointment out of the hands of the president and Senate for a broad range of offices and thereby enable Congress to regulate removal in those cases. Thus, both Beck and Taft sought a broader constitutional ground for executive removal power, and Madison and his associates in the First Congress supplied just that.

Congressional Delegation

Now we turn to the briefs for the appellant and the dissenters in *Myers* to understand the logic of the congressional delegation position. We include here the arguments of Edward Corwin in his monograph on the removal power written shortly after the *Myers* decision. Just as the executive power theorists relied on constitutional clauses like the vesting clause and the take care clause to make their case, the partisans of congressional delegation relied on the inferior appointments clause and the necessary and proper clause of Article I, Section 8 to ground their arguments. We will see slightly different versions of this position emerge, with Brandeis and Corwin comprising one version of congressional delegation, and McReynolds and Senator Pepper comprising another, perhaps more radical, version.

Senator Pepper's brief contains an exceptionally clear statement of the congressional delegation position, which points implicitly to both the relevant constitutional clauses and the core assumptions about the separation of powers scheme. He wrote:

> Whether or not a certain office shall be created is a legislative question. The duties of the official, the salary which he is to receive, and the term during which he is to serve are likewise matters for legislative determination. Provision for filling the office is in its nature legislative, and so is provision for vacating it. The fact that the Constitution makes a specific provision in connection with the filling of the office works no change in the nature of the provision for vacating it. *The actual removal is an Executive act; but if it is legal it must be done in execution of a law — and the making of that law is an act of Congress.*[79]

Pepper contrasted the power expressly vested in Congress through the necessary and proper clause with what he saw as the much more modest language of the Inferior appointments clause of Article II, which merely declares that the president has a duty to make appointments. Everything related to removal, up to the actual act of dismissing the incumbent from office, flows out this legislative power of Congress. Thus, Pepper rejected both executive power and advise and consent, because the latter just as much as the former denied to Congress the power to state the terms of removal that flows from its legislative power to create the offices in the first place. Thus, Pepper argued that though the Tenure of Office Act may have been unwise, it was perfectly constitutional. Further, during oral argument Sutherland asked Senator Pepper if Congress could pass a law that vested the removal power in the Senate alone: "undoubtedly" was his reply.[80] Another telling exchange came shortly thereafter with Justices Edward Sanford and Harlan Stone. Sanford asked the senator what happened to the removal power if Congress declined to pass any language related to it. Stone refined the question by asking where the president's power to remove comes from in the face of congressional silence: Would it flow from statute or from the Constitution? Pepper argued that it came from the statute, and that in that case "there is an inference of the intention to confer the power upon him."[81] Thus, Pepper did not concede there was *any* constitutional basis for the executive power to remove, *only* a statutory one.

Neither Brandeis nor McReynolds went this far, though perhaps McReynolds came closer than Brandeis. Like Pepper, McReynolds quoted a passage from a speech of John Calhoun in support of his contention about the relevance of the necessary and proper clause:

> Congress shall have power to make all laws, not only to carry into effect the powers expressly delegated to itself, but those delegated to the government or any department or officer thereof, and, of course, comprehends the power to pass laws necessary and proper to carry into effect the powers expressly granted to the executive department. It follows, of course, to whatever express grant of power to the executive the power of dismissal may be supposed to attach, whether to that of seeing the law faithfully executed, or to the still more comprehensive grant, as contended for by some, vesting executive powers in the president, the mere fact that it is a power appurtenant to another power, and necessary to carry it into effect, transfers it, by the provisions of the Constitution cited, from the executive to Congress, and places it under the control of Congress, to be regulated in the manner which it may judge best.[82]

For Calhoun, then, the necessary and proper clause trumps both the take care clause and the vesting clause of Article II. As we saw in Chapter 3 ("Jackson to Johnson: The Rise of Congressional Delegation"), Henry Clay made this same argument.[83] Prescribing the conditions of removal is central to carry into execution the will of the government. The necessary and proper clause grants to Congress the power to carry into execution not only its own powers but also those of the other branches. In his gloss on this passage from Calhoun's speech, Corwin argued that the take care clause must be understood as a "duty," not as a "power." Other powers crucial to carry into execution the laws of the government are assigned to Congress. "No one would contend," argued Corwin, "that the president could appropriate money, or erect courts, or create offices, or enlarge the military forces, on the justification that such action was necessary in order to assure the enforcement of the laws."[84] Assuming sole executive removal power would be a similar error, in Corwin's view. It is Congress, not the executive, through the necessary and proper clause, that is given further latitude to carry into effect the enumerated powers.

One can see the difference in emphasis in the Brandeis and McReynolds opinions by recalling the two central holdings of the Court in *Myers*. First, the Court held that if an official is appointed by the president with the advice and consent of the Senate, the power to remove that official is the president's alone and Congress may not involve itself in removal.

Second (and here, of course, Taft went much further), the Court argued that a broader class of executive officers—those officers exercising executive functions whose actions are not merely ministerial in nature—are removable at the discretion of the president. Both Brandeis and Corwin suggested that Taft's mistake was in assimilating the case for executive control of cabinet-level or superior officers with the case for executive control of all officers. This was why the inferior appointments clause was central to Justice Brandeis's dissent. History demonstrated Congress's steady role in prescribing the conditions for the removal of these inferior offices, and this longstanding practice revealed that Taft was wrong that strict executive control was necessary to the functioning of the executive branch.

But the inferior appointments clause alone could not solve the constitutional question for those who were inclined to limit the role of the executive in removal. If this were the only basis for Congress's power, one would have to rely on the principle that removal is incident to appointment. But this principle cuts both ways: It leaves the president with significant power. It also would seem to indicate that although Congress could vest appointment (and thus removal) in the president alone, the courts of law, and the heads of departments—it could not involve itself in the removal. Though this might have worked as an argument against Taft's more radical contention in *Myers*, it would not have saved the statute at hand. Thus, Brandeis was driven to the conclusion aptly stated by Corwin: "Congress's power to stipulate the qualifications and tenure of inferior officers rests on precisely the same basis as its power to stipulate the qualifications and tenure of superior officers. It rests upon the 'necessary and proper' clause."[85]

One can see Brandeis working through this problem in his dissent. He maintained that the executive removal power over inferior offices always comes from the statutory authority granted to the president by Congress; again the distinction between statutory and constitutional authority is key. But then Brandeis added this: "It is true that the exercise of the power of removal is said to be an executive act, and that, when the Senate grants or withholds consent to a removal by the president, it participates in an executive act."[86] Brandeis was treading carefully here. The *power* is not executive, but the *exercise of the power*—or the act—is. In other words, though the inferior appointments clause enables Congress to vest appointment and removal, something inheres in the action of removal that is executive. But that something, according Brandeis, is fairly insignificant. Brandeis knows this because the "Constitution has confessedly granted to Congress the legislative power to create offices, and to prescribe the tenure thereof, and it has not in terms denied to Congress the power to control removals. To prescribe the tenure involves prescribing the conditions under which incumbency shall cease."[87] Pepper characterized his position in remarkably similar terms during oral argument: "[Henry] Clay took precisely the ground which I am feebly attempting to take here, that the act of removal is an executive act, but that the power to determine the conditions under which removal may be made is a great legislative power and is resident in Congress."[88] Though Brandeis seemed to want to carve out a more moderate version of congressional delegation theory than Pepper, he ended up with a congruent understanding of the necessary and proper clause and Congress's role in removal.

Shortly after Pepper's encapsulation of the position above, Sutherland asked him about his contention that Congress could vest the power of removal in the Senate alone: "If that were done, would that be fixing the terms of the removal or the conditions upon which removal could be made, which probably would be a legislative power, or would it be conferring the power itself?"[89] Pepper did not have clear answer as to how one could make a principled distinction. Thus, to concede the legitimacy of Pepper's understanding of the meaning of the necessary and proper clause and its relation to the removal power seemed to grant to Congress wide latitude in limiting and even conferring the power.

Conclusion

So just as Justices Brandeis and McReynolds must have been troubled during oral argument by Beck's affirmation of an extensive executive removal power (despite his insistence on the possibility of a more moderate middle ground for the decision), Justices Taft, Sutherland, and the others joining the majority must have recoiled from Pepper's affirmation of a broad congressional removal power. Both Taft, writing for the Court, and the dissenters in *Myers* looked not just to the narrow ground of the appointments clause to make a more moderate middle ground. Each party to the dispute was driven to other constitutional clauses to counter the claims of their antagonists. Neither the executive power position nor congressional delegation in *Myers* could admit of a middle ground rooted in particular constitutional clauses.

Each side in *Myers* also had strikingly different visions of the place executive power held within the broader separation of powers scheme. The partisans of congressional delegation held a very narrow view of execution in the sense that executive authority was primarily — if not solely — derived from the statutory grants of Congress. Brandeis, in concluding his dissent, appealed to an understanding of the separation of powers that emphasized the lack of autonomy granted to each branch. Foreshadowing modern scholars and jurists who today are often described as "functionalists," Brandeis argued that the Constitution "left each [branch] in some measure dependent upon the others, as it left to each power to exercise, in some respects, functions in their nature executive, legislative and judicial."[90] Congress occupied the center of this system due to its powers to create offices and appropriate the funds necessary for those offices to function. But Brandeis also made a normative claim about the separation of powers closely linked to his constitutional argument. This principle was not put in place for the sake of "efficiency" but rather to forestall the "exercise of arbitrary power." According to Brandeis, "In America, as in England, the conviction prevailed then that the people must look to representative assemblies for the protection of their liberties."[91] For Brandeis, then, Congress was ultimately a safer repository of power: It was the more republican branch due to its close connection with the people.

Taft argued that Brandeis made the same error that was vigorously disputed by executive power theorists at the First Congress. It is, wrote Taft,

> a fundamental misconception that the president's attitude in his exercise of power is one of opposition to the people, while Congress is their only defender in the Government. . . . The president is a representative of the people just as the members of the Senate and of the House are, and it may be, at some times, on some subjects, that the president elected by all the people is rather more representative of them all than are the members of each body of the legislature, whose constituencies are local, and not countrywide; and, as the president is elected for four years, with the mandate of the people to exercise his executive power under the Constitution, there would seem to be no reason for construing that instrument in such a way as to limit and hamper that power beyond the limitations of it, expressed or fairly implied.[92]

Taft's linkage of democratic mandate with constitutional duty echoed the arguments of presidents such as Andrew Jackson and Grover Cleveland. And like other executive power theorists before him, Taft also emphasized the importance of the relationship between a president and his subordinates. Here he sought to counter the idea that because executive officers were bound via the statutory authority granted to them by Congress they could not be understood as agents of the president. For Taft, the removal power had to be understood in the context of the president's power to superintend the construction of the statutes to be executed by his subordinates. He argued that to the extent that any statute granted an executive officer discretion in the administration of the law, it would be all the more crucial for the president to have the removal power. Because these subordinates acted in the president's stead, the "unitary and uniform" execution of the law demanded he be able to judge their conduct and take action accordingly.

But as Taft well knew, and as subsequent history would demonstrate in the vast expansion of federal power, this problem of executive superintendence was exceedingly complex. Taft granted that Congress could prescribe a specific action of an executive officer; in that case, the action would be ministerial rather than discretionary and would not be subject to presidential control.[93] But there were two other instances in which presidential control of subordinates might be limited. As Taft wrote,

> There may be duties so peculiarly and specifically committed to the discretion of a particular officer as to raise a question whether the president may overrule or revise the officer's interpretation of his statutory duty in a particular instance. Then there may be duties of a quasi-judicial character imposed on executive officers and members of executive tribunals whose decisions after hearing affect interests of individuals, the discharge of which the president cannot in a particular case properly influence or control. But even in such a case, he may consider the decision after its rendition as a reason for removing the officer, on the ground that the discretion regularly entrusted to that officer by statute has not been, on the whole, intelligently or wisely exercised. Otherwise, he does not discharge his own constitutional duty of seeing that the laws are faithfully executed.[94]

What is striking here is that even though Taft granted the possibility of limits to direct presidential supervision of the discretion of subordinates, he still maintained a presidential removal power over those same subordinates.

It was Corwin, anticipating the Court in *Humphrey's Executor v. United States* (1935), who countered Taft by claiming that the degree of executive removal power over an office would change according to the nature of the office. For Corwin, the president's removal power would rise or fall along with the degree to which superintendence of execution was appropriate. It was Corwin's claim that an unlimited removal power in either Congress or the president was equally mistaken. He argued, "It is the essential nature of the office under consideration, as shown by its characteristic duties, [that] determines the scope of the removal power in relation to the power of congress, in creating an office, to fix its tenure."[95] Corwin's examples included, at one end of the spectrum, a Secretary of State, and, at the other end, judicial officers. The former he called "a mere instrument of presidential prerogative," whereas the latter were irremovable. But we notice that even though Corwin grounded the congressional power to limit removal in the necessary and proper clause, he offered no parallel constitutional ground for executive control over an officer such as the secretary of state. Indeed, he made the case against the significance of the vesting clause and the take care clause using Calhoun's analysis of the necessary and proper clause.

Yet Corwin's primary concern was not so much to protect congressional power from executive encroachment, but rather to protect the newly emerging administrative state and its functionaries: the independent regulatory commissions. A member of the Interstate Commerce Commission, argued Corwin, "exercises no power within presidential authority, either constitutional or statutory, and is designated neither by the constitution nor by custom to be an instrument of presidential policies or a recipient of presidential confidences. His powers are none of them a subtraction from presidential prerogative, but are, on the contrary, derived from a delegation by congress of its own express constitutional powers."[96] These broad delegations had been found tolerable by the Supreme Court, according to Corwin, only on the assumption that such bodies had due regard for proper procedure and deliberate, disinterested policy analysis. Such regard is guaranteed by one thing: true independence. But how, asked Corwin, is independence of decision "to be reasonably predicated of an officer over whose head the Damocles sword of removal is ever suspended?"[97] Here, then, emerges the debate that we will examine fully in the next chapter: the rise of the expert administrator and his place in (or outside of) the separation of powers scheme.

Members of independent regulatory commissions were not the only officers Corwin and others thought worthy of protection from the scope of executive removal power. We recall the Comptroller General and his assistant as outlined in the Budget and Accounting Act. As Will King argued in his brief on behalf of Myers, the duties of the Comptroller were not executive in character but rather semijudicial.[98] The regulation of such an officer and his activities belonged, therefore, under the domain of Congress. Accounting officers, King argued, had long been thought to have a special nature. King recalled Madison's description of the Comptroller during the debate over the Treasury Department at the First Congress. Though placed in the Treasury Department over Madison's objections, finally these officers were being given the sort of independence suitable to their tasks. The sort of executive removal power being recommended by the government and defended by the Court, according to Corwin and the dissenters in *Myers*, would threaten the delicate, semijudicial, administrative tasks increasingly being demanded of governments. The Comptroller was only a particularly recent and telling example of the phenomenon.

Chapter Five

The Progressive Era and Independent Regulatory Commissions

Here we examine the 1935 Supreme Court case *Humphrey's Executor v. United States* in light of Congress's creation of independent regulatory commissions. Because IRCs were a means of buffering administration from presidential control over removals, scholars have long argued that the rise of IRCs can be explained as a victory of the Progressive movement in American politics (1890–1920). According to many Progressive reformers during this period, administration ought to be liberated from accountability to any *political* branch of government so that scientific expertise could design efficient forms of regulation. There is much to this story, but it does not wholly explain the way the Court treated the removal power in 1935. As we show below, the creation of the IRCs took a path similar to previous manifestations of advise and consent doctrine, particularly that suggested by Elbridge Gerry during the congressional debates in 1789 and later by Daniel Webster in the nineteenth century.

The history surrounding the creation of IRCs shows that neither Congress nor the president really regarded IRCs as truly independent. As in the case of Daniel Webster's evolution from advise and consent to congressional delegation in the 1830s, Congress was most emphatic about the "independence" of regulatory commissions only when challenging the president's claim over the administration. Members of Congress in the twentieth century wanted IRCs to function as legislative adjuncts. In particular, what might have been a desire for a truly nonpolitical agency of government became in fact an effort by Congress to shield officers from removal in areas where Congress wanted to retain authority over administration. Presidents, by contrast, believed that the regulatory commissions should aid the president in executing the law. This contest between congressional delegation and executive power theory can be seen in Justice George Sutherland's opinion in *Humphrey's*.

Lastly we look to President Franklin Roosevelt's efforts to reinvigorate the executive administration in 1937. Roosevelt hoped to reorganize the executive branch so that it could carry out his ambitious and unprecedented

141

economic plans under the New Deal. But Roosevelt was conscious that he faced a new set of challenges in doing this when Congress, also increasingly sensitive to administrative issues, had denied the White House a free hand in controlling many of the most important regulatory agencies of government. Consequently, Roosevelt would bring together Madison's argument for executive responsibility as well as the Jefferson-Jackson arguments for democratic accountability to a new level of intensity.

Introduction

The emergence of independent regulatory commissions around the turn of the twentieth century complicates our framework for the study of the executive removal power. IRCs assign their members tenure for a limited period and immunize them from at-pleasure removal by the president. For most historians, IRCs are regarded as the brainchild of the Progressive Era, when many political thinkers had come to the conclusion that modern economic regulation required a new style of governing outside of the traditional separation of powers scheme. IRCs, according to Progressives, would be shielded from the political influence of Congress and the president so that their members could employ their expertise and specialized knowledge over the regulation of the economy. As Stephen Skowronek has argued, the American "state" emerged in a patchwork fashion because of the competition between "the constancy of the Constitution of 1789 and the destructive consequences of constructive reform initiatives." Even as this haphazard construction resulted in "operational confusion," the IRCs represented the "signal triumph" of the Progressive state-building aspiration to disjunction rather than continuity with the past. "The national administrative apparatus was freed from the clutches of party domination, direct court supervision, and localistic orientations only to be thrust into the center of an amorphous new institutional politics."[1] To be sure, the literature on state-building that took place during the first half of the twentieth century is rich. Daniel Carpenter, for example, has argued that the key variable in the development of the state was not the emergence of IRCs, which he sees as too wedded to a Progressive interpretation of the period, but rather the abilities of executive agencies to enhance their reputations and build networks.[2] Below we focus on the way the IRCs affected the removal power in this period.

In 1935 the Supreme Court legitimized the anomalous arrangement surrounding IRCs in *Humphrey's Executor v. United States*. It reasoned that the members of these commissions derived their immunity to presidential removal from the unprecedented need for a new kind of power in the administration of government. Lying outside the scope of the traditional

tripartite system of government, these administrators were not to be considered an arm of the executive; instead, they exercised "quasi-legislative"
and "quasi-judicial" powers.[3] Consequently, the IRCs do not seem to fit
any of the positions we have outlined among the debates of 1789.

We also raise some doubt over whether the president or Congress really conceived of the IRCs as a new frontier in organization of the bureaucratic administration in relation to the removal power. Although we
acknowledge that their independence from congressional and executive removals represented an innovation on the main positions put forth in 1789,
we also argue that neither Congress nor the president embraced the idea
of a bureaucracy that is removed from politics. Rather, the debate over
the IRCs is best understood as a new version of an older debate between
Congress and the president, but this time changes in the presidency itself
required new arguments.

The Decision of 1789, Hamilton, and Progressives

The only position we have examined that comes close to resembling the
Progressive argument for the IRCs was that of Alexander Hamilton. As
we discussed above in Chapter 1 ("The Decision of 1789"), Hamilton
hoped that the Senate's involvement in removal would actually frustrate
presidential ambition and protect administrators from the popular passions that accompany a national election of the president. For Hamilton,
the undulating nature of political life, tossed to and fro by the incessant
fluctuation of public opinion, posed a threat to the steady administration of
law. Immunity from presidential removal had a twofold benefit. Not only
would it liberate bureaucracy from democratic politics in order to effectively undertake the sensitive and complicated tasks of executing federal
policy; in addition, unlike those democratic politicians who acquire office
by means of "the little arts of popularity," administrative offices would attract men with real talent and elite qualities.

Though their institutional design differed from that of Hamilton, the
IRCs (at least in the minds of the Progressives) achieved the same purpose:
creating a class of expert administrators immune from the vicissitudes of
democratic politics. The resurrection of Hamilton's vision near the turn
of the twentieth century could be explained by the unique challenges that
government faced with the rise of modern industrialization. The Industrial Revolution had produced a host of complicated regulatory issues that
seemed to require the knowledge and abilities of experts specialized in the
subjects they would supervise.[4] But democratic politics in America was not
entirely conducive to scientific administration. The most prominent offices
of government were elective, and most administrative posts continued to

be distributed according to the political interests of the parties. Progressive intellectuals at the time argued that the country would be prepared to meet the challenges of the new century only if the nation was willing to rethink its previous assumptions about democratic politics, including such traditional limits on power as the Constitution's separation of powers and doctrines like the rule of law. Independent regulatory commissions offered a pathway for this kind of reform, for it was here that one could carve out a space for scientifically trained experts who would be free from the ebb and flow of popular opinion. Progressives began by drawing a novel distinction between political power and what they termed "administration." "Administration," explained Woodrow Wilson in 1886, "lies outside the proper sphere of *politics*. Administrative questions are not political questions."[5] In the past, the primary concern of democratic countries consisted in finding intricately designed limitations on political power. At that time, argued Wilson, "the weightier debates of constitutional principle are . . . no longer of more immediate practical moment than questions of administration. It is getting to be harder to *run* a constitution than to frame one."[6]

Hamilton's vision for administration became the model of political thought among Progressive reformers, as exemplified in the formula coined by Herbert Croly for the Progressive plan of reform: Hamiltonian means to Jeffersonian ends.[7] In fact, their vision of the political reform was strikingly similar to Hamilton's original hopes for the Constitution of the executive office explained in Chapter 1 ("The Decision of 1789"). Both agreed that democratic forms of government would be successful only if they could attract and utilize the talents of an expert elite. But, more important, both seemed to agree that the Constitution of 1787 was at least partly inadequate to achieving this end. Hamilton did, of course, defend the proposed Constitution in his contributions to *The Federalist Papers*. But his argument, carefully read, really points to a very different constitutional vision than that embodied in the original document. In his ostensible defense of the presidency in *The Federalist*, Hamilton praised the Constitution for combining two seemingly antithetical but essential elements of a well-designed executive branch: "energy" and "stability."[8] The difficulty in structuring the executive office, according to Hamilton, is to render it sufficiently energetic so that it can act with immediate decision while making it sufficiently stable to secure the uniform administration of law over time. Hamilton's solution, as we have already described, was to include the Senate's participation in the removal power in order to shield executive administration from the influence exerted by a popularly elected president. Although the Constitution vests the sole power of the executive in the president, Hamilton's argument anticipated a bifurcated executive branch—one political and one administrative. Consequently the Hamiltonian vision of executive power anticipated not one but two executives.[9]

That Hamilton knew he was departing from the constitutional design of the executive office can be seen from his innovative account of the Electoral College in *The Federalist* No. 68. Here, Hamilton described the method of presidential election as a device whereby electors would refine public opinion distinguishing the "sense of the people" from the passion and whims of temporary majorities.[10] Yet in the debates of the Convention (where, of course, Hamilton was present), no delegate suggested that the Electoral College served any function other than registering in a convenient mode the electoral choice of the nation at large.[11] Though exaggerated in their criticism, Jefferson and Madison may not have been far off the mark in thinking that Hamilton was seeking to transform the original Constitution.

The Progressives thought this vision of the presidency would prove a serviceable model for reconciling democratic politics with the rising need for administrative expertise in the twentieth century. In the age of modern industry with its horizontal command over the economic resources of the nation, democracy and expertise were becoming harder to reconcile. The Progressives feared that political parties under the control of powerful unelected bosses threatened to eviscerate the nation's institutions of democratic government. Their solution was a more energetic and popular executive office capable of resisting the political machines and protecting the national government from special interests.[12] At the same time, the regulation of a modern economy would require experts in scientific management shielded from the influence of popular opinion. Thus we might say of their binary proposals such as direct primaries, on the one hand, and independent regulatory commissions on the other — that they too believed that there was a need for not one *but two executives*. By sequestering "administration" from politics, the Progressives aimed at realizing Hamilton's design within a narrower space — federal regulatory policy.

Yet Hamilton's ingenious solution to the problem of executive power would probably not prove to be so facile in practice. If the Senate and the president remained deadlocked over the removal of a supposedly negligent administrator, whom would the people hold periodically accountable for the execution of the law? How could the president be held accountable every four years if he is not free to remove those whom he entrusts to carry out his commands? Perhaps Hamilton's argument was never adopted because many thought that in reality the joint participation of the Senate and the president in removal would have crippled the executive branch, undermining its unity and jeopardizing its independence. The Progressive case for the IRCs, we believe, suffers from similar problems. With their commissioners immunized from at-pleasure removal, the IRCs would theoretically occupy a neutral territory in the national government immune from the political branches of government. But, as we will show, neither branch has ever really treated them as such, either in their statutory origins or in their subsequent operation.[13] Our study of the historical development of the IRCs in the twentieth century reveals that the IRCs were never simply admired for employing nonpartisan experts. Rather, they were regarded in the eyes of Congress as a political arm of the legislature and, in the eyes of the president, as an agent of the executive.[14] Their so-called independence, consequently, amounts in the end to an uneasy compromise between the two branches, one that has proved awkward under our constitutional form of government.

Progressivism and the Independent Regulatory Commission

While every position in the debate of 1789 adopted a different interpretation of the removal power, they all shared a single common ground: Each was conceived within the framework of the separation of powers, and they all allocated the removal power according to a certain interpretation of that core principle. By contrast, the Progressives argued explicitly that new institutions of governing were necessary in order to circumvent the defects in this constitutional division of powers. In particular, they believed that the system of checks and balances in the Constitution hampered the nation's ability to address the evolution of economic developments throughout the country. As Woodrow Wilson complained: "The trouble with the theory is that government is not a machine, but a living thing. It falls, not under the theory of the universe, but under the theory of organic life. It is accountable to Darwin, not to Newton. It is modified by its environment, necessitated by its tasks, shaped to its functions by the sheer pressure of life."[15] Wilson's comments here reflect the general sentiments of the period: The Constitution was a noble but now antiquated design that limited political authority in an age that needed more concentrated forms of power to deal with the challenges of interstate commerce and industry. A more thorough critique of the original constitutional order found expression in the writings of Herbert Croly, who would eventually help to write part of the Progressive platform of 1912. Croly believed that the nation's traditional principles embodied in the central doctrine of "government by law" was now responsible for America's lagging political development in regulatory administration. The Constitution, according to Croly, had been the keystone for realizing this public philosophy in practice because the document both established a fundamental set of rules for governing political life and served as a model for all future laws. In an advanced industrial economy where corporations had taken the place of individuals and regulations had to address the ever changing and infinitely complex undertakings of businesses, the rule of law, according to Croly, was unable to meet the challenges of governing for three reasons. First, Congress's procedures for lawmaking, designed to promote slow, careful deliberation after extensive debate, rendered most economic regulations obsolete as soon as the bill came into effect in the fast-paced economic world of the twentieth century. Second, laws are of a general nature and therefore cannot be written to address the complex dimensions of economic activity when the activities engaged in by a corporation or industry could change over night. Finally, many Progressives like Croly thought that economic activity could not be captured by terms like "fair" versus "unfair" or even "legal" versus "illegal." Law, applied uniformly to every citizen or corporation, can only proscribe certain activities in these abstract moral terms since its efficacy rests on the moral authority behind its punishments. For Croly, then, real reform would require both a thorough overhaul of the traditional constitutional arrangements as well as the nation's assumption that the fundamental purpose of government lies in the protection of equal rights.

Progressives, Congress, and the Independent Regulatory Commissions

The example on everyone's mind during this period had been the Sherman Anti-Trust Act. Section 1 of the act stated: "Every contract, combination in the form of trust or otherwise, or conspiracy, in restraint of trade or commerce among the several States, or with foreign nations, is declared to be illegal."[16] The problem with the law, according to most Progressives, was how broadly it stated the scope of activity that was defined as illegal.[17] Because almost any activity performed by a corporation amounted to some restraint of trade, it was impossible according to the wording of the law to distinguish between activities that constituted a trust or conspiracy and normal business activities. In Croly's view, the trusts had indeed engaged in some suspect business practices, but their control of the market was really only the consequence of the fact that they were more efficient and productive than their competitors. The defect in the rule of law in this case was that it did not permit administrators to distinguish between undesirable and desirable combinations in industry. The problem, according to many at the time, lies in the very idea of the rule of law. Whereas most Americans insisted that law treat people equally because everyone had the same rights, Progressives like Croly advocated for a more utilitarian treatment of the trust issue — one where experts would judge ex post facto the economic impact of certain activities before determining whether they should be prohibited or not. Unlike legislators, regulators would be pragmatic in their approach to public policy–making, crafting their rules in terms of experience rather than a priori assumptions about justice or fairness.[18] Under a Progressive order, regulatory agencies would address each activity on a case-by-case basis, thereby maintaining the efficiency and productivity present among some of the trusts while preventing those same corporations from leveraging their market advantage for the sake of personal gain. Once the constraints on American government imposed by the doctrine of individual rights and the rule of law were loosened, it would be possible to institute this type of administrative state.

As mentioned before, Croly even assisted George Rublee, future architect of the Federal Trade Commission, in crafting the Progressive Party platform of 1912 in which they proposed to amend the Sherman Act along these lines and to create an IRC for the regulation of corporate activity.[19] In a letter to Learned Hand explaining the defects of the Democratic Party's position on the trusts in 1912, Croly argued: "What Brandeis [author with Wilson of the Democrats' campaign platform on the regulation of trusts] proposes to do is to prejudge the issue of the conflict between large scale & small scale production and to discriminate against the former.... The question is not yet settled how far and in what industries each is more efficient, and it should not be pre-judged."[20] When Croly says "it should not be pre-judged," he meant that it is better to make a determination on the desirability or undesirability of certain economic activities post facto on the basis of utility rather than a priori assumptions about justice. The problem with the Wilson-Brandeis position for the regulation of the trusts is that it would attempt to define good and bad before we have seen whether the activity is useful or harmful. This was precisely the problem with the rule of law for the Progressives.

In 1914, Congress created the Federal Trade Commission. Section 5 of the FTC Act gave the commission broad discretion for both determining and pursuing unfair methods of competition. The FTC would be composed of five politically independent, nonpartisan commissioners who would possess the necessary business expertise to regulate modern industry in the interests of the general welfare. The membership of the commission was to be allotted in a bipartisan manner (no more than three members from one party), appointed for seven-year terms (following an initial period of staggered terms). Commissioners, according to the enabling act, could be removed only for "inefficiency, neglect of duty, or malfeasance in office."[21] Under the indeterminate wording in Section 5 of the act, the commissioners were granted wide latitude for regulation. They could enforce these regulations according to their own standards and pursue cases according to their own discretion. Finally, the act also made it possible for the commission to mete out less punitive punishments on offending corporations than those that would have been imposed under criminal law or in civil liability.[22]

If we look to the origins of the FTC in 1914, however, the historical record suggests that its independence was really an expedient compromise in the struggle between the executive and legislative branches for control of a burgeoning regulatory state rather than a common conviction that the nation's constitutional form of government needed to be restructured. In fact, the FTC statute (particularly Section 5, which gave broad discretionary authority to the commission), was forged by a Congress that was deeply fractured over how to regulate modern corporate activity. The one thing members could agree upon was that they did not want the president to have sole authority over this sort of regulation. Since the creation of the Sherman Anti-Trust Act, members of Congress and various presidents had adopted sharply different approaches to regulation in the antitrust area.[23] A divided Congress was unclear about the real meaning of "unfair methods of competition" and yet unwilling to relinquish authority to the president. Congress would thus design an FTC that over time could work out an effective regulatory policy under the watchful eye of the legislature.

The Sherman Act forbid "every contract, combination in the form of trust or otherwise, or conspiracy, in restraint of trade or commerce among the several States, or with foreign nations."[24] Passed into law in 1890, the act did little to stop a boom of mergers near the turn of the century.[25] As one historian reports, "During those years at least 303 firms disappeared annually through mergers; 1,208 disappeared in 1899. . . . Consolidation piled on consolidation, as the American Tobacco Company, for example, absorbed what once had been 250 firms."[26] One of the chief causes of discontent over the enforcement of the Sherman Anti-Trust Act had been the construction that the law had received at the hands of the Supreme Court between 1897 and 1899. In *United States v. Trans-Missouri Freight Association* (1897), the Court held that the Sherman Act prohibited a contractual arrangement among railroad companies for setting prices despite the fact that Congress had created an exemption in the Interstate Commerce Act that made such activity immune from prosecution.[27] Though many scholars have depicted the Court as probusiness and hostile to federal regulation during this period, it was actually the Court's insistence on a strict reading of law and its refusal to favor one kind of activity over another that drew the ire of so many critics and members of Congress.

While there was much criticism of the Court's literal reading of the Sherman Anti-Trust clause, there also existed a wide disagreement in Congress over how to distinguish between reasonable and unreasonable restraints of trade. Martin Sklar summarizes the dilemma over regulation of the trusts during this period in the following way: "The conflict in policy and law may be defined as follows: neither the executive branch nor Congress was prepared to impose upon the market the law as construed by the Court; neither branch wished to require unrestricted competition, and each was either unwilling or unable to undertake statist command."[28] Between the adoption of the act in 1890 and the creation of the FTC in 1914, the diversity of interpretations adopted by different presidents mirrored the variety of interpretations held by members of Congress.

Roosevelt, Taft, and Wilson on the Problem of Administration

Naturally, the task of defining the meaning of the Sherman Anti-Trust Act fell to the president whose duty it was to enforce the law. In doing so, presidents faced one of two choices: Either read the law literally and prosecute every restraint of trade, or interpret it with a certain discretion based on a broader conception of the public good. But a strict interpretation had its own risks in that it might simply remind Congress of how poorly it had done in first undertaking the task of economic regulation and how little it had accomplished in antitrust regulation since then. Having experienced the inconveniences of a broad construction of executive power under Theodore Roosevelt and a more narrow one under William Howard Taft, Congress decided that neither served its interest in the end. Woodrow Wilson's election in 1912 presented an opportunity for Congress to respond, since Wilson's attempt to straddle both Roosevelt's and Taft's construction of executive power made him more pliable to the will of Congress.

During his first term, Theodore Roosevelt came to believe that large corporations and trusts were neither products of nefarious business dealings nor threats to economic progress but natural parts of the evolution of an efficient and productive industrial economy.[29] In 1908, he attempted to find a way for the executive branch to distinguish harmful versus beneficial activity when he worked with the National Civic Federation to develop a strategy for the regulation of corporations and trusts with the aid of a newly empowered Bureau of Corporations located under the Department of Commerce. The proposal would have given the bureau, under the direction of the president, investigatory powers and responsibility for the registration of corporations and publicizing their financial activities. As Arthur Johnson explains: "Since [the bill] provided no yardstick by which the president was to be guided in deciding whether or not to release information gathered by the Bureau of Corporations, he was seemingly in a position to wield the big stick of publicity against corporations that he decided were 'bad' while shelving adverse information about those that he thought were 'good.'"[30]

Roosevelt was not unaware of the implications for executive power in his own proposal. As he explained to one correspondent: "I want full power given to *Executive* officers in the matter of the Sherman Anti-Trust Law."[31] Having "full power" was essential to Roosevelt's particular understanding of the executive office. "My view," he explained, "was that every officer, and above all every executive officer in high position, was a *steward of the people* bound actively and affirmatively to do all he could for the people."[32] Contrasting his position to that of his successor's more restricted view of executive power, Roosevelt found a precedent for his own view in the example of Andrew Jackson.[33] From our perspective, this appears to be an apt analogy. Roosevelt's stewardship theory fits well with Jackson's expansion of the way Madison and his allies defended executive power theory in 1789. This was particularly true of the way Roosevelt defended his removals: "In every such case I stood by the official and refused to recognize the right of Congress to interfere with me excepting by impeachment or in other Constitutional manner. On the other hand, wherever I found the officer unfit for his position I promptly removed him, even although the most influential men in Congress fought for his retention."[34] Congress, having been persuaded by testimony like that of Henry Towne, president of the Merchant's Association of New York, of the degree to which the president's powers might trespass upon their own, ultimately rejected the bill. Towne explained to the House Judiciary Committee: "Instead of fixed and definite laws we would have a set of rules made by . . . the president, subject to change without notice by him . . . at pleasure. In brief we would have personal government and instability in place of law and order."[35] Roosevelt's proposals for the regulation of interstate corporations were defeated in Congress, and by 1907–1908 Congress was chipping away at his executive powers in numerous ways.[36]

Like Roosevelt, William Howard Taft also believed that reasonable restraints of trade should be distinguished from unreasonable restraints under the Sherman Anti-Trust Act. Though Taft is often remembered as more conservative than Roosevelt on the trust question, particularly during the 1912 campaign for the presidency, Taft actually shared Roosevelt's view that the size of the corporation should not determine whether it constituted a restraint of trade, and he even supported the creation of a licensing program for corporations under the Bureau of Corporations.[37] However, Taft did depart from Roosevelt over the place of executive discretion. Responding to Roosevelt's later criticism of his limited use of discretionary executive power, Taft argued "the president can exercise no power which cannot be fairly and reasonably traced to some specific grant of power or justly implied and included within such express grant as proper and necessary to its exercise."[38] For Taft, Roosevelt's method of enforcement under the Sherman Anti-Trust Act had wandered into a dangerous area of constitutionally undefined power that made a mockery of Congress's legislative authority. Yet Taft actually prosecuted many more antitrust cases than did the Roosevelt administration. In fact, Taft's strict interpretation of his executive responsibilities compelled him to do so. As the existing antitrust statute did not explicitly provide for a more selective form of enforcement, Taft prosecuted *all forms* of corporate malfeasance even to the point of betraying the gentlemen's agreement between the Department of Justice and U.S. Steel Company made under President Roosevelt. Taft's consistency incurred the eternal ire of the former president, and it ruptured his party within Congress by fomenting the question of what legislative standards ought to define antitrust law.[39]

Woodrow Wilson emerged the winner in the 1912 presidential election, adopting a conservative platform on the trust question. During the election, Wilson argued that Congress should simply define illegal trade practices in law and provide stiff criminal sanctions rather than trusting regulatory authority lawyers and experts in the administration.[40] Seemingly closer to Taft's argument conception of executive power, Wilson attacked the discretionary exercise of power like that of Roosevelt. "Must we fall back on discretionary executive power? . . . The government of the United States was established to get rid of arbitrary, that is, discretionary executive power. . . . If we return to it we abandon the very principles of our foundation, give up the English and American experiment and turn back to discredited models of government."[41] It seemed like a massive reversal in the direction of his former scholarship on the presidency, though perhaps one he could defend as a matter of expedient accommodation under his theory that constitutional practice evolves over time. But Wilson changed his policy direction again in 1914 when, like Taft before him, he found it impossible to get Congress to adopt any legislative standards for the enforcement of the Sherman Anti-Trust Act. Between 1911 and 1914, Congress had repeatedly tried to define the terms of legitimate competition from the forms it hoped to proscribe. After a protracted effort failed to win a consensus on a new trust bill, Congress turned instead to the idea of a commission.

Wilson and the Birth of the FTC

The impetus for a more urgent legislative effort to find more precise standards in antitrust law was the May 1911 Supreme Court decision *Standard Oil v. United States*. Ironically, the Court in *Standard Oil* had in fact adopted a distinction between reasonable and unreasonable restraints of trade that had been supported by many in Congress as well as by Presidents Taft and Roosevelt. Yet the decision by the Court was received in Congress in the same way as was Roosevelt's enforcement of the law. Some members believed that all restraints on trade should be punished under the Sherman Anti-Trust Act. Others feared that the Court's understanding of "reasonable and unreasonable" restraints might be different from their understanding—thus, they accused the Court of making law on its own. Finally, others agreed with the distinction the Court had drawn but believed that the sanctions were either too harsh or too lenient. As had been the case under Taft, any attempt to consistently enforce one interpretation of the Sherman Anti-Trust Act's "restraint of trade" provision would suddenly ignite the divisions within Congress.[42] Whatever the merits of the decision, it was clear that the legislature believed that it and not the courts should define those standards. This seems to have been the case, too, with respect to executive discretion. In creating an IRC, Congress coupled a limitation on the president's removal power with a limitation on judicial review over the commission's decisions as well.

Under Wilson's presidency, Congress was once again mired in a sea of conflicting views over how to define fair standards of competition. Desperate to deliver on his party's campaign promise to do something about the trusts, Wilson became more amenable to the idea of a commission that would provide information and aid to the Justice Department in its prosecutions of unfair trade practices.[43] On January 20, 1914, Wilson delivered an address to a joint session of Congress calling for more legislation, but this time with an appeal for a commission. Unlike Croly, Wilson believed that more specific legislation was needed to better define the meaning of the Sherman Anti-Trust Act. "Surely we are sufficiently familiar with the actual processes and methods of monopoly and of the many hurtful restraints of trade to make definition possible, at any rate up to the limits of what experience has disclosed. These practices, being now abundantly disclosed, can be explicitly and item by item forbidden by statute in such terms as will practically eliminate uncertainty, the law itself and the penalty being made equally plain."[44] Certainly the knowledge was there, but Wilson also seemed less confident that a consensus on the terms of a statute could be reached in the legislature. In light of this fact, Wilson added a proposal for the creation of "an interstate trade commission" because "the business men of the country desire something more than that the menace of legal process in these matters be made explicit and intelligible. They desire the advice, the definite guidance and information which can be supplied by an administrative body."[45] With the midterm elections not far off, Wilson needed some visible form of achievement in the area of antitrust to tout for the party. Nevertheless, Wilson's commission differed from the Progressive Party's proposal for a strong IRC in 1912. His commission would serve as a type of "sunshine agency" that would provide public information for business activity, investigate anticompetitive activity, and offer advice. But it would not have enforcement power. Wilson dismissed the proposal of the 1912 Progressive Party platform that had called for an administrative body of experts as government by "a smug lot of experts."[46] "God forbid that in a democratic country we should resign the task and give the government over to experts. What are we for if we are to be scientifically taken care of by a small number of gentlemen who are the only men who understand the job?"[47] Rather, the commission Wilson initially proposed would supply the Justice Department information on corporate activity only in order to facilitate the department's own administration of the law.

On April 13, 1914, James Covington of Maryland of the House Committee on Interstate Commerce proposed a bill to create an Interstate Trade Commission and transfer to it the existing powers of the Bureau of Corporations. As Wilson had contemplated in his "Address on Monopolies and Trusts," the new commission would have had no enforcement authority. Instead, it would be authorized to conduct investigations into "unfair competition or practices in commerce" and to publish reports with recommendations for further investigation by the Justice Department or legislation by Congress. However, Covington's bill did add an important provision that would prevent the proposed commission from playing the same role that the Bureau of Corporations had under Roosevelt: The commission was to be removed "entirely from the control of the president and the Secretary of Commerce."[48] Over the years, Congress had discovered how weak its legislative authority over antitrust matters was in the hands of an executive who could prosecute offenders at his own discretion. As Senator James Reed of Missouri declared:

> I am not prepared to charge bad faith to past Attorneys General of the United States, but I am prepared to say that, in my humble judgment, the same zeal has not been back of the enforcement of this law many times that has been back of the enforcement of the laws aimed at the poor fellow who makes moonshine whiskey or sells a box of cigars without having the correct number of stamps upon the box. As to any law that has been so enforced that monopoly has grown like a green bay tree, so that its evil roots have spread into every State and every community, I am prepared to say that you need some more enforcement and you need some independent action by independent men.[49]

In the House, Representative Dick Morgan (Republican from Oklahoma), who introduced the original bill to create a commission and has come to be regarded as "the Father of the Federal Trade Commission," argued: "It is unsafe for an . . . administrative officer representing a great political party . . . to hold the power of life and death over the great business interests of this country. . . . That is . . . why I believe in . . . taking these business matters out of politics."[50] Wilson did not voice any objections, particularly since the bill provided that an investigation by the commission could be triggered by the president or the U.S. Attorney General and because the commission in Covington's proposal was not empowered to prosecute.[51]

Among those who played an important role in the creation of the FTC, it was the congressional outsider George Rublee who held the strongest progressive convictions about the role of IRCs. Like Croly, Rublee believed that the decision whether to prohibit a particular trade practice could not be defined by the rule of law or by some a priori notion of right and wrong. Rather, corporate regulation depends in each case upon particular circumstances that are better managed by experts than politicians. Rublee pressed the administration to support what would eventually become Section 5 of the FTC Act giving the commission broad discretionary powers to issue restraining orders prohibiting unfair competition.[52] As he explained in his testimony before Congress: "The [Federal Trade] commission by reason of its knowledge of business affairs and the concentrated attention it will give thereto, its facilities for investigation, its rapid summary procedure, will be able to protect business against unfair competition in much more effective and timely fashion than Department of Justice can do."[53] By June, Rublee had convinced Wilson to have Section 5 incorporated into Covington's bill, thereby setting the stage for the adoption of a stronger commission than either Wilson or the Congress had heretofore supported. Section 5 of the FTC Act of 1914 read as follows:

> Whenever the Commission shall have reason to believe that any such person, partnership, or corporation has been or is using any unfair method of competition or unfair or deceptive act or practice in or affecting commerce, and if it shall appear to the Commission that a proceeding by it in respect thereof would be to the interest of the public, it shall issue and serve upon such person, partnership, or corporation a complaint stating its charges in that respect and containing a notice of a hearing upon a day and at a place therein fixed at least thirty days after the service of said complaint.[54]

Although most commentators find Wilson's conversion to a strong commission with the power to hold hearings and issue injunctions both startling and inexplicable, it is most likely he understood how expedient Section 5 of the FTC Act was in this particular political environment.[55] As Wilson biographer Arthur Link explains, by June 1914 "Wilson concluded that the Stevens bill [for a strong rather than weak commission] offered a way out of the dilemma created by the failure of the Clayton bill [which attempted to define legislative standards for fair competition] and a perfect answer to the critics of the weak trade commission." A trade commission armed with broad powers under Section 5 offered an expedient means for reconciling the insurmountable differences in Congress with enough time to give the Democratic Party something to brag about come the midterm elections. But, more important, it ingeniously resolved the standoff in Congress. Section 5 did not explain what constituted fair or unfair trade practices, so the problem of legislative standards went unresolved. But it could now pass this problem on to the FTC without unduly inflating the authority of the executive branch.

Some leading members of Congress, like Senator Francis Newlands, disclaimed any intent to undermine the Justice Department's enforcement of the Sherman Anti-Trust Act but said they wanted an independent agency that would at least cohabit this space with the president.[56] However, Congress's desire to insert itself into the field of executive power is revealed in statements like that of Senator Albert Cummins, one of the bill's leading sponsors in the Senate, who only a few days after having defended the proposed trade commission as a committee of experts removed from the normal politics of the executive office, now explained:

> What we propose to do here is not to arrest the enforcement of the antitrust law . . . but to add to the Department of Justice an investigating tribunal of high character, of greater experience well equipped to bring to the attention of the Attorney General those instances which may have escaped the inquiries carried on in that department, and thus secure through the Department of Justice a more efficient enforcement of that law.[57]

There is something suspect in Cummins's statement that we need an independent body of experts removed from the politics of the executive branch in order to "add" to the Department of Justice a more qualified tribunal. If Congress wanted a "tribunal of high character" and with greater expertise, why not authorize the president to hire more experts in the Department of Justice? If the previous appointments in the department were insufficiently qualified for the task, why not pressure the president to remove them and then either refuse to consent to future appointments until the president has nominated sufficiently fit candidates or, in the case of lower officials, place the appointment in someone capable of making a wise choice? Finally, why would one need to make the commission independent if the commission was merely designed to "bring to the attention of the Attorney General" cases that might have escaped his inquiry? What kind of cases escape the attention of the Department of Justice other than those cases that the executive branch had chosen to ignore? Obviously, the proponents of the bill were seeking to obscure the fact that the issue here, which they claimed to be sui generis to the regulatory challenges of the twentieth century, was really part of a long-standing controversy in American politics over congressional-executive relations. The president enjoys a certain degree of independence in the discretionary enforcement of law by having the support of a national majority. Congress clearly hoped that a body of commissioners immune from the influence of the president might give it a better chance at controlling the administration of law.

Congressmen certainly could have anticipated a number of tools at their disposal for controlling the FTC. First, like any other executive office, it would have continuous authority to redefine its policies and procedures. Congress could also control the behavior of the agency through the appropriations process, showing its approval or disapproval of its work in the details of the budget.[58] Though it has been decided that Congress cannot retain for itself a role in the removal of the independent regulatory commissioners,[59] Congress did something akin to this when it terminated the terms for commissioners on the Federal Tariff Commission in 1930.[60] Alternatively, Congress has used appropriation riders as a means of removal.[61] Whether the Congress that crafted the FTC was fully conscious in 1914 of all of these tools at its disposal, none of them were wholly unprecedented.

In many important respects, then, the FTC was not the nonpolitical expert agency envisioned by the Progressives.[62] As even the most Progressive proponent of the bill in Congress, Senator Newlands, argued:

> This trade commission bill is a very different one from that urged by the Progressive movement and by Mr. Roosevelt as head of that movement. This commission is organized for the enforcement of the Sherman antitrust law by aiding the courts in the preparation of decrees and in the dissolution of these trusts, by aiding the Attorney General in his work in enforcing the antitrust law, by investigations under which it is the duty of the commission to call the attention of the Attorney General to any violation of the antitrust law with a view to securing his action as to its enforcement.[63]

The bill thus differed from the Progressive agenda on a number of important fronts. First, the commission could stop trusts in their embryonic form. Those who are accountable to the president in the executive branch generally lack the incentive to pursue trusts at their incipient stage because presidents cannot capitalize on the publicity that comes from prosecuting a firmly established and notorious corporation. But in enabling the commission to pursue trusts in their embryonic form, Congress made a substantial departure from the thinking of Progressives like Hebert Croly who believed that regulation should not proscribe corporate activity until their effects on the economy could be fully evaluated. To pursue a trust in its embryonic form assumes that all trusts are bad; it assumes that there are a priori standards of right and wrong that can be applied at all times. Finally, this approach to economic regulation assumes that the economy can be governed by the rule of law even when Congress authorizes the enforcement of that law under an independent commission. Related to this is the astonishing fact that Congress could not muster a majority for the bill until it included a provision for judicial review of the commission's decisions. Given that the original impetus for the adoption of the bill was a widely shared animus in Congress toward the Court's role in reviewing trust cases, it is remarkable that this became the sine qua non of the bill. In the end, congressmen would not accept a commission whose decisions were final, because they could not stomach a procedure that might arbitrarily deprive citizens of rights without due process of law.

It would be difficult to conclude, then, that Congress imagined that it was embarking upon the revolutionary departure from the traditional constitutional order that the Progressives envisioned. What they did establish was an arrangement similar to that which might have grown out of Hamilton's proposal in *The Federalist*—a bifurcated executive under which regulation would be administered by an independent body of experts and the remainder of the executive power exercised through the political office of the president. But as we have seen here, Congress's intentions differed from those of Hamilton in one important respect. For Hamilton's version of advise and consent, the legislature played no direct role in administration. Even the Senate's role in advising and consenting to removals was designed to merely thwart the president's influence over the administration, not to enhance the powers of Congress. In the case of the IRCs, Congress hoped to control one side of administration through this multimember body, while the president would continue to carry out the prosecution of law on the other under his singular direction in other areas.

The potential defect in this arrangement was thoughtfully anticipated during the debates by Senator Harry Lane of Oregon:

> The provision in the bill which allows the president, when there is a failure upon the part of the commission to execute the law, himself to take action is a wise one and a good one. It is the surest provision in the bill. In the president lies individual responsibility and direct action. Commissions walk slowly. Commissions are composed of a body of men; they are not of a single mind; they cannot be brought to decide on speedy action; they are cumbersome. The president is unfettered by the views of others. He represents more nearly what the people want; they look to him as the head of government, and they have confidence in him.[64]

As Senator Lane anticipated, most of the FTC's achievements were accomplished under the direction of the president and not from the institution's prestige as a nonpartisan body of expert administrators. The FTC's record of projects undertaken by its own initiative during its initial years of existence was paltry. George Rublee ultimately concluded that "what was once thought a very promising experiment in the regulation of big business instead proved to be a disheartening failure."[65] The FTC ultimately lost the competition Congress hoped it would win by failing to control the direction of the prosecutorial powers of the executive office. Wherever the agency did not function as a mere supplement to the president, President Wilson lost any interest in its future. Under Presidents Harding, Coolidge, and Hoover the FTC's subsequent performance remained dismal. As Marc Winerman concludes, "A multi-member structure can produce creative synthesis at best, but, at the Commission, it produced discord and flip-flopping policy changes — both on issues that were primarily in the FTC's bailiwick and on issues where it interacted with other agencies, such as the DOJ."[66] Designed to be nonpartisan by arranging the membership of the commission so that it was bipartisan, the commission in the end reflected the makeup of Congress.

In the end, however, it is neither Hamilton nor the Progressives who offer the best model for the historical evolution of the IRCs. Rather, the advise and consent theory as articulated by Elbridge Gerry and Alexander White in the debates of 1789 is more analogous. As Gerry explained in defense of this position: "We [Congress] have the power to establish offices by law; we can declare the duties of the officer; these duties are what the legislature directs, and not what the president; the officer is bound by law to perform these duties."[67] For Gerry, executive removal was dangerous because the intention of Congress might go unheeded if the president were free to determine how the law ought to be enforced. This was the same concern that animated the proponents of the FTC in Congress. But as we can see in the case of the creation of the trade commission, the advise and consent position does not really amount to an agreement to "share" power in practice; rather it is an assertion by Congress of power over the administration on the grounds that it is Congress's duty to oversee the administration of its own laws. Here advise and consent is in perfect accord with congressional delegation theory. From the perspective of Madison and other proponents of executive power theory in 1789, Senate involvement in removal would neither preserve the independence of the branches nor offer a salutary check by Congress on executive power; rather it would upset the balance of the separation of powers and enable the legislature to aggrandize itself at the expense of the executive.[68]

Humphrey's Executor v. United States

There were only a few IRCs prior to the inception of the New Deal. Two years after Franklin Roosevelt's election, Congress created the Federal Communications Commission (FCC), the National Labor Relations Board (NLRB), and the Securities and Exchange Commission all in one year and with others soon to follow. With the explosion of the regulatory programs under Roosevelt, the constitutional status of the IRCs took on a new sense of urgency given the prominent role that these regulatory agencies would play under the New Deal order. Until 1935, the constitutionality of these IRCs had been unclear particularly since the *Myers* decision in 1926 seemed to imply their removal provisions were suspect. In 1935, the Court was finally faced with a direct challenge to the statutory limitations on executive removal, when Franklin Roosevelt attempted to fire Federal Trade Commissioner William Humphrey.

Assuming that the trade commissioners were really just another agency under the executive branch, Roosevelt's first order of business after taking office was to restaff the FTC so that it could be trusted to undertake a number of important new responsibilities in the New Deal's regulatory program. The commission had performed dismally under previous administrations, but Roosevelt believed that the agency could be reinvigorated under his direction and could function as a critical administrative arm of New Deal policymaking.[69]

Roosevelt first planned to utilize the FTC's administrative capacities under the 1933 Securities Act,[70] which the commission did until Congress amended the act in 1934[71] and transferred its administrative duties to the newly created Securities and Exchange Commission (SEC).[72] Originally, the FTC was responsible for registering sellers engaged in the issue of securities by a procedure that would publicize their information and make the buying and selling of stock more transparent. It was a critical task given that the subterfuge of security traders was thought to have caused the stock market crash in 1929. Empowered under the draft bill to issue and revoke securities' registration, the FTC would have taken on a role analogous to Theodore Roosevelt's program for the registration and licensing of corporations through the Bureau of Corporations.[73]

FDR seemed unaware of the fact that the FTC had been constituted in order to prevent executive control of the commission's regulatory authority when he fired William Humphrey over disagreements about how the administration of the agency ought to be conducted. But many members of Congress seemed to have forgotten as well. During his time as chief commissioner of the FTC, William Humphrey was notorious for his opposition to the federal regulation of the economy, and he was widely considered an anathema to New Deal principles. "By the time Franklin D. Roosevelt had won election in 1932," William Leuchtenburg observed, "Humphrey had become the symbol of all that the Progressives abhorred in the Old Order."[74] His position as commissioner of the FTC bitterly annoyed many New Dealers in both the executive and legislative branches who thought that his ultimate intention was to subvert the regulatory function of the commission altogether. According to Pendleton Herring, "Congressman Wright Patman of Texas sounded a popular note when he voiced the hope that when Roosevelt entered the White House he would 'certainly change the policy of the Federal Trade Commission and put it back to its original function or intent.'"[75] For Roosevelt, Humphrey was not just a lingering embarrassment from a former administration; he was an impediment to FDR's plans to make the FTC the premier administrative agency of the New Deal's regulatory program. Roosevelt fired Humphrey a few months before the securities bill went before Congress, partly to raise confidence in Congress that such an important program could be well-administered, and partly because it would not be administered to his liking with a commissioner like Humphrey among the staff. Were FDR to have prevailed in the case, he might have succeeded in acquiring the "full executive power" that Theodore Roosevelt had been denied by Congress in 1908.

The FTC would also serve a central role in Roosevelt's signature New Deal program — the National Industrial Recovery Act (NIRA). The act had been signed into law on June 16, 1933, a little over a month before Roosevelt asked for Humphrey's resignation. The NIRA allowed competitors to meet and propose industrial codes of fair competition that would then be approved by the code administrators. Recall that the FTC Act had given the commission broad authority to determine standards of fair competition because Congress could not come to a consensus on those standards. However, George Rublee's vision of a commission of economic experts empowered to exercise broad discretion for rulemaking had never materialized due to both adverse court decisions and the FTC's own internal failures. The NIRA attempted to accomplish what neither Congress nor the commission had so far been able to. Under the National Recovery Administration, experts from industry would meet to determine the standards of fair competition, and the FTC would then administer the codes once they were approved by the president. Part of Congress's justification for the FTC's independence was that only an independent, nonpartisan agency could win the respect of businesses as well as the general public in determining fair standards of competition. The NIRA's arrangement for creating those same standards through the voluntary cooperation of business and government rendered the independence of the FTC irrelevant in this respect. Roosevelt's administration even went so far as to promote the codes as a patriotic form of solidarity during tough times — holding public parades in support of the program and even adopting a patriotic symbol — the Blue Eagle — which buyers and participating businesses could rally around. The FTC would now be tasked with the duty of administering and enforcing these codes of fair competition. This kind of innovation was precisely the type of activity that the conservative William Humphrey would have resisted.

In *Humphrey's Executor*, the Court rejected FDR's assertion of executive removal power over the commissioners and sided with the statute's limitations on the president. In its opinion, the Court reasoned that the members of the FTC — though appointed by the president — exercised

powers that were "quasi-legislative" and "quasi-judicial," *not* executive.[76]
The decision came as a surprise — as well as a personal affront — to Roosevelt, who assumed he could remove any subordinate officer appointed by
the president (President Coolidge had appointed Humphrey to the FTC,
and President Hoover reappointed him). Because the Court, less than a decade before, had affirmed in *Myers* that the president had sole power of
removal over those officials appointed by the president with the consent of
the Senate, he seemed to be on solid legal ground.[77] While Taft did remark
in *Myers* that there might be some room for Congress to delegate tasks to
particular officers exercising quasi-legislative and quasi-judicial powers
outside the direct supervision of the president, the Chief Justice still argued that the president could remove such officers after the fact. Even activity partaking of a "quasi" legislative or judicial nature is still in essence
"executive," according to Taft, because it ultimately falls under the president's duty to faithfully enforce the law. The political challenge the Court
faced in *Humphrey's Executor* was to square their decision in *Myers* with the
proliferation of IRCs that had come into existence since 1887. Sutherland
tried to carve out an exception aimed at balancing the interests of Congress
with the previous court's ruling.

Sutherland's opinion in *Humphrey's Executor* made convenient use of
the language of Progressivism as a justification for an expert commission
without invoking its revolutionary implications for the traditional separation of powers system:

> The commission is to be nonpartisan, and it must, from the very na-
> ture of its duties, act with entire impartiality. It is charged with the
> enforcement of no policy except the policy of the law. Its duties are
> neither political nor executive, but predominantly *quasi*-judicial and
> *quasi*-legislative. Like the Interstate Commerce Commission, its
> members are called upon to exercise the trained judgment of a body
> of experts "appointed by law and informed by experience."[78]

A trained body of experts has to be free of the political influence of Congress and the president in order to impartially enforce the law. Because political decisions are not always made in the interest of efficiency, nor are
they informed by a truly knowledgeable assessment of the facts of industry
or commerce, it is best to leave those decisions to experts who can make
them without being influenced by the political pressure that comes from
electioneering. To do their work efficiently, these administrators must be
shielded from the political influence of the president. Though Sutherland
invoked the language of Progressivism, he did not believe that the independence of the FTC undermined the traditional separation of powers in
the Constitution. "The fundamental necessity of maintaining each of the
three general departments of government entirely free from the control or

coercive influence, direct or indirect, of either of the others has often been stressed, and is hardly open to serious question."[79]

However, Sutherland characterized these unique quasi-judicial and quasi-legislative duties as "the enforcement . . . of the law." Such a characterization posed some potential problems since it sounded a lot like executive power:

> The Federal Trade Commission is an administrative body created by Congress to *carry into effect legislative policies* embodied in the statute in accordance with the legislative standard therein prescribed, and to perform other specified duties as a legislative or as a judicial aid. Such a body cannot in any proper sense be characterized as an arm or an eye of the executive. Its duties are performed without executive leave, and, in the contemplation of the statute, must be free from executive control.[80]

An "administrative agency created by Congress *to carry into effect legislative policies*" seems no different than any other executive department that administers law. On what grounds, then, could commissions be regarded as anything other than executive? Ultimately, the only argument Sutherland could find to support his contention for the independence of the commission here was Congress's assertion that regulatory commissions were different.

Sutherland's argument on behalf of the quasi-legislative and quasi-judicial status of the commission seems equally unconvincing. The commission's quasi-legislative duties included making investigations and reporting to Congress. Sutherland not only failed to note that the statute also provided a reporting requirement to the president; regardless, even the duty to report its finding to Congress hardly made the agency a legislative aid given that the president and executive department heads are also required to make recommendations to Congress. At its most extreme, Sutherland's argument would seem to reduce the entire executive branch to a ministerial instrument of Congress. In regards to the supposedly quasi-judicial function of the FTC, Sutherland cited the authority that the statute confers upon the commission to investigate and issue injunctions. Yet even though a court may issue an injunction pursuant to a legal finding, a court may not seek an injunction incident to a power to prosecute—something that the FTC does in fact have the power to do.[81] The Department of Justice, in contrast, does issue such injunctions, though no one would conclude that the DOJ therefore is a quasi-judicial agency immune from presidential control.[82]

Even scholars critical of the Court's decision in *Myers*, like Edward Corwin, found Sutherland's designation of quasi-legislative and quasi-judicial power in *Humphrey's* puzzling. In Corwin's view, it seems to have done more to confuse the issue rather than clarify it, especially because Sutherland might just have easily labeled the regulatory commissions—"agents of Congress."

> The dictum seems to have been the product of hasty composition. . . . If a Federal Trade Commissioner is not in the executive department, where is he? In the legislative department, or is he forsooth in the uncomfortable halfway situation of Mahomet's coffin, suspended 'twixt Heaven and Earth? . . . Nor is Justice Sutherland's endeavor to make out that [Federal Trade Commissioners] are any more "agents of Congress" than is a postmaster at all persuasive. Both officials get their powers—such as they are—from an exercise by Congress of its constitutionally delegated powers; there is no other possible source.[83]

Indeed, in the absence of more compelling evidence for limiting the president's removal power, Sutherland had to rely simply on the wording of the statute: "not to be subject to anybody in the government" and to be "free from 'political domination or control' or the 'probability or possibility of such a thing.'"[84] As Hadley Arkes puts it, "Sutherland seemed to offer the argument that the commission must be independent because it is different, and it must be different because it is independent."[85]

Sutherland's decision, in the end, really seems closer to the position of congressional delegation theorists in the debates of 1789 than to the Progressive argument for genuine independence from the political branches of government. There is some good evidence for this speculation on our part. Perhaps the most able critic of the FTC Act during the debates in the Senate in 1914 was none other than George Sutherland, senator from Utah. Though one should approach any comparison of Sutherland's views as a justice and senator with trepidation, we believe that there are some helpful clues about his general understanding of executive power that can be gleaned from this examination. When asked which element of the commission he opposed, Senator Sutherland responded, "I object to pretty nearly everything in the bill. If I had my way about it, I would simply strike out all of the bill after the enacting clause and then drop the enacting clause into the wastebasket."[86] Sutherland opposed the trade commission in the form that it was proposed because he thought it unconstitutionally conferred the judicial responsibility to issue injunctions on an essentially legislative commission. "Suppose," he explained, "that Congress instead of undertaking to devolve this power upon an administrative body were itself to make an investigation of some particular case where it is claimed that unfair competition existed [could] Congress issue an injunction against the continuance of that practice?"[87] Sutherland's criticism of the trade commission proposal was as interesting for what it did not argue as for what it did argue. All of Sutherland's objections to the bill assume that it is the usurpation of legislative power or judicial power that is at stake in debate over the constitutionality of the bill. But Sutherland never considered the possibility that the regulatory commissions might actually exercise executive power when commissioners adopt particular rules or hear individual cases. Rather, Sutherland assumed that administrative commissions were creatures of the legislature. As such, they overstep their constitutional domain when empowered to issue injunctions because that was the job of a court. Sutherland also objected to the scope of the FTC's authority under Section 5. Without clearer legislative guidelines for determining fair standards of competition, Congress might abdicate its legislative responsibility to the commission. The Interstate Commerce Commission, according to Sutherland, was a better model of a "legislative commission" because its ratemaking authority was more clearly defined by a legislative standard.[88] But in neither case did Sutherland consider the possibility that the commissions, which apply general laws to particular cases, might be engaged in a form of executive power. When another member of the Senate pointed out that the Bureau of Corporations had just as broad an authority to investigate corporate activity, Sutherland reminded him that the Bureau of Corporations was an executive office and that, in his opinion, the delegation of investigative authority conferred by Congress in that case violated the nondelegation doctrine.[89] In light of his argument in the Senate, we can see how Sutherland might have arrived at his argument in *Humphrey's Executor*. The administration of law is a power created by Congress and accountable to Congress. Broad delegations of power are unconstitutional and dangerous because they jeopardize Congress's legislative prerogatives. Even though Sutherland might have once opposed the creation of the FTC in its current form, he could at least take comfort in the fact that the commission's authority and its immunity from executive removal were under the control of the legislature.

The political context of the New Deal and the changes it threatened to wreak upon congressional-executive relations during this time also help us understand Sutherland's change of heart over the constitutional status of the IRCs. One commentator nicely captures the burlesque contrast between the *Humphrey's Executor* decision and the historical circumstances of this case, explaining: "There is more than a touch of irony in Humphrey's appeal to the court and the ground upon which he was sustained. Here was the most partisan-minded member of the Commission upheld in his position by the courts on the ground that the president had no right to intervene in the affairs of a quasi-judicial agency."[90] The irony was not lost on Roosevelt, who did not believe that administration could exist separately from politics. One of his first actions as president was to transfer all legal authority in the administration to the Justice Department.[91] But it was not enough to regroup the power of prosecution under the control of the president. Roosevelt knew that the administration of the regulatory programs would require the expert resources of the regulatory commissions. Prior to the New Deal, the IRCs had played a very limited role in the administration, and most had seen their powers curtailed over the years.[92] The FTC was originally granted very broad jurisdiction and flexibility under Section 5, but its regulatory role had been displaced by the Department of Justice.[93] In fact, Coolidge's and Hoover's reasons for appointing Humphrey to chair the commission in the first place probably had less to do with their ideological agreement with his views on regulation and more to do with the benefit they gained by appointing a commissioner who would narrow the scope of the FTC's jurisdiction. By 1935, however, a major ideological shift in the regulatory policy of the national government had made bureaucratic organization an even more critical issue. There was a new sense of urgency in defending the IRCs, because under the New Deal these agencies would no longer be marginalized. The future of congressional-executive relations now hung in the balance of this case.

The Court's decision in *Humphrey's Executor* was handed down on the same day as *Schechter Poultry Corp. v. United States*, in which the Court struck down the code-making procedures of the National Industrial Recovery Act. When examined together, the two decisions make a great deal of sense out of the political situation the Court faced in 1935.[94] Roosevelt's effort to gain control over the FTC was really part of a more ambitious project undertaken by the executive branch. As Sidney Milkis explains, "The administrative program of the New Deal would combine executive action and public policy, so that the president and the administrative agencies would be delegated authority to govern, thus making unnecessary the constant cooperation of party members in Congress and the states."[95] Congress was set to renew NIRA on May 28, 1935, when the Court struck down the act the day before, finding that the legislative powers delegated by the act to the president were without any effective limitations and therefore in violation of the nondelegation doctrine.[96] Justice Hughes observed that the purpose of the statute was not to administer a preexisting law or to create new means of enforcing the law, but "rather . . . the purpose is clearly disclosed to authorize new and controlling prohibitions through codes of laws which would embrace what the formulators would propose, and what the president would approve, or prescribe, as wise and beneficent measures."[97] Armed with removal power over the FTC, Roosevelt would not only be able to approve the codes once they were agreed upon; he would also be able to influence the administration of these standards through his influence over the commission's membership.

With enormous authority to direct the course of corporate regulation, Roosevelt looked to gather administrative control over those remaining features of the national economy that were most publicly visible: securities, stock exchanges, and the public utility holding companies. By 1934, Congress had passed the Exchange Act, which required the registration of publicly traded securities, though its administration had now been transferred from the FTC to a new independent regulatory agency — the SEC.[98] In 1935, Congress also passed the Public Utility Holding Company Act of 1935, which gave the SEC regulatory authority over this industry as well.[99] If the Court had concluded that Congress could not impose statutory limits on the executive's removal power, then Roosevelt would have unified control in the administration over a vast portion of the government's economic regulation. In light of these developments, Sutherland's decision makes more sense politically than it does jurisprudentially. The two decisions of the Court on May 27, 1935, taken together, signaled to the president that Congress would continue to control the terms of policy-making and the courts would continue to be the primary institution for the adjudication of rights in the United States.

Whether we accept the Progressive account of modern political reform in whole or not, it is true that the administration of economic regulation requires experts who possess the authority to create new rules on a discretionary basis. In this case, the FTC offered a convenient solution to the challenges of legislating amid a complex industrial economy. Rather than delegate this authority to a rival branch of government, Congress could create an institution populated by experts that would be less hostile and therefore a safer repository for its own delegation of power. Sutherland's reasoning assured congressmen that they were within their constitutional rights when they treated these administrative agencies as aids to Congress. Even though modern legislation required substantial delegation of rulemaking authority to administrative agencies, this did not mean that Congress would be left out of the loop in the future by another political branch when it came to policymaking. In the end, Sutherland's decision really only paid lip service to the IRCs. Its real purpose was to advance the cause of a Congress desperate to maintain some degree of control over the emerging administrative state.

FDR and Executive Power

For Roosevelt, the Court's rebuff of his assertion of his removal power over the FTC was as much a setback as was the Court's finding that the New Deal's signature program was unconstitutional. Most of Roosevelt's success during his first term had been achieved by means of bypassing the current administrative organization and implementing relief programs through ad hoc appointments and agencies.[100] Roosevelt's "second New

Deal," which included his legislative programs for regulatory reform, could not be administered in the same way. Without greater control over the sprawling administration that had mushroomed under New Deal legislation, Roosevelt's administration over the economy would likely prove to be a political disaster. Following his landslide reelection in 1936, Roosevelt famously joked that the Republican Party might have defeated his administration had it focused on his administrative record. The solution lay in an ambitious program for the reorganization of the executive branch, one that included eliminating the IRCs and subordinating their powers to the president. Already in 1935 Roosevelt had assembled a new committee of public administration experts (including Charles Merriam, Luther Gulick, and Louis Brownlow) to study the issue of administrative organization and to formulate a proposal to Congress for the reorganization of the executive branch under a more centralized plan. This group, the President's Committee on Administrative Management, would come to be known as the Brownlow Committee. The purpose of the study was to recommend legislation to Congress that would hopefully be enacted according to the president's wishes.[101]

Unlike former reorganization efforts by previous presidential administrations, which concentrated exclusively on achieving efficiency and cost-savings, the report of the Brownlow Committee emphasized the need for more responsiveness to the national interest.[102] The Brownlow Report described the presidency's relationship to the administration in terms similar to those of James Madison in 1789, when he argued that the removal power vested in the president alone was essential to a responsible and accountable administration. The Brownlow report thus began: "The efficiency of government rests upon two factors: the consent of the governed and good management. . . . Administrative management concerns itself in a democracy with the executive and his duties, with managerial and staff aides, with organization and personnel, and with the fiscal system because these are indispensable means of making good the popular will in a people's government."[103] As Corwin noted, the plan was Jacksonian in its call for a muscular presidency attached to the popular will, but it went further in its presumption that the popular will had to be managed.

The proposed plan of reorganization had essentially four features. First, it asked Congress for the necessary appropriations to reorganize 130 agencies into twelve departments that would make the administration more responsive to presidential leadership. The proposal would restructure the executive branch so that each agency's specialized knowledge could be coordinated across the administration and directed from a central authority. Six new assistants, who would be chosen for their "high competence, great physical vigor, and a passion for anonymity," served a critical role in this plan of reorganization. They would combine the necessary expertise and specialization necessary for the administration of a modern government with a centralized organization that was directly accountable to a popularly elected president. As experts in the science of administration, they would ensure "that all matters coming to the attention of the president have been examined from the over-all managerial point of view, as well as from standpoints that would bear on policy and operation."[104]

Second, the president asked Congress to expand the merit system "upward, outward, and downward." As in the case of the reorganization of the departments, the extension of the merit system to cover almost everyone except those in "high executive and policymakers."[105] In order to assure Congress that it was serious about improving the quality of administrators, the report, while proposing to eliminate the Civil Service Commission, did offer to place responsibility in a single Civil Service Administrator who would be shielded from the influence of the president. What seems odd here is that this part of the proposal runs counter to the whole tenor of the report in which the central goal was the accountability of the administration to the president. Sidney Milkis argues that this was part of a grand strategy by Roosevelt to establish a permanent administration that would continue to administer New Deal programs regardless of who was elected to office. We think that it is more likely that the president and the Brownlow Committee were trying to mask the devastating effect this proposal would have on congressional participation in political patronage. For some members of Congress, this part of the proposal was probably the most damaging to the legislature because it deprived Congress of an important customary privilege. As we have seen above in other chapters, the spoils of patronage in administrative posts had served as a battleground between Congress and the president. Congress, unable to limit the president's removal of officers since the repeal of the Tenure of Office Act, nevertheless continued to enjoy an extralegal form of participation in the appointment power through the influence of the parties.[106] Roosevelt's civil-service reforms would be a major boon to the president by relieving him of the custom whereby he shared the appointment power with Congress; and with lower-level officers completely free of congressional interference, it would actually intensify the loyalty of his administrators. The Brownlow Report's proposal to transfer the administration of the merit system to a single Civil Service Administrator who would be immune from presidential influence was really just a means of cloaking the president's ambition to wrest control of the appointment process from Congress under the guise of reforming civil service along nonpolitical lines.

Third, the Brownlow Report's most controversial feature was its proposal to curb the authority of the Comptroller General in order to give the president sole authority over fiscal expenditures. "Sound fiscal management is a prime requisite of good administration. The responsibility of the Executive for the preparation of a fiscal program in the form of a budget for submission to Congress and for the direction and control of expenditures under the appropriation acts must be carried on faithfully, effectively, and under clear-cut authority."[107] To correct this defect in the budget process, the report proposed a number of reforms, including the enhancement of staffing in the Bureau of the Budget (as well as making that bureau more responsive to the White House by moving it from the Treasury Department to the Executive Office of the President). The bureau, created by the Budget and Accounting Act of 1921, had been a step in the right direction, but if the president was to take full responsibility for the proposal of the federal budget and the control of expenditures, then the institution would need to be staffed with more experts and given closer proximity to the president. The Brownlow Report strongly criticized the role of the Comptroller, who could control expenditures using a pre-audit procedure under which he could disapprove of spending. In fact, Roosevelt had tussled many times with the Republican-appointed Comptroller General, John McCarl, over the increased expenditures under the New Deal.[108] The Report argued that the Comptroller's duties of accounting and auditing had been wrongly fused into an instrument of controlling executive expenditures that, not being responsible to the president, posed an unconstitutional intrusion upon the powers of the executive office. But the report treaded carefully here in its criticism before Congress. It argued that the problems posed by the Comptroller had evolved accidentally rather than by the intention of the Budget and Accounting Act of 1921. In what it knew would be a highly controversial proposal, the Brownlow Report attempted to argue that restoring control over the expenditures to the president was necessary in order to make the president "more accountable" to Congress.[109] But as the Brownlow Committee admitted, the initial reason for the legislation had been to give more independence to the Comptroller. In fact, the act itself had been a compromise between President Harding's desire to modernize the accounting procedures and Congress's continued effort to control presidential administration. Hoping that Congress would accept some consolation for its loss, the report recommended that the Comptroller continue to be a nonpolitical officer who would report to Congress under a newly created Government Accounting Office and who would be empowered to audit expenditures but not control them through a pre-audit procedure.[110] With all of its deferential language to Congress, the Brownlow Report in the end was direct about the constitutional issue at stake here in the president's mind:

> The removal from the Executive of the final authority to determine the uses of appropriations, conditions of employment, the letting of

contracts, and the control over administrative decisions, as well as the prescribing of accounting procedures and the vesting of such authority in an officer independent of direct responsibility to the president for his acts, is clearly in violation of the constitutional principle of the division of authority between the Legislative and Executive Branches of the Government. It is contrary to article II, section 3, of the Constitution, which provides that the president "shall take Care that the Laws be faithfully executed."[111]

The final proposal of the report was to eliminate the IRCs and place their regulatory authority under the president.[112] If an independent science of accounting constituted an intrusion upon executive duties, then the concurrent administration of economic regulation by the IRCs was even more problematic. The report stated the problem starkly: "Governmental powers of great importance are being exercised under conditions of virtual irresponsibility. We speak of the 'independent' regulatory commissions. It would be more accurate to call them the 'irresponsible' regulatory commissions, for they are areas of unaccountability. . . . Power without responsibility has no place in a government based on the theory of democratic control, for responsibility is the people's only weapon, their only insurance against abuse of power."[113] This "headless fourth branch," as the report called the IRCs, posed a threat to the very existence of the executive branch. Given the increase in responsibilities being undertaken by the federal government since the inception of the New Deal, the report predicted that in a few years we would have "40 to 50" such commissions. The consequence would be a "relative weakening of the Executive" in which Congress (the report prudently did not explicitly say "Congress") would transfer the administrative duties of the president to the regulatory commissions. Instead of a single executive, the president would become only "one of many executives." In light of these dangers, the report recommended simply relocating the IRCs to the appropriate departments — something that the report assumed would be easy to do as the commissions really exercised powers that were no different than any other executive branch official.

The president's proposal for reorganization threatened to undo many of the things that Congress had achieved at the beginning of the twentieth century when it first grew concerned over the extent of executive power under Theodore Roosevelt.[114] FDR enthusiastically endorsed all of the Brownlow Committee's report and announced to Congress:

I would not have you adopt this five-point program, however, without realizing that this represents an important step in American history. . . . But in so doing, we shall know that we are going back to the Constitution, and giving to the Executive Branch modern tools of management and an up-to-date organization which will enable the Government to go forward efficiently. We can prove to the world that American Government is both democratic and effective.[115]

By April 1938, Congress defeated the original proposal by leaving it to languish in committee.[116] The debates in the congressional records do not contain a coherent portrait of members' reasoning or their general understanding of interbranch relations on these issues, but there are still some important explanations for the demise of the proposal that can be discerned from the events. First, congressional attention at the time was also focused more on FDR's notorious "court-packing plan." Coupled with the recommendations of the Brownlow Report, members of Congress thought they detected a grand plan to aggrandize the executive branch at the expense of the other two. Congress began to cry "dictatorship."[117]

The proposal that provoked the strongest reaction in Congress was the Brownlow Report's recommendation to remove the Comptroller from its role in the executive branch.[118] Senator Harry Byrd, chairman of the Senate Select Committee on Government Organization, led the attack on the reorganization proposal in Congress. He stated:

> In my opinion it is the duty of Congress to see that all appropriations are disbursed in accordance with the provisions of law. . . . If the majority concedes that the Congress has the responsibility for demanding that Federal expenditures be made in the manner and for the purposes set forth in its appropriation acts. . . . Even faithful execution of the laws by the president does not minimize to any degree the responsibility placed upon the Congress in Article I of the Constitution to pay the Nation's debts and to see that no money SHALL be drawn from the Treasury but in consequence of the appropriations made by law.[119]

Byrd's response here is revealing because it helps to explain the logic behind Congress's antipathy to this part of the reorganization proposal. Byrd argued that Congress could be certain that its appropriations were properly executed as expenditures only if it had the tools to carry them out. In other words, the Comptroller, as an agent of Congress, was a more trustworthy means to faithfully execute the law than was the president. How else, argued Byrd, could Congress be confident that it had discharged its own constitutional duties? Byrd's argument here extends to Congress's reservations about the whole of the Reorganization proposal. Each assertion of the proposal that sought to concentrate executive responsibility over the administration of law posed a threat to Congress's own responsibilities in making the law.

Congressional concerns about the proposal over the accounting and budget procedures were extended in particular to the president's proposal for bringing the IRCs within the orbit of the executive branch. Members of the IRCs testified in the hearings before the Select Committee on Organization of Government against the proposal. In summary, their arguments were:

> (1) these commissions are agents of Congress, and are not a part of the executive branch; they have been setup to fill in the details of legislation and to carry out the policies adopted by Congress; (2) to place them within an executive department would subject them to political pressures and control by constantly changing, politically selected, cabinet officers while at present they are removed from partisan influence; (3) the work of these commissions is of such a nature that they should not be made subject to any supervision or direction from the president; and (4) to place them within the executive branch would greatly hamper and impede their work.[120]

Again, the testimony of the IRCs' representatives is revealing because they argue that, on the one hand, the IRCs are agents of Congress and yet, on the other, that they must retain their independence to avoid being politicized. The contradiction here can be resolved only if we conclude that their independence is really a grant of Congress and not something to which they are entitled by virtue of the kind of work that they do. Congress appears to have agreed with the testimony of the representatives for the commissions and insisted that any form of reorganization would have to exempt the IRCs and keep them separate from the control of the president.

The IRCs and Unfinished Business

Despite the fact that the first proposal was defeated, Congress did pass a watered-down version in 1939. Congress rejected the proposal to allow the president to place the regulatory commissions under executive departments. As for the restructuring of the cabinet, Congress did give the president authorization to do so by executive order, but each order was subject to legislative veto. Congress did permit the creation of the Bureau of the Budget to aid the president but left the Comptroller's powers intact. Finally, the independent agencies would be exempted from the control of the president.

The debate over the FDR's reorganization proposal represents a culminating moment in the debates over the removal power in the early twentieth century. Though Progressivism may have inspired many in politics to look outside the constitutional separation of powers scheme for a new mode of regulating the economy following the inception of the Industrial Revolution, the differences between Congress and the president over administrative control remain much the same as the arguments first presented in the debates of 1789. In the case of the IRCs, Congress never desired independence — it wanted to control the administration of law and deny to the executive discretion in carrying out legislative mandates. In short, Congress wanted to secure its place in the burgeoning administrative state and prevent executive ascendance in this sphere. Its vociferous resistance to Roosevelt's reorganization plan reflects the entrenchment that had taken place following Congress's early assertion of control over economic regulation by the administration. Congress was not going to lose what it had worked so long to secure.

Many parts of FDR's proposal for executive reorganization would eventually be realized either during his presidency or under subsequent presidents. By executive order, Roosevelt created the Executive Office of the President, which, as Elena Kagan explains, "established the infrastructure underlying all subsequent attempts by the White House to supervise administrative policy."[121] During his administration, he also achieved some of his objectives in regards to civil-service extension partly through executive order and partly by weakening some patronage in Congress by securing the passage of the Hatch Act, which prohibited federal employees from participating in campaigns.[122] Roosevelt's hopes were realized with the passage of the act in 1940 that extended civil-service classification throughout the executive branch.[123] Congress also permitted the transfer of the Bureau of the Budget from the Treasury Department to the Executive Office of the President; and beginning with President Dwight Eisenhower it became an effective tool for unifying executive administration as a whole. Transformed into the Office of Management and Budget under President Richard Nixon, it would become the supreme instrument of the president's coordination of policy in the future. But the most controversial issues between the president and Congress remained essentially the same. Roosevelt was unable to eliminate the Comptroller's influence in the administration, and the regulatory commissions remained independent institutions of policymaking under the oversight of Congress. President Harry Truman, by executive order, was able to have the FTC's authority consolidated in the hands of a single administrator whom he could nominate, but his authority remained limited. The Court, for its part, continued to affirm its ruling in *Humphrey's Executor* when in 1958 it again unanimously decided that the president did not have authority to remove a member of an independent commission when Congress had specifically limited the president's removal power by law.[124] As the Brownlow Report anticipated, the commissions would proliferate over the next few decades due to greater demands on the federal government for regulation as well as Congress's continued desire to find a means of exercising some control over presidential administration. This unfinished business, at least from the perspective the Brownlow Report, would set the stage for another major battle between the president and Congress.

Even though Franklin Roosevelt did not achieve everything he set out to accomplish in the reorganization of the executive office, his efforts would establish the bar to which other presidents must measure up. Corwin was right to label Roosevelt a "Jacksonian," for FDR attempted to embody the daily needs of average citizens in the presidency. He also claimed that his own responsibility as the unmediated embodiment of the popular will allowed the president to deploy those unilateral and executive responsibilities to the fullest extent. Congress would tenaciously resist losing what control it could still retain over the administration as modern presidents pushed this Jacksonian argument to more intense levels. As we will see in the latter half of the twentieth century, this controversy at the heart of the debate over the removal power would become the defining issue in legislative and executive relations to this day.

Chapter Six

The New Unitarians

Below we examine the rise of the Unitary Executive Theory, which is commonly thought to have originated under President Ronald Reagan's time in the White House (1981–1989). However, the rise of the unitarians had an important precursor in the events that unfolded under Richard Nixon's presidency (1969–August 9, 1974). In this chapter we also explain the origins of the latest version of executive power theory. It, too, would have its counterpart in a new form of congressional delegation theory. Unitarians take their name from James Wilson's statement at the Constitutional Convention when he proposed vesting the executive power in a single individual: "that *Unity* in the Executive instead of being the fetus of Monarchy would be the best safeguard against tyranny."[1] Hence, unitarians claim fidelity to the Framers' original intent. The argument is also very straightforward and economical.[2] Unitarians all share the same essential premise: *The president is vested by the Constitution with all executive powers.* Any other official in government who executes the law must be under the president's control. As Saikrishna Prakash puts it: "Whenever an official is granted statutory discretion the Constitution endows the President with the authority to control that discretion."[3] According to unitarians, this is also the optimal arrangement for a democratic political system. The Framers of the Constitution wanted a popularly elected executive who would be the sole representative of the nation-at-large in government.

One problem with the unitarian argument is that it ignores the political development behind the articulation of executive power theory and even fails to observe that it is part of that ongoing evolution.[4] As we have seen in previous chapters, each reconstructive president brings a new conception of presidential accountability in his defense of executive removal power. The reason we think many unitarian scholars overlook these considerations is due to the fact that they do not sufficiently pay attention to the double meaning of the term "accountability." "Accountability" can be understood in two ways. In one sense, an officeholder acts with accountability when he has the ability and determination to act responsibly — that is, others are able to judge his actions and hold him to account. In another sense, accountability implies that an officeholder acts as an instrument of another party. In the case of the president that party is the people. But who are "the people?" The answer often depends on how presidents attempt to balance the two types of accountability: accountability *to* and accountability *for*. This twofold meaning of the word, then, is partly responsible for the various forms that executive power theory has taken under different presidents. In the case of Thomas Jefferson, he steered a middle course by replacing members of the bureaucracy with fellow Republicans in order to claim an office that proportionally reflected the votes of the people while at the same time resisting the movement toward popular parties that might have suppressed his independent judgment. Jackson went much further in adopting a popular role for the president, instituting the system of rotation in office whereby the president's party was entitled to administrative posts so it could better reflect the will of the people. Franklin Roosevelt's reconstruction in the 1930s subordinated the party to the programmatic ambitions of the president himself.[5] How, then, could presidents claim to embody popular will without the discipline of a party organization to register it? For FDR it was straightforward. Most Americans thought of themselves as beleaguered as a result of the Great Depression. Yet his campaign rhetoric also hinted at the problem that future presidents would face. The "forgotten man," ironically, was a description of almost every man or woman in the 1930s, and Roosevelt knew it: "the forgotten, the unorganized but *indispensable* units of economic power."[6]

The key to claiming the authority to act in the name of the people and thereby establish one's authority over bureaucracy in the modern age required rhetoric that could appeal to everyone without admitting that it was impossible to discern what everyone thinks or wants. Nixon adopted his own version of this: the "silent majority."[7] He hoped the phrase would initiate his own reconstruction, but instead his ambitious effort to vindicate his popular claim to authority would prove to be one of the final gasps in the expression of executive power that began with FDR's reconstruction. Entering office less than a decade after Nixon's downfall, President Reagan would try to reestablish the executive's control over the bureaucracy with a new formulation of executive power theory. Resisting conservatives that simply wanted to reenact Nixon's tragic effort to bring the bureaucracy under his personal authority, Reagan would find in the unitary school the kind of principled clarity of constitutional law that might cement his efforts to resurrect the presidency for the future. This chapter concludes with a treatment of *Morrison v. Olson* (1988). This case illustrates the fact that this revolution was far from complete, as it, too, was opposed by an equally forceful assertion of congressional delegation theory.

Richard Nixon and the Plot That Failed

The struggle for control of the bureaucracy between Congress and the president reached a climax under Richard Nixon. Most remembered among the battles between Nixon and Congress was the final moment when the president fired Watergate Special Prosecutor Archibald Cox, leading to the resignations of the Attorney General and one of his deputies. In addition to Andrew Jackson's removal of Treasury Secretary William Duane and Andrew Johnson's removal of War Secretary Edwin Stanton, it stands as one of the most dramatic exercises of the removal power in history. Nixon's removals during Watergate followed his sustained efforts as president to gain control of the administration. The spectacle of Watergate, as most commentators have observed, was fueled at least in part by Nixon's intensive efforts to claim the administrative state for the executive. The Watergate firings fueled the perception that the presidency had become an imperial institution unchecked by the people's representatives in Congress. As the title of Arthur Schlesinger's treatment of Nixon— *The Imperial Presidency* — reminds us, Watergate had become a monument in the minds of many to the danger of executive aggrandizement.

Nixon stood at the point of a massive collision between two very different paths of administrative development since the presidency of Franklin Roosevelt. One path included FDR's reorganization efforts—the creation of a centralized body of leadership in the Executive Office of the President (EOP) and the strengthening of executive management of federal fiscal policy through the reorganization of the budget process. Another path was created by FDR's failure to gain control of the IRCs for the executive branch. IRCs not only continued to exist after FDR; by the time of Nixon, they had tripled in number. Furthermore, Nixon himself found his efforts to clean house in the bureaucracy fettered by entrenched bureaucrats under civil-service protections. Between the rising expectations for popular leadership in the executive branch and the statutory limitations that had been imposed upon his removal power, Nixon faced a colossal task if he was to unify control.

After FDR, presidents were particularly worried about the political liability they might incur with statutorily imposed limitations on their removal power over IRCs. Harry Truman (1945–1953) tried to gain some control over the independent agencies through executive reorganization but was rebuffed on a number of occasions by Congress.[8] Dwight Eisenhower (1953–1961) lost a Supreme Court case in which the Court reaffirmed its ruling in *Humphrey's Executor* upholding restrictions on the removal power.[9] Lyndon Johnson (1963–1969) was stymied in his efforts to reorganize the Departments of Commerce and Labor, a move designed to give the executive branch much greater control over regulation.[10] But apart from these efforts, presidents rarely challenged the removal limitations Congress had placed upon IRCs. The fact that there had been no open confrontation between presidents and the Congress demonstrates the remarkable resilience of the uneasy, institutional legacy of FDR's New Deal. As long as both presidents and Congress continued to support programs in the spirit of New Deal liberalism, neither branch had much reason to dispute the independence of the regulatory commissions.[11]

Nixon's actions to gain control of the bureaucracy would shatter the fictions that had formerly sustained some modicum of harmony between the two branches and had sustained the appearance that regulatory agencies were autonomous from politics. Nixon thought he had entered office with a mandate to change the course of the nation now that the New Deal coalition was beginning to dissolve. Challenging the fundamental premises of the New Deal, Nixon boldly declared in his 1971 State of the Union Address:

> The idea that a bureaucratic elite in Washington knows best what is best for people everywhere and that you cannot trust local governments is really a contention that you cannot trust people to govern themselves. This notion is completely foreign to the American experience. Local government is the government closest to the people, it is most responsive to the individual person. It is people's government in a far more intimate way than the Government in Washington can ever be.[12]

The current bureaucracy did not embody the people's will — but Nixon's would. It was an ambitious agenda to abolish preexisting institutional arrangements and reconstruct a new order on the basis of the silent majority's support of the no-nonsense, law-and-order policies he campaigned on. To implement this vision, Nixon needed to overcome the sclerosis that had developed within the bureaucracy. Nixon undertook his own three-part reorganization plan to combat New Deal liberalism. First, he would restructure the existing administration to make it more responsive to the leadership of the president. Second, he would reorganize the Bureau of the Budget. Third, he would employ the traditional prerogative of executive enforcement of the law to structure federal policy.[13]

To restructure the executive's power to embody the latest popular mandate, Nixon first needed to find some means of eliminating the entrenched bureaucracy that existed in Washington when he entered office in January 1969. Nixon was not shy about his intentions regarding the removal of bureaucrats with the director of the Office of Management and Budget (OMB), George Shultz: "You've got to get [us some discipline,] and the only way to get it, is when a bureaucrat thumbs his nose, we're going to get him. There are many unpleasant places where civil service people can be sent. . . . Maybe [the recalcitrant bureaucrat] is in the regional office. Fine, demote him or send him to the Guam regional office. There's a way. Get him the hell out."[14] According to Richard Nathan, "Nixon proposed to cut in half the number of executive officer personnel reducing staff from 4,250 employees in the 1973 budget to 1,668 in 1974."[15] Yet during his first term Nixon nearly doubled the size of the U.S. government bureaucracy.[16] The reason for this seeming paradox had to do with the limits on the president's ability to remove a large portion of federal employees under the civil-service extensions begun under Roosevelt's reorganization.[17] Since then it had become more and more difficult to remove officials with these protections. Nixon therefore inherited the reforms of Roosevelt in a form that now trapped the president. As the former Nixon speechwriter William Safire later put it: "The reform of the spoils system threatens to become a spoiler system, capable of frustrating the initiatives of the newly elected . . . diffusing responsibility, and, above all, capable of protecting itself."[18] For Nixon, almost the entire administration, with the exception of his personal staff and cabinet heads, would seem as immovable as members of the IRCs.[19] Consequently, his strategy, which greatly increased the size of the administrative bureaucracy, was aimed at installing an entirely new level of administration that would be responsive to his directives.

Like FDR, Nixon concentrated on organization and structure within the administration before personnel.[20] Following the model of top-down administration as proposed in the Brownlow Report for Franklin Roosevelt, Nixon's efforts were essentially premised on executive power theory as well: Any president who lacked unified control of the administration could not fulfill his constitutional responsibility to the people. In his 1971 Special Message to Congress on Executive Branch Reorganization, Nixon explained:

> Perhaps the most significant consequence of scattered responsibility in the executive branch is the hobbling effect it has on elected leadership — and, therefore, on the basic principles of democratic government. In our political system, when the people identify a problem they elect to public office men and women who promise to solve that problem. If these leaders succeed, they can be reelected; if they fail, they can be replaced. Elections are the people's tool for keeping government responsive to their needs. . . . No wonder bureaucracy has sometimes been described as "the rule of no one." No wonder the public complains about programs which simply seem to drift. When elected officials cannot hold appointees accountable for the performance of government, then voter's influence on government's behavior is also weakened.[21]

Nixon's criticism of the bureaucracy as a whole reflected Madison's criticism of the argument during the Debate of 1789 that executive officers should be removable only through impeachment: "The danger to liberty, the danger of mal-administration has not yet been found to lay so much in the facility of introducing improper persons into office, as in the difficulty of displacing those who are unworthy of the public trust."[22] When Congress later proposed a bill that effectively would have amounted to a legislative removal of his OMB director and deputy director, Nixon vetoed the bill, directly citing Madison's argument in 1789.

Nixon's Advisory Council on Executive Organization, known as the Ash Council, also released a 1971 report that directly addressed the IRCs ("A New Regulatory Framework — A Report on Selected Independent Regulatory Agencies").[23] The report of the Ash Council proposed to group the existing commissions into four agencies under a single administrator appointed by the president. The report echoed the statements of the Brownlow Report, even citing its derogatory sobriquet for the IRCs: "a headless fourth branch."

Nixon knew a proposal to place the independent agencies within the executive department would be dead on arrival in Congress. Instead, the key to maintaining control over a new level of bureaucracy while marginalizing the former layer was the Ash Report's call for a new Office of Management and Budget to replace the existing Bureau of the Budget, which Nixon did accomplish by Executive Order in 1970.[24] During his first term, Nixon really did experience the difficulties of working with an unresponsive and intractable bureaucracy. The Ash Report's proposal would ameliorate this problem by permitting the president to punish or reward departments and agencies through his control over budgeting and discretionary spending. To head the OMB, Nixon appointed George Shultz, an economist who had proven political credentials, successfully heading up a Republican Party task force to develop economic proposals during the 1968 election. The OMB would be designed to provide the president with a powerful tool for political management over the rest of the administration by controlling the purse strings.

Once the OMB was in place, Nixon could begin to routinely use an extraordinary device: executive impoundment of appropriated funds. As Judith Michaels observes, "[Nixon's] new strategy was designed to do more and to do it more quickly."[25] But an impoundment was also a bold assertion of executive power, the use of which was likely to put the president into intense conflict with Congress. Previous presidents had only employed this power to correct minor discrepancies in which Congress's original intent for having appropriated certain amounts of funding would have been wasted due to the fact that the circumstances had changed.[26] Nixon, by contrast, used impoundments as a political means of transforming policy by refusing to spend congressionally appropriated sums on programs that were staffed by recalcitrant programmatic liberals like the community housing project.[27] Nixon claimed that the power to impound, regardless of whether it was used in routine administrative ways (as in the past) or in his admittedly more vigorous manner, was an inherent constitutional prerogative of the president to faithfully enforce the law.[28] Though the extent of Nixon's use may have been different from previous presidents, the principle in both cases, he argued, was the same: The president was merely interpreting two conflicting laws—one that required saving money, and the other that required spending it. High economic inflation justified the president's vigilance against waste.[29]

Congress did not sit by idly as Nixon concentrated power in the executive branch. Most notably, Congress attempted to remove Nixon's OMB director and the deputy OMB director by abolishing their positions and then reestablishing them subject to Senate confirmation. The congressional bill led to an early showdown over executive power between Nixon and Congress. As Calabresi and Yoo report, "Although Nixon did 'not dispute Congressional authority to abolish an office or to specify appropriate standards by which the officers may serve,' Nixon vetoed the bill because 'the power of the Congress to terminate an office cannot be used as a back-door method of circumventing the president's power to remove.'"[30] In an attempt to rein in the president's influence through the OMB over the regulatory agencies, Congress proposed that IRCs submit their budgets directly to Congress, hoping to weaken the president's ability to use the OMB to manage the legislature's policymaking powers. Although this legislative effort failed, Congress did curtail the president's capacity to impound funds and also weakened the influence of the OMB's budgetary authority by creating a rival institution, the Congressional Budget Office (CBO). Seeing Nixon's aggrandizement of power as part of a long-term trend in executive-congressional relations, Senator Alan Cranston of California commented to his colleagues in 1973: "Those who tried to warn us back at the beginning of the New Deal of the dangers of one-man rule that lay ahead on the path we were taking toward strong, centralized government . . . may not have been so wrong."[31] As the events of Watergate brought down Nixon, Congress turned to secure its long-term interests as an institution by going after the most powerful weapon in the executive's discretionary arsenal—the president's budgetary authority.

Congress reasserted its authority in a number of ways over the next few years. In 1973, Congress sought to repair the perceived disproportion of power between the branches in foreign affairs by passing the War Powers Resolution to "insure that the collective judgment of both the Congress and the President will apply to the introduction of the United States

Armed Forces into hostilities."[32] In 1974 Congress passed the Congressional Budget and Impoundment Control Act, under which it hoped to protect its appropriations power by assuming responsibility for imposing its own controls on excess spending.[33] Finally, though not officially passed into law until Jimmy Carter's presidency (1977–1981), Congress proposed the creation of an independent counsel so that it could effectively compel the investigation and prosecution of high-ranking executive officials. Let us take a brief look at these latter two congressional initiatives.

Prior to the passage of the Budget and Impoundment Act in 1974, Congress lacked a unified budget process whereby it could discipline its members and set its own fiscal priorities. Consequently, Congress had to rely upon the president to establish the budget and thereby set legislative priorities for spending. It is not necessary here to examine the budgetary procedures of the act, but we note that a process whereby Congress might impose its own restraints on spending would aid the legislature in restoring both its credibility as an equal branch of government while reducing the president's ability to impose spending limitations on the legislature. Controlling the budget, however, for Congress was only a means to a more important end: reducing the president's discretionary powers of impoundment.[34] Congress then put the Comptroller General in charge of reviewing the executive's use of impoundment. The Comptroller was still shielded from the removal power of the president as legislatively prescribed by the Budget and Accounting Act of 1921, but presidents had not viewed the office as a serious threat to their control of the budget since Roosevelt's confrontation with the Comptroller in the 1930s. Under 1974's Budget and Impoundment Act, however, the Comptroller would now serve the important task of distinguishing routine administrative impoundments ("deferrals") from impoundments that canceled spending in whole ("rescissions").[35] Deferrals were generally an innocuous and routine form of impoundment, whereas rescissions, though not unheard-of in previous administrations, constituted a more extraordinary exercise of executive power. Congress was intent on taming the discretionary powers of the president by giving the Comptroller — over whom it controlled the removal power — the authority to make the determination of which impoundments were routine and which were extraordinary. The act then made deferrals subject to a legislative veto by one house; rescissions could not be done at all without the approval of both houses of Congress. Though the act did not really clarify the constitutional question, the implication of the law from the congressional perspective was clear: Impoundments were not an Article II power but were a delegation by Congress and always subject to the approval of Congress.

Finally, Congress proposed the establishment of an independent counsel whereby Congress could instigate the investigation of high-ranking executive officials. Most observers thought of it as simply a correction to the perceived lessons of Watergate, an effort to prevent other broad claims for executive privilege like that of Nixon or the firing of another special prosecutor as was done in the case of Archibald Cox. But, as we will demonstrate, there was a lot more at stake here than Congress's fear of a potential repeat performance of the "Saturday Night Massacre." Just as Congress hoped to limit Nixon's assertions of discretionary authority to impound appropriated funds under Article II, we think that Congress also hoped to limit the discretionary authority of the executive in the field of prosecution. An independent council would not only correct the problems that had prevented Congress from easily subduing Nixon; it would also set a precedent whereby the legislation would assert its right to share in the power of investigation and prosecution.

Following the discovery of the Watergate break-in, Congress had demanded the appointment of a special prosecutor by Attorney General Elliot Richardson, who in turn appointed Archibald Cox to investigate the Nixon administration. Nixon's firing of Archibald Cox in the Saturday Night Massacre supposedly revealed the inadequate protections afforded by the special prosecutor procedure. In the mind of Congress, these events illustrated the need for a new system of checks and balances by which the legislature could initiate an investigation of high-level executive officers without the interference of those same officials.

Among the legislature's boldest efforts to challenge the president's influence over the administration in the wake of Watergate, Senator Sam Ervin introduced a bill to create an independent Justice Department. Under this proposal, the Attorney General, deputy attorney general, and Solicitor General would serve six-year terms and would be removable by the president only for "neglect of duty or malfeasance of office."[36] Although the title of Ervin's subcommittee hearing for the proposed legislation paid lip service to the Progressive belief that administration should be separated from politics — *Hearings on Removing Politics from the Administration of Justice* — his opening statement revealed that the real motive was to advance the interests of Congress over the executive's powers of prosecution, and to restore congressional power to its proper place.[37]

> All powers of the Attorney General and of the Department of Justice flow from acts of Congress. There can be little doubt — in fact I have no doubt at all — that what Congress gives, Congress can take away. The constitutionality of an independent Department of Justice or of an independent permanent Special Prosecutor cannot be validly disputed. I am aware, of course, that some commentators argue that

because the Constitution says that the President has a duty to take care that the laws be faithfully executed, the administration of justice is inherently executive and cannot be altered by the Congress. I firmly reject that notion. There is not one syllable in the Constitution that says that Congress cannot make the Justice Department independent of the President. After all, Congress has established the General Accounting Office, as well as the independent regulatory commissions, all of which "execute" certain laws independently of the President. No one can validly argue that those agencies are contrary to the Constitution.[38]

Sensing their opportunity to finally restore some balance between the legislature and the executive, Ervin and members of Congress went all in. They put forth a strong version of the congressional delegation doctrine akin to the one put forward by Senator Pepper in the *Myers* case. Ervin's argument also made explicit what we believe had always been implied in the argument for IRCs: Congressional limits on removal are not deduced from an abstract theory of administration like that advanced by Progressive intellectuals, such as Herbert Croly, but from the interests of Congress in controlling executive power.

Congress simply could have celebrated the departure of Nixon in 1974 and congratulated itself for a job well done as it pressured the Department of Justice to continue investigations under the existing procedures for a special prosecutor. Had Nixon refused to resign from office, there were always the constitutional provisions for impeachment by the legislature. Why, then, did Congress proceed to dig deeply into traditionally core areas of executive power in order to prevent the recurrence of an episode that had, in the end, been handled to its satisfaction? The short answer: perhaps for the same reason that Congress felt it must prevent another impoundment episode under the president. Leading congressmen like Senator Ervin and Senator Cranston thought that the specter of Nixon was not a momentary anomaly in executive-legislative relations but the logical culmination of the presidential order that had been set in motion under Franklin Roosevelt. As Peri Arnold explains: "In reorganization planning Richard Nixon followed the path of his predecessors in the presidency; he understood reform in power terms, seeing that values of good government and ambitions for increased presidential control over government were intermixed within American government."[39] Control over the discretionary resources of executive power was the key feature of Nixon's efforts to make the federal administration reflect the popular will. Nixon may have indeed seemed paranoid to some scholars (and he probably was), but his paranoia reflected the real dilemma he faced as a conservative president who followed in the footsteps of the institutional model set by Roosevelt.

Congress sought to severely curtail the discretionary powers of the president to prevent such control.

Reagan and the Unitary Executive Theory

From one perspective, the Reagan administration (1981–1989) began where Nixon had ended. Reagan came to office with an agenda to shrink the size of government and to devolve many of the federal government's regulatory responsibilities to the states. Reagan also faced the same institutional obstacles as Nixon. To accomplish a substantial reduction in the size of the bureaucracy and the scope of its regulatory authority, he would also need to centralize executive power over the administration. As a modern president in the mold of Franklin Roosevelt, Reagan would invoke the presidency as an embodiment of popular will in order to justify the exercise of unilateral powers in pursuit of his administration's goals. Moreover, Reagan's confrontations with Congress involved the same two areas of discretionary executive power: control over expenditures in the budget process, and law enforcement through executive prosecution.

Unlike Nixon, however, Reagan would survive his battles with Congress and establish a lasting legacy that would define the presidency in the future. Reagan had two advantages when he entered the presidency that Nixon did not. First, there was nowhere to go but up in terms of the popular image of the presidency in 1981. The institution was at an all-time low following Watergate, as well as Gerald Ford's and Jimmy Carter's dismal performances as executive managers. Second, he entered the presidency at a time when the New Deal coalition had nearly dissolved both inside of Washington and in public opinion. More broadly, Reagan was able to use his administration's unified ideological vision to speak loudly, but in domestic matters he tended to carry a small stick. Reagan proved to be more willing than Nixon to accommodate Congress and the status quo of the entitlement state.[40]

Another important advantage for Reagan was the ideological unity within his administration. With the help of conservative think-tanks like the Heritage Foundation, Reagan recruited a coherent cadre of appointees who would work together to create this vision of a unified executive. Conservative task forces were employed to train new members through seminars, and, unlike previous administrations, the EOP insisted that it be informed of even low-level noncareer appointments by cabinet members. Thus, Edwin Meese and E. Pendleton James had already begun the process of recruiting members of the Unitary Executive School for the administration six months before the presidential campaign of 1980 had gotten under way.[41] Unlike Nixon, who focused on "machinery" rather than personnel, the Reagan administration aimed at both unified accountability as well as a common ideological vision among subordinates.

These seminars included a new understanding of separation of powers, including in particular the doctrine of the unitary executive.[42] As Solicitor General Charles Fried has written, "The Reagan administration had a vision about the arrangement of government power: the authority and responsibility of the President should be clear and unitary. The Reagan years were distinguished by the fact that that vision was made the subject of legal, rather than simply political dispute." Recalling his time as director of the Office of Legal Counsel (OLC), Samuel Alito (now Associate Justice Alito) told the Senate Judiciary Committee, "We were strong proponents of the theory of the unitary executive, that all federal executive power is vested by the Constitution in the president. And I thought then, and I still think, that this theory best captures the meaning of the Constitution's text and structure."[43] Proponents of the unitary executive school occupied posts throughout the Department of Justice under the direction of Attorney General Meese, who headed Reagan's transition efforts following the election. Steven Calebresi, a member of Reagan's OLC, described their vision of the executive's role in the separation of powers scheme in the following terms:

> (1) The President has a right co-equal with that of the Supreme Court to interpret the Constitution; (2) all employees of the Executive Branch are legally the President's subordinates and obtain all their constitutional power by implicit or explicit delegation from the President; and, therefore, (3) all employees of the Executive Branch holding legal jobs should follow the President's line in every respect on all constitutional issues, and it is the job of the Attorney General (and maybe the White House Counsel) to ensure that every lawyer in every administration toes the President's line in every respect.[44]

The emphasis on the legal authority of the executive in cases like the exercise of unilateral powers or the removal of members of the administration constituted a significant departure from Roosevelt's and Nixon's emphasis upon the popular authority of the president. Though Reagan did believe that he possessed a popular mandate to advance his policies, he made a distinction between his political role as the chief representative of the people and his constitutional duty to protect the office of the presidency. That distinction would be a key part of Reagan's overall strategy and the critical difference between him and Nixon. Nixon conflated the political and legal authority of the president, leading to his political suicide in the end. By keeping the two separate, Reagan could compromise on policy questions related to his popular mandate, while being unyielding in fulfilling his constitutional duties as president. For this reason, most of

Reagan's biggest battles would be fought out in the courts rather than on Capitol Hill.

To this end, Reagan was fortunate enough to recruit a legal staff of like-minded individuals who shared a strong conviction that the post-Watergate presidency needed to be reinvigorated.[45] Under the direction of Attorney General Meese, the Reagan administration hired a sizeable cadre of legal experts who have now been dubbed collectively the "unitary executive school."[46] Meese led the charge with an important speech soon after taking office in which he directly attacked the IRCs, those same institutions that had been obstacles to Nixon's efforts to unify the executive branch. But Meese's speech put the issue in a broader context than just executive control of the federal government's regulatory apparatus. He focused on the issue of constitutional responsibilities and the accountability of the president in the separation of powers scheme:

> The men who wrote the Constitution were keenly concerned with accountability. They were too familiar with the dangers of despotic authority and with the weaknesses of an unwritten constitution to leave the spelling out of authority and the accumulation of power to chance. . . . They created a federal government of three well defined branches. And they carefully enumerated the powers and responsibilities of each. Increasingly, the real law making power in Washington is wielded neither by the Congress nor the President, but by relatively anonymous members of federal agencies . . . excessive agency independence serves to defeat accountability in government.[47]

As we noted earlier, the two areas of discretionary power that had most concerned Congress were prosecution and budgetary expenditures. There were good reasons for Congress's jealousy over these two forms of executive power. Among the responsibilities of the president in the arena of domestic politics, law enforcement and spending were the most powerful means by which he could concretely affect the policy of the national government. Congress feared that the executive's interpretation of law paved the way for the potential subversion of law. But by the New Deal, the duties and responsibilities of the federal government over the public welfare had become so extensive and complex that Congress was forced to legislate in broad strokes and leave much authority to executive-branch officials to fill in the details. Congress would find new means of retaining control such as independent prosecutor statutes and the legislative veto to counter the increased power of the executive. Unfortunately for Congress, these new weapons of self-defense have not worked to the degree it had hoped.

Under Reagan, Congress would find itself in a similar position to the one it occupied under Nixon. With the Court now taking the defense of Congress under its wing in cases like *Morrison v. Olson*, a new formula for the separation of powers would be introduced into the debate over the removal power — one that did away with the former pretensions of the independent regulatory commissions. It referred to the old separation of powers idea as "formalism" — perhaps intended to suggest that this view was as antiquated as someone who would go to a discothèque in a tuxedo. The discourse over the removal power turned away from the quasi-legislative and quasi-judicial functions to a more naked discussion of *how much* executive power Congress could withdraw from the president to maintain a balance of powers. Scholars call this approach "functionalism."[48] Regardless of the merits of either position, the evolution reveals the naked truth behind the IRCs and their limitations on presidential removal. Congress feared the consequence of discretionary executive power more acutely in the twentieth century, especially when its own capacity to restrain the president's power had been severely handicapped.

Bowsher v. Synar and Budgetary Control

Bowsher v. Synar (1986) marked one of the major moments in the constitutional debate over the removal power under the Reagan presidency.[49] The case arose from a challenge to the constitutionality of the Comptroller General's role in the budget process. According to the Balanced Budget and Emergency Deficit Control Act of 1985, also known as Gramm-Rudman, Congress would set deficit reduction goals for the annual budget over a series of years.[50] If Congress failed to reach the target in its annual appropriations budget, the Comptroller General was required under Section 251 of the act to reconcile the estimates of the CBO and OMB and, based on his independent study, direct the president to make across-the-board cuts in discretionary spending. The legislation was an attempt to improve the Congressional Budget Act of 1974, which had failed by the 1980s to keep down spending.[51] But instead of relying upon presidential impoundments to control Congress's appropriation levels, the act utilized the office of the Comptroller General for the same purpose.

Gramm-Rudman was an attractive political tool for Congress. Congressmen who disliked Reagan's powerful influence on Capitol Hill could score some points with the public by passing fiscally responsible legislation. Reagan, for his part, did not focus on balanced budgets as much as cutting taxes and increasing defense spending. "I did not come here to balance the budget," explained Reagan, "at the expense of my tax cutting program and my defense program."[52] By utilizing an "independent" officer from the Government Accounting Office to enforce the provisions for sequestration, Congress appeared more serious about fiscal discipline; the president, they hoped, would appear to be a political ideologue indifferent to the deficit problem.

Congress also hoped Gramm-Rudman would be an improvement over the previous budget acts in actually cutting spending. It dispensed with the open-ended budgetary guidelines in the 1974 act and instead imposed concrete spending caps that were designed to extend over a series of years rather than a single fiscal year. The Comptroller General served two critical functions for remedying the defects in the former act. First, the cancellation or deferral of spending imposed by the sequestration order would be integrated into the process of the budget without the involvement of the president. Congress would also not have to rely upon moral persuasion to get members to act collectively in order to vindicate its repudiation of the impoundment device. Rather, it could threaten spendthrifts in Congress with a sort of impoundment devise of its own wielded by the independent Comptroller General. Second, the Comptroller's independence from the executive made him an ideal candidate in Congress's scheme to give the CBO the respectability it may not have earned on its own. Since the Comptroller was required to reconcile the differences in the CBO and OMB numbers, the former would have to be taken more seriously as an integral feature of the overall budget process.

Soon after its passage, the legislation did have its dissenters both among some members of Congress and the president himself. Representative Henry Waxman noted, "We are betraying [the public] trust by handing our jobs over to bureaucrats, triggers, and automatic decisions."[53] Reagan supported the bill in general terms given how popular it was among most conservatives. But, in his signing statement, the president expressed some reservations regarding the constitutionality of the bill's sequestration provisions which gave executive powers to the Comptroller in the budget process.[54]

In 1981, President Reagan had launched his own budget reform through Executive Order No. 12,291.[55] It mandated that agencies submit all proposed and final regulations to the OMB's Office of Information and Regulatory Affairs for review.[56] Like Nixon before him, Reagan looked to the OMB for exerting presidential leverage in the budget process as a means of gaining control over the administration.

As the Reagan administration began to tighten its control over administrative agencies falling within its area of political control, the IRCs continued to stand in the way of a unified executive branch. As one member of the Justice Department explained, the IRCs' "independence of presidential authority was considered the extreme example, a kind of emblem, of one of the biggest obstacles to the administration's program."[57] Here Reagan had limited control over personnel selection and limited removal power. In order to avoid a massive turf war with Congress, the executive order described above was not applied to the IRCs.[58] As Peter Strauss explains: "To exempt the independent agencies from regulatory review must have been a great source of annoyance for the Reagan administration given that their efforts to centralize control elsewhere would have made the IRC's even more obviously 'a headless fourth branch.'"[59] A Court decision declaring the Comptroller General's role in the budget process a violation of the Constitution on separation of powers grounds would have enormous ramifications at this point in the Reagan presidency. It would liberate the president from the control of the Comptroller under Gramm-Rudman, and it might even give the OMB constitutional authority to regulate the IRCs if the court found that they, too, were unconstitutional by implication.

In *Bowsher v. Synar*, the Court addressed the question of whether the assignment to the Comptroller of these powers in the budget process violated separation of powers. At stake in the case were two questions. First, were the duties of the Comptroller under the act executive in nature? Second, did Congress's participation in the removal power over the Comptroller abridge the separation of legislative power and executive power under the Constitution? The Court's opinion, authored by Chief Justice Warren Burger, answered affirmatively to both questions. The act vested the Comptroller with "executive" powers, and it granted Congress the power to remove the Comptroller through a joint resolution. "Congress," the opinion held, "cannot reserve for itself the power of removal of an officer charged with the execution of the laws except by impeachment."[60]

As straightforward as Burger's opinion may seem, both the concurrence and the dissents in the case observed that the opinion of the Court actually went to great lengths to avoid what would seem like a clear implication of the decision. If Congress could not control a federal officer with duties like those of the Comptroller, how could it limit the president's removal of the independent regulatory commissioners? As the petitioners in the case argued, "All the independent agencies . . . would be over the side, particularly if you adopt [the] theory that it is not the removal power in those statues which would have to be invalidated but the function that is to be performed."[61] Burger's opinion tried to obfuscate this potential conclusion by focusing narrowly upon Congress's role in the removal. By focusing on Congress's control of the Comptroller first, he could concentrate attention on that problem without having to discuss the obvious corollary: whether Congress was also prohibited from limiting the removal power over an officer who was *executive*. Of course, Burger could not avoid some mention of the tension between the precedent set in *Myers* and the one in *Humphrey's Executor*, because the decision rested heavily upon the former precedent. Burger dealt with this enormous constitutional question with a single blithe statement about the relevance of the latter: "*Humphrey's Executor* involved an issue not presented in the *Myers* case or in this case —i.e., the power of Congress to limit the President's power of removal of a Federal Trade Commissioner."[62] But if the legislature violated the constitutional precedent set in *Myers* by assigning executive powers to an "agent of Congress," it bordered on equivocation to argue that the only constitutional violation that had occurred in this case was Congress's retention of a role in the removal process. The next logical step in the reasoning should have led to the conclusion that any such limit on the executive was a violation of the president's duty to faithfully enforce the law. As Justice Byron White responded in his dissent, the case here and the constitutional question at stake in the IRCs were exactly the same. Burger simply asserted, and then only in a footnote, that this case posed no future challenge to the constitutional status of the IRCs:

> Appellants therefore are wide of the mark in arguing that an affirmance in this case requires casting doubt on the status of 'independent' agencies, because no issues involving such agencies are presented here. The statutes establishing independent agencies typically specify either that the agency members are removable by the President for specified causes . . . ('for inefficiency, neglect of duty, or malfeasance in office'), or else do not specify a removal procedure. . . . This case involves nothing like these statutes, but rather a statute that provides for direct Congressional involvement over the decision to remove the Comptroller General.[63]

Both Justice John Paul Stevens's concurrence and Justice White's dissent objected to Burger's formal use of the separation of powers doctrine as the basis of reasoning for the removal authority. Assigning what appeared to be forms of executive power to officials who were not responsible to the president, according to Stevens, was not new; neither did the Court conclude in its opinion that for Congress to do so is always unconstitutional. "As our cases demonstrate, a particular function, like a chameleon, will often take on the aspect of the office to which it is assigned."[64] Stevens dismissed the premise of the plurality's opinion and argued that no "bright line" can be drawn between executive and legislative power. In the absence of clear demarcations between the powers of government, the justice believed that the best guarantee of democratically responsible legislation is the constitution's provision for bicameralism and presentment. The problem with Gramm-Rudman, from this point of view, was that Congress's delegation of authority to the Comptroller did not comport with this procedure and thus posed a danger to responsible democratic legislation. Stevens believed that his reasoning more adequately reconciled the apparent contradiction between the majority's claim that the Comptroller's role in the budget process was unconstitutional and the Court's *obiter dictum* asserting that the IRCs were constitutional. In one way he had resolved the issue by eliminating the contention over the location of executive power. The Comptroller's duties were really no different than the power wielded by an independent regulatory commissioner. But Stevens also assumed that IRCs were constitutionally valid because their enabling statutes were passed under the bicameral and presentment clause requirements of the constitution. The problem here was that Gramm-Rudman had been created in the same manner.

White's dissent was perhaps the most consistent among the opinions in the case for its reasoning. Like Stevens, White dispensed with bright-line distinctions over executive and legislative power. But White went further and actually rejected almost any formal limitations on Congress's authority to tailor new initiatives to meet emergency needs. Commenting on the origins of the IRCs, White concluded:

> In an earlier day, in which simpler notions of the role of government in society prevailed, it was perhaps plausible to insist that all "executive" officers be subject to an unqualified Presidential removal power, but with the advent and triumph of the administrative state and the accompanying multiplication of the tasks undertaken by the Federal Government, the Court has been virtually compelled to recognize that Congress may reasonably deem it "necessary and proper" to vest some among the broad new array of governmental functions in officers who are free from the partisanship that may be expected of agents wholly dependent upon the President. The Court's recognition of the legitimacy of legislation vesting "executive" authority in officers independent of the President does not imply derogation of the President's own constitutional authority.... As Justice Holmes put it: "The duty of the President to see that the laws be executed is a duty that does not go beyond the laws or require him to achieve more than Congress sees fit to leave within his power."[65]

Similar to the arguments that had been made during the Progressive era, White claimed that modern budgetary and regulatory concerns had rendered the formal requirements of the separation of powers doctrine obsolete. In particular, "the advent of the administrative state" required innovative responses from Congress to manage its own duties.

White's dissent seemed to imply that there were no constitutional limitations to Congress's power to create and assign this "new array of governmental functions." "Perhaps as a matter of political science we could say that Congress should only concern itself with broad principles of policy, and leave their application in particular cases to the executive branch. But no such rule can be found in the Constitution itself, or in legislative practice. It is fruitless, therefore, to try to draw any sharp and logical line between legislative and executive functions."[66] But one wonders if there are any limits to the scope of legislation if we follow White's exhortation to avoid "unduly constrict[ing] Congress' ability to take needed and innovative action pursuant to its Article I powers."[67] What limitations are there to Congress's legislative powers? White did recognize that the branches were in fact accountable to voters for the success of their policymaking and therefore needed the requisite authority to carry it out. Consequently, White offered a new standard for reviewing congressional allocations of executive authority when placed beyond the reach of the president. "In determining whether a limitation on the President's power to remove an officer performing executive functions constitutes a violation of the constitutional scheme of separation of powers, a court must focu[s] on the extent to which [such a limitation] prevents the Executive Branch from accomplishing its constitutionally assigned functions."[68] In this case, according to White, there had been no disruption of executive power, because appropriations are a duty entrusted to Congress under Article I, Section 9.

White aspired to dispense with considerations of formal powers assigned to the branches, but in the end it is clear that his argument had a certain legislative bias.[69] How does one know when "too much" executive power has been restricted from the control of the executive? White offered a clue in his reflections on the merits of the budget procedure in Gramm-Rudman: "To be sure, if the budget-cutting mechanism required the responsible officer to exercise a great deal of policymaking discretion, one might argue that . . . Congress had some obligation based upon Art. II to vest it in the Chief Executive or his agents."[70] The compatibility of the Comptroller's responsibilities with the constitutional authority of Congress, according to White, could be seen in the legislation's careful attempt to eliminate discretionary policymaking in the budget process. The "automatic" budget-cutting measures were designed to provide a tightly controlled institutional mechanism for enforcement so that Congress's legislative intent would not go adrift during the course of its implementation. But, if this were really the case, Congress could have done that itself — as it in fact planned to do under the "fallback provision" of the law in the event the reporting procedure was declared invalid.[71] White's description of the Comptroller's duties as merely mechanical implementations of the law was thus misleading. According to the statute, the Comptroller must first anticipate revenues and expenditures in order to ascertain the gross amount that must be cut from the budget to meet the required level of spending. Second, he must specify how to meet that level by deciding what items of spending ought to be reduced and by how much. The district court's original decision in this case was more direct than Burger's opinion in its characterization of these activities as executive: "The first of these specifications requires the exercise of substantial judgment concerning present and future facts that affect the application of the law — the sort of power normally conferred upon the executive officer charged with implementing a statute. The second specification requires an interpretation of the law enacted by Congress, similarly a power normally committed initially to the Executive under the Constitution's prescription that he 'take Care that the Laws be faithfully executed.'"[72] White mischaracterized the powers of the Comptroller in the same way that leading congressmen also misrepresented the operation of the automatic budget cuts. In Congress's view, the process was supposed to operate as an institutionalized mechanism for carrying out the will of Congress in regard to the budget. But what the act tried to obscure was the fact that any articulation of a budget is a political action. As David Nichols explains: "It is also important to remember that even though Gramm-Rudman tried to make the goal of a balanced budget more realistic by creating a process of gradual deficit reduction, it did nothing to counter the fact that "the budget" is a very elastic concept."[73]

White's characterization of these provisions in Gramm-Rudman reflected a viewpoint common to adherents of the congressional delegation school. According to that argument, Congress had the right not only to create laws but also to insert itself into the execution of law in order to make sure that its intent was realized in its enforcement. In the end, the Comptroller really was an aid to the legislature regardless of the degree of congressional removal power. Congress needed someone who could enforce its own rules without being a member of the legislature; normally that individual would logically be the executive, but in this case, as in the case of the IRCs, Congress wanted an alternative source. Given White's criticism, Burger might have found a better way of reconciling the tension between his use of the *Myers* precedent and that of *Humphrey's Executor*. One possibility would have been to argue that the duties of an independent regulatory commissioner were quasi-judicial, whereas the responsibilities of the Comptroller were executive. To be sure, it might not have been entirely persuasive, especially given that in 1789 Madison had made an exception for the Comptroller General's office on the grounds that it was not executive but quasi-judicial. But it would have been more plausible than the mere assertion that what appears contradictory is not. Why didn't Burger and the other members of the plurality simply opt for this solution?

Legal historian Bernard Schwartz offers a possible answer in his examination of the Court's conference reports and correspondence during the case. According to Schwartz, Burger initially drafted an opinion that relied heavily upon the *Myers* precedent. But other members objected to the implications of the draft opinion, pointing out that his reasoning would erode the Court's precedents supporting the constitutional status of the IRCs.[74] Consequently, Burger wrote a second draft that merely used the *Myers* precedent for the purpose of making the case against congressional removal of an executive officer. The second draft then attempted to distin-guish between the Comptroller's executive powers and the quasi-judicial powers of the IRCs. Justice William Brennan, however, objected to the usage in a letter to the Chief Justice:

> My concern is that reintroducing such notions as whether some func-tion is 'quasi-legislative' or 'quasi-judicial' will encourage claims that all sorts of independent agency activity is neither, and that it must therefore be under the President's control. In other words, I am afraid that reintroducing this analysis will cast doubt upon the legality of much of the work of independent administrative agencies. . . . This problem can easily be avoided simply by not using this terminology in discussion.[75]

For Brennan, the holding in *Humphrey's Executor* actually detracted from Congress's authority to place nearly any limitation it desires on the presi-dent's removal power. Brennan's objections were ultimately incorporated into the final draft by Burger, which explains why the opinion seemed so evasive about the relationship between *Myers* and *Humphrey's Executor*.[76]

As we have argued, White's dissent was far more consistent and per-haps truer to the logic behind the IRCs. If Congress wanted to limit the president's power, according to White, it ought to be able to do so as long as it did not impose a limitation that might embarrass the president in exe-cuting an assigned task. But "embarrassing" the president was a phrase that should not be made too strict a standard here, because that was precisely the issue that arose in the next significant legal test of the removal power. In fact, White's argument for a new standard of review would in fact be-come the criteria employed by the majority opinion in the case of *Morrison v. Olson* (1988).

Morrison v. Olson

Reagan was more accommodating to Congress's demands than Nixon had been. Reagan signed Gramm-Rudman as well as the two bills reauthorizing the independent counsel statute (though he included in a signing statement to Gramm-Rudman as well as the second reauthorization bill for the inde-pendent counsel statute serious reservations about the constitutionality of both laws). However, the administration's attempts under Reagan to imple-ment its unitary executive vision put a strain on its relations with the legis-lature. The case of *Morrison v. Olson* arose out of one of the many quarrels between the administration's use of discretionary law-enforcement powers and Congress's desire to constrain that discretion. But unlike in the case of Nixon's impoundments, Congress had a more robust weapon to wield in challenging the Reagan administration's implementation of policy. The independent counsel provision of the Ethics in Government Act of 1978 gave Congress the means to do more than simply haul members of the administration before a hearing.[77] Under the act, Congress could compel the Attorney General to conduct a preliminary investigation of high-ranking executive-branch officials.[78] The Attorney General was then required to determine whether further investigation was warranted and to report the results of his investigation to a special division of the United States Court of Appeals for the District of Columbia Circuit. If the circumstances did warrant further investigation, he was compelled to request the appointment of a special prosecutor by the panel, or, if not, a report of his reasons for not seeking the appointment.[79] The special division would then select the independent prosecutor and define the prosecutor's jurisdiction.[80] Finally, the Attorney General's power to remove the special prosecutor was limited to "good cause," and the court could then review the Attorney General's decision upon request of the special prosecutor.[81]

The independent prosecutor statute now offered a convenient test case where the escalating tension between the branches post-Nixon could be aired before a neutral Court. By upholding the statute, Congress would finally have its authority to control executive law enforcement vindicated, and it would even possess some prosecutorial authority over those who attempted to interfere with its efforts to do so. Since the act effectively reserved to Congress some executive power, a favorable decision would set an important precedent and perhaps instruct the president that Congress was always free to take more.

The facts of this particular case neatly capture in a microcosm the broader constitutional disagreements between the Reagan administration and Congress. The case arose from an acrimonious dispute between Congress and the president over the Environmental Protection Agency's (EPA) enforcement of the "Superfund" law that dealt with the cleanup of toxic waste sites. Then as now, enforcement of environmental law was a sensitive matter. The EPA directed the enforcement of environmental regulations in a manner that had concrete effects upon congressional districts, yet the scientific expertise needed to formulate policy compelled Congress to legislate in very broad strokes.[82] Lloyd Cutler, former head White House counsel under President Carter (and eventually recruited to the same post under Democratic President Bill Clinton), shared the same view of the presidency as did the unitarians in the Reagan Justice Department. Addressing the administration of environmental protection matters, Cutler explained:

> Expert advice and the independence of those who give this advice are still of great importance, and ultimate decision makers cannot be

without such counsel. However, as we are beginning to recognize, regulation today involves political choices between competing interests — concerning which economic and social goals to pursue, how far and at what economic and social cost. Under our constitutional scheme, these are choices that only politically accountable officials who are "dependent" rather than "independent" and "generalists" rather than "experts" should be making. The regulatory agencies should not have more independence from the political process and more opportunity to apply expertise to nontechnical decisions than is consistent with effective, democratic government.[83]

In this area, Congress was especially sensitive to the discretionary law-enforcement powers of the executive given the highly publicized effects that the EPA's policy decisions would have in congressional districts. Because Congress could not control much of the details of the policy, the EPA was a prime interest of congressional oversight. The EPA therefore was much like the FTC in that Congress lacked both the policy expertise and the capacity to form a general consensus on what specific policies ought to be written. But as was the case with antitrust policy in the early part of the twentieth century, Congress knew something had to be done in environmental matters given growing public concerns by the late twentieth century.

This case illustrated the mounting tension between Congress and the president in a very public manner. As Kevin Stack relates, by 1982 two House subcommittees had begun investigations of the EPA's actions with respect to Superfund. In the process, "The Subcommittees had obtained information from current and former EPA employees suggesting that partisan political considerations had influenced the EPA's handling of Superfund enforcement actions." In particular, according to Stack, EPA staff had claimed that political appointees within the EPA had "delayed a proposed agreement on cost sharing between the federal government and California concerning the clean-up of the Stringfellow Site until after the November elections," presumably to help Republican Pete Wilson's chances in the 1982 Senate election.[84] When the House Judiciary Committee attempted to subpoena members of the EPA staff to testify in this case, assistant attorney general for the OLC Theodore Olson recommended invoking executive privilege on the grounds that the information included material sensitive to executive law enforcement.

Congress did not have the power to compel prosecution or enforcement, but it now had the ability to effectively compel the appointment of someone who could prosecute the prosecutors. The Ethics in Government Act, as mentioned before, created an independent counsel armed with investigatory and prosecutorial powers that could be wielded against certain high-ranking government officials.[85] When the Reagan administration's Office of Legal Counsel invoked executive privilege against Congress's request for documentation of EPA enforcement of the Superfund statute, the legislature could now direct the Attorney General to request the appointment of an independent prosecutor to investigate the same issue it had been pursuing through subcommittee hearings. Once the Attorney General found that there were "reasonable grounds" for further investigation, he would be required to submit a request for the appointment of counsel by a special division of the United States Court of Appeals for the District of Columbia Circuit. The special division, in turn, would choose the counsel and define jurisdiction for the investigation and potential prosecution of high-level administration officials.[86]

Theodore Olson was not the first member of the Reagan administration to be investigated by an independent counsel. Many top officials, including Attorney General Edwin Meese, had found themselves on the receiving end of this procedure. Congress suspected that Olson had been guilty of giving misleading or inadequate response to Congress's investigation of the EPA's enforcement of the Superfund statute.[87] Olson was also not the first to attempt to challenge the independent counsel statute in court. During the period of time in which Olson had moved to quash the subpoena issued by the independent prosecutor, Alexia Morrison, most attention in Washington was actually being paid to a more high-profile independent prosecutor case against Oliver North during the investigation of Iran-Contra.[88] But Olson's was the first case on this issue to be heard before the Supreme Court.[89] Furthermore, as one of those strong advocates of the unitary executive recruited by Meese to work in Reagan's OLC, Olson believed it was a top priority to protect the president's reserved powers of discretion in the execution of law from attempts by Congress to weaken that authority.[90] Olson insisted on regularly invoking executive privilege in order to protect the president's control of law enforcement.[91] Given that part of the reason for the independent counsel law was to minimize the executive's capacity to invoke this privilege, *Morrison* would provide the opportunity for Reagan to vindicate his administrative strategy while getting rid of a very pesky congressional device. Even after his service during Reagan's first term when he returned to private practice, "Ted Olson [was] looking for a case in which to make the attack on the independents as a private litigant."[92]

The challenge to the independent counsel law in *Morrison* was the perfect place to make inroads against the IRCs in the courts. Unlike *Bowsher*, where the Court could avoid the broader issue by focusing on congressional removal, *Morrison* compelled the Court to decide a landmark case that would have to take the issue of the IRCs head-on. The Reagan administration's chances of prevailing in court over the independent counsel law seemed good at the time. The Court's previous decisions lent some support for a separation of powers vision congruent with the ideas of the unitarians. The Court had lent partial support in *Bowsher*, and in the case of *Immigration and Naturalization Service v. Chadha* (1983),[93] the Court declared that Congress's use of a single-house legislative veto to reverse a decision of the Attorney General violated separation of powers. The Reagan administration certainly welcomed such a decision. Not only had the independent counsel been an effective weapon of harassment by Congress; the administration was also trying to tighten its control over a large portion of the administrative agencies. In a similar way to Nixon's attempt to control the bureaucracy in his second term through internal devices and rules promulgated through the OMB, Reagan had attempted to unify executive management of rulemaking and policy under the same agency. The administration's chances looked even better in 1988, when the United States Court of Appeals for the District of Columbia Circuit found the independent prosecutor statue to be unconstitutional. Employing the term "unitary executive" throughout the decision, the Court of Appeals explained:

> Central to the government instituted by the Constitution are the doctrines of separation of powers and a unitary executive . . . and yet the independent counsel interprets the appointments clause as if those doctrines were nonexistent. Understanding that the President could not fulfill his constitutional role by himself, the Framers envisioned that the Executive Branch would be divided into departments whose officers would be appointed by the President and who could be removed by Congress only through the impeachment process.[94]

Confident that the Court might finally deliver the blow to the law that the administration's lawyers had long desired, Reagan prepared the way with a signing statement to the 1987 reauthorization of the independent prosecutor statute:

> Continuance of these independent counsel investigations was deemed important to public confidence in our government. Nevertheless, this goal, however sound, may not justify disregard for the carefully crafted restraints spelled out in the Constitution. An officer of the United States exercising executive authority in the core area of law enforcement necessarily, under our constitutional scheme, must be subject to executive branch appointment, review, and removal. There is no other constitutionally permissible alternative, and I regret that the Congress and the President have been unable to agree under that framework on a procedure to ensure impartial, forthright, and unimpeded criminal law investigations of high-level executive branch officials.[95]

The Court's decision in *Morrison* upholding the independent counsel statute provision must have come as a surprise to many of the members of the unitary executive school in the Reagan administration. Charles Fried, who argued the case during his tenure as Solicitor General, reported that the justices remained almost entirely silent during his oral argument, which he believed was an early indication that they were not going to engage in much discussion of the legal questions for the president's side. Instead, the majority, in an opinion written by Chief Justice William Rehnquist, concluded that all of the provisions of the law were not only constitutionally defensible but reasonable means of ensuring a balanced system of government.

What was peculiar about the decision was the fact that even though the case raised central removal-power questions, it only briefly mentioned *Myers* and *Humphrey's* and never discussed the Decision of 1789. To understand how the case fit into the history of the removal power at this culminating moment requires some examination of the majority's reasoning. The Court divided its treatment of the constitutional challenge to the independent counsel into three essential questions. First, did the act violate the appointments clause of the Constitution when Congress vested the appointment of an independent counsel in a special division of the judiciary? Second, did the powers of the special division impermissibly assign nonjudicial duties to Article III judges? Third, did the act violate separation of powers by interfering with the president's duty to faithfully enforce the laws? For our purposes, the Court's examination of questions 1 and 3 are the most relevant and, as we will see, instructive for understanding the current state of the removal power debate.

The appointments clause raised the thorniest question of the case. The Court could not approach the question as it had in *Bowsher*. In that case it had narrowed its finding to the constitutionally suspect practice of congressional participation in the removal power; here, no such issue was presented. Neither could it take the approach of *Humphrey's*, because prosecution was not a quasi-legislative or quasi-judicial function but clearly an executive one. Yet to declare the independent counsel statute unconstitutional on executive power grounds would raise enormous problems for the legal status of the IRCs. As the Ash Council's report had observed years before during Nixon's tenure, the distinction between the duties of the IRCs and normal executive responsibilities was impossible to discern in reality because many agencies that were independent appeared to exercise powers that were also assigned to executive departments. Members of the *Bowsher* majority, as we have seen, were still present on the Court when it decided *Morrison*. They essentially agreed with Nixon, but they were eager to avoid a decision that called into question the constitutionality of the IRCs.[96] Finally, the case also raised another serious constitutional question:

Could Congress vest the appointment of an executive officer in another branch of government?

The first question regarding the appointment and removal power, then, was whether the legislature had violated this part of the Constitution by shielding the independent prosecutor from removal by the Executive. The form of the question seemed to raise the principle appealed to by many participants in the removal power debate and by the Court in its removal power jurisprudence: "The power to remove follows from the power to appoint." The Court of Appeals had framed the issue this way and concluded that the limitations on executive removal violated separation of powers. Congress's statutory limitations upon the executive's removal power — in this case the Attorney General's removal power — violated the executive's duty to faithfully enforce the laws. Drawing on reasoning in *Myers*, the Court of Appeals decision had made an important distinction between superior (or "principal") officers and inferior officers. According to Chief Justice Taft in *Myers*, one could limit the president's capacity to remove the inferior officers through something like civil-service laws but not principal officers because they have duties for which the president is directly accountable for faithful execution of the law.[97] Independent Counsel Morrison, according to the Court of Appeals, was a principal officer having powers that were directly accountable to the president.

The Court of Appeals had also dismissed the continued relevance of the *Humphrey's Executor* precedent with its exception for an official exercising quasi-legislative and quasi-judicial powers — the traditional legal buffer for the IRCs:

> To be sure, Supreme Court Justices have expressed dissatisfaction with the distinctions drawn in *Humphrey's Executor*. They contend, not without force, that the FTC Commissioners' duties included law enforcement responsibilities and so *Humphrey's Executor*'s reliance on the Commissioners' quasi-judicial and quasi-legislative functions is inadequate to explain the case — and to limit its future applicability. Even under this alternative reading, which recognizes certain executive functions performed by the FTC, *Humphrey's Executor* cannot, it seems to us, sanction the Act's good cause removal limitation. In *Humphrey's Executor*, the Commissioners were described as a "body of experts" whose purpose was "to carry into effect legislative policies embodied in the statute in accordance with the legislative standard therein prescribed, and to perform other specified duties as a legislative or as a judicial aid."[98]

In *Morrison*, the Supreme Court eschewed such formal distinctions in constitutional law, declaring that the distinction between principal officers and inferior officers had never been made with any clarity. Rehnquist argued that the distinction depended on what function the officer had in the executive branch and how important the function was. Inferior officers were not that important and therefore could be, on occasion, shielded from removal, whereas principal officers were important and therefore could not. According to the reasoning here, a number of features of the independent counsel's duties supported the interpretation for her inferior status in the executive branch. Among the list the Court cited were the office's limited tenure (Morrison served only as long as she had something to prosecute); the fact that she had a specific and limited set of duties defined by the Attorney General; the fact that her jurisdiction was defined to a limited extent by the special division; and finally, the fact that she was ultimately removable by the Attorney General "for good cause." Added together, these elements qualified the officer as "inferior."

What was astounding in this reasoning was that the Court argued that the prosecutor's independence from the president was constitutionally defensible by virtue of the fact that she was "squarely in the hands of" and completely subordinate to the directives of the Attorney General. In his dissent, Justice Antonin Scalia mocked this argument, asking if by this reasoning the ruler of Liechtenstein is an inferior officer due to the fact that he rules a country with very restricted borders. In this case the Court held that the independent counsel was in fact an inferior officer because she was required to follow the policies of the Department of Justice and thus lacked discretionary policymaking powers of her own. But this, too, was a weak argument because the Attorney General also followed the policies of the Justice Department but could not be regarded as an inferior officer. In fact, by this standard Morrison was even superior to the Attorney General, because her duties exempted her from department protocol in certain instances. As Scalia observed in his dissent: "The Court points out that the Act directs the independent counsel to abide by general Justice Department policy, except when not 'possible'. The exception alone shows this to be an empty promise."[99] The central problem with the court's argument was that it treated an independent prosecutor as a ministerial officer—an understanding that has proven, in the experience of later independent counsel prosecutions, to be very naive.

In the dissent, Scalia offered an instructive lesson from a famous speech by the late Supreme Court Justice Robert Jackson on the nature of prosecution:

> If the prosecutor is obliged to choose his case, it follows that he can choose his defendants. Therein is the most dangerous power of the prosecutor: that he will pick people that he thinks he should get, rather than cases that need to be prosecuted. With the law books filled with a great assortment of crimes, a prosecutor stands a fair chance of

finding at least a technical violation of some act on the part of almost anyone. In such a case, it is not a question of discovering the commission of a crime and then looking for the man who has committed it, it is a question of picking the man and then searching the law books, or putting investigators to work, to pin some offense on him. It is in this realm — in which the prosecutor picks some person whom he dislikes or desires to embarrass, or selects some group of unpopular persons and then looks for an offense, that the greatest danger of abuse of prosecuting power lies. It is here that law enforcement becomes personal, and the real crime becomes that of being unpopular with the predominant or governing group, being attached to the wrong political views, or being personally obnoxious to or in the way of the prosecutor himself.[100]

From this perspective, what was truly naive about the Court's decision was not just that it failed to anticipate what kind of havoc an independent counsel's prosecutorial authority can wreak in the executive branch, but how it failed to see how well Congress knew this all along. As Scalia noted in his dissent:

Thus, by the application of this statute in the present case, Congress has effectively compelled a criminal investigation of a high-level appointee of the President in connection with his actions arising out of a bitter power dispute between the President and the Legislative Branch. Mr. Olson may or may not be guilty of a crime; we do not know. But we do know that the investigation of him has been commenced, not necessarily because the President or his authorized subordinates believe it is in the interest of the United States . . . but only because the Attorney General cannot affirm, as Congress demands, that there are no reasonable grounds to believe that further investigation is warranted. The decisions regarding the scope of that further investigation, its duration, and, finally, whether or not prosecution should ensue, are likewise beyond the control of the President and his subordinates.[101]

Rehnquist's assumption that the independent prosecutor played a merely ministerial role made it easy to answer the rest of the legal questions posed to the Court. The Court defended Congress's decision to vest the appointment of a purely executive officer in the judiciary on the grounds that doing so logically facilitated the narrow purposes of the office. The executive could not be trusted to appoint a prosecutor to investigate himself, so the courts, familiar with many prosecutors, were a reasonable place to lodge the appointment power. The act also gave the special division in the judiciary the power to define jurisdiction, but the majority argued that this, too, was essentially ministerial in that the jurisdiction for investigation was limited to the original complaint as determined by the Attorney General. There were, of course, limits to what Congress could assign to the judiciary when it came to a purely executive officer: "We do not think that Congress may give the Division unlimited discretion to determine the independent counsel's jurisdiction."[102] "Incongruity" would be the guiding principle in this balancing test. Congress may assign to the courts appointment and supervision of an independent executive officer as long as it is congruous to both its function as a judicial body and the narrowly defined ministerial duties of the officer.

But as Jackson's speech on prosecution illustrated, determining the jurisdiction for an investigation was an awesome discretionary power, the exercise of which bore enormous ramifications for individual rights and policies of the government. Defining the scope of a prosecutor's jurisdiction was the most significant discretionary power implicit in prosecution. As the Court of Appeals opinion had explained: "Definition of a prosecutor's jurisdiction is . . . crucial to the whole enterprise of executing the criminal law, for in practical terms, it determines who may be subject to prosecution and for what crimes. Deciding to target certain people and certain acts, and to exclude others, necessarily involves a balancing of factors and a setting of priorities."[103] In fact, Morrison had petitioned the special division on numerous occasions to extend the scope of her investigation in order to execute her duties of investigating Olson's role in the EPA controversy.[104]

Finally, separation of powers was the central issue of the case and the focus of both Morrison's and Olson's briefs submitted to the Court. Whereas the Supreme Court's opinion here concluded with this issue, the Court of Appeals decision began with this because it was the fundamental issue of the case. In light of the doctrine of the separation of powers, the Court of Appeals concluded:

> Not merely an abstract idea of political theory, the Presidents accountability is a hallmark of our democracy. . . . The constitutional scheme is as simple as it is complete — Congress passes the criminal law in the first instance, the President enforces the law, and individual cases are tried before a neutral judiciary involved in neither the creation nor the execution of that law. The Ethics in Government Act, it seems to us, deliberately departs from this framework in both its particular provisions and in its general purpose, which is to authorize an officer not accountable to any elected official to prosecute crimes . . .[105]

Because the officer was not quasi-legislative or quasi-judicial but purely executive, then limiting the removal power abridged the constitutional scheme of separated powers whereby each branch retained control of its own power except where the Constitution explicitly provided otherwise (e.g., impeachment or the veto power). Olson's brief also emphasized separation of powers, arguing that within our constitutional scheme "the President alone must discharge that power."[106] Even the petitioner's brief in *Morrison* led with separation of powers, arguing that if the Court were to decide that the independent counsel act was unconstitutional, then nearly every IRC has been constituted on unconstitutional grounds.[107] By treating this issue last, it almost seemed that the question was an afterthought in the reasoning in the opinion of the Court.

In some ways, the majority opinion's treatment of separation of powers was in fact an afterthought. Rehnquist's opinion treated the doctrine as an archaic understanding of the Constitution that had clearly been superseded by years of evolutionary development in constitutional reasoning. Instead of relying upon these formal demarcations between the powers of government, he introduced a new standard: "The analysis contained in our removal cases is designed not to define rigid categories of those officials who may or may not be removed at will by the President"; but those past precedents were merely a warning that future courts must prevent Congress from "*unduly* trammel[ing] on executive authority."[108] According to this new standard of review, Congress could reserve certain executive powers for itself as long as it did not reserve *too much*. Hence the new standard was not absolute but a matter of degree. In the case of the independent counsel, the degree had not been violated because the Attorney General still had *some* control.

The act's provision restricting the Attorney General's power to remove the independent counsel to only those instances in which he can show "good cause," taken by itself, does not impermissibly interfere with the president's exercise of his constitutionally appointed functions. Here, Congress has not attempted to gain a role in the removal of executive officials other than its established powers of impeachment and conviction. The act instead puts the removal power squarely in the hands of the executive branch.

Of course, the special division could always overturn a removal decision by the Attorney General. In his dissent, Scalia remarked that the Court's conclusion (that the limitations on removal were constitutional because the Attorney General had the power of removal) was disingenuous. According to the law, if the Attorney General were to remove for good cause, he would also have to report his reasons for doing so to both the special division and both congressional judiciary committees.

But the Court's reasoning does not appear so suspect if viewed from the perspective of the new standard introduced here in the separation of powers jurisprudence of the Court. In fact, the standard was not altogether new. It was articulated by Byron White in his dissent in *Bowsher*. According to White, Congress's interest in making laws justified its intrusion into the executive branch because it was the legislature's duty to see that the law was executed. The rule that both the *Morrison* Court and White argued for was famously stated by the Court in its 1977 decision *Nixon v. Administrator of General Services* (written by William Brennan).[109] There, Brennan criticized the notion that the branches each control their own powers: "We therefore find that appellant's argument rests upon an archaic view of the separation of powers as requiring three air-tight departments of government. Rather, in determining whether the Act disrupts the proper balance between the coordinate branches, the proper inquiry focuses on the extent to which it prevents the Executive Branch from accomplishing its constitutionally assigned functions."[110] Though Brennan relied on the distinction between the formal and functional approach to discern the president's constitutional duties, he did not offer any analysis of the text of Article II. Rather, he argued that the constitutional duties of the president included only those responsibilities that *Congress* had explicitly entrusted the president with carrying out. For Brennan, as long as Congress does not entrust the president with a duty that it makes impossible to fulfill, it is always within its authority to claim certain executive powers for itself.

The Unitarians in Context

Even if we put aside the question whether Scalia's reading of the vesting clause is persuasive, his dissent perceived that the "functionalist" reading has a clear legislative bias. In that sense, he may have perceived what had been happening for a long time. By the time of *Morrison*, it was very difficult to discern any difference between the powers exercised by executive officers and those exercised by the IRCs. White's dissent in *Bowsher* and the majority opinion in *Morrison* may have been right on this point. Both cited positively a dissent by Jackson in 1952 (*FTC v. Ruberoid*) where he bitterly criticized the rationale behind the IRCs: "Administrative agencies have been called *quasi*-legislative, *quasi*-executive, or *quasi*-judicial, as the occasion required, in order to validate their functions within the separation of powers scheme of the Constitution. The mere retreat to the qualifying '*quasi*' is implicit with confession that all recognized classifications have broken down, and '*quasi*' is a smooth cover which we draw over our confusion, as we might use a counterpane to conceal a disordered bed."[111] But if this were true, how can one still constitutionally support the existence of the IRCs? The answer? On the same grounds that the Court approved the independent counsel: Congress thought it needed it. Though seemingly inapt as a statement of constitutional reasoning, Scalia's provocative declaration in his *Morrison* dissent neatly summed up the issue: "That is what this suit is about. *Power*."[112]

Although some might be inclined to regard the Ethics in Government Act's failure as a well-meaning law derailed in practice, we believe that the partisan use of the independent counsel reflects the problem in the original conception of the act itself. The title of the congressional committee hearing in which the independent counsel provisions of the Ethics in Government Act were initially proposed — *Removing Politics from Government* — reflected the ostensible purpose of the act. The IRCs were supposedly created on the same premise — that is, some forms of administration were better executed outside the political influence of the president. But as we argued in Chapter 5, in the case of the IRCs the independent counsel was really a pretext that, despite its legislative purpose, was neither as independent nor apolitical as Congress advertised. Regardless of whether Olson offered misleading testimony before the House Judiciary Committee in March 1983, the right of the legislature to control the execution of law was clearly the underlying motivation that prompted and sustained the independent counsel statute.

If judged according to its professed purpose to restore public trust and confidence in government, the law's subsequent history demonstrates that it was a failure in practice. As Nick Bravin explains, "The Act gives pause as to whether the cure was worse than the disease."[113] In practice, it was employed in partisan attacks by majorities in Congress against the president — often emboldening the president's enemies to go where representatives would not dare to tread solely under Congress's impeachment powers. As one commentator put it succinctly, "When the Republicans controlled the White House, Democrats loved it because counsels could give the White House fits. Now that Democrats control the White House, the Republicans love it."[114] When Republicans won both houses of Congress in 1994 for the first time in more than four decades, they, too, sought a revolution in balance of powers. But their attempt to use the independent counsel provisions to strengthen their hand backfired, and the institution came crumbling down after Kenneth Starr's investigations of President Bill Clinton. Once regarded as a solution to the specter of the "imperial presidency," the independent prosecutor statute, after eleven more investigations following the case of *Morrison*, became a symbol of odious witch-hunting and petty politics. Congress let the act expire once and for all in 1999.

Compared to the Ethics in Government Act, the story of the unitarians and the removal power is yet unfinished, but there is nonetheless an important lesson. As *Free Enterprise Fund v. PCAOB* reveals, even conservative members of the Court are reluctant to apply the unitarian position to overrule *Humphrey's*. Perhaps this is because of something larger about executive power that the unitarians and their critics have overlooked.

Article II does not provide the kind of certainty that the unitarians or their critics presume. Even if they did, interpretations that profess to be nothing more than faithful interpretations of the text emerge inevitably within a certain political context. This does not mean that political context determines everything, but it may mean that forging an agreement over textual puzzles requires attention to politics, both past and present.

Conclusion

In summer 1789, before partisan differences were institutionalized in the form of political parties, an extraordinary debate and decision took place in Congress. Four interpretations of the removal power were aired. And even though the executive power interpretation prevailed, we argue that the question was not settled, as subsequent political actors and commentators contend. Rather, four positions were enunciated and gave shape to a debate that endures today. Three of those initial positions would continually resurface in American political life, offering presidents, members of Congress, and federal judges a bountiful resource to formulate their own constitutional logic, a logic defining the terms of institutional integrity, determining the conditions for the efficient operation of power, and articulating the ends of republican government itself.

Despite their power, these initial positions were modified, perhaps even transformed, during the course of American history. Presidents continued to promote executive power theory, but changes (the development of the party system, for example) altered the institutional consequences. Congress, in turn, responded with a more forceful and radical version of congressional delegation theory as the institutional stakes were raised. The rise of the Progressive movement and its chief institutional innovation—independent regulatory commissions—marked another pivotal moment when the terms of the debate were altered. The Supreme Court may have legitimized an administrative state at least partially insulated from executive authority, but neither Congress nor the president have fully embraced the terms of its settlement. Consequently, members of the unitarian school of executive power, officially born during the Reagan era, have made it their cause to legally question the rationale behind this institutional legacy of the Progressive era in order return the debate to the original bases of 1789. Others, worried that power concentrated in the hands of the executive may fail to check an overly politicized administration, have concluded that we need to pay less heed to form in our constitutional considerations and give more attention to rendering the functions of administrative government stable and immune to partisan zeal. As the 2010 *PCAOB* Supreme Court case illustrates, both sides still have far to go in finding a satisfactory way to balance the benefits of independence and stability versus accountability and responsiveness. Doing so within the parameters of our constitutional order remains elusive. Nowhere is this ongoing problem more acute and visible as in the continuing struggle over the removal power.

Let us look back, then, and survey the trail we have traveled. Seventeen eighty-nine set forth different visions of separation of powers and the place of the executive within the constitutional system. On one hand we can trace the vision of a powerful and independent executive—its powers vested by the Constitution itself, in control to a great degree over its own officers and accountable chiefly to the people. On the other we can make out a more clerical conception of the chief executive—indebted primarily to Congress and endowed with a very limited scope of discretionary power, less in charge of its own officers and strictly accountable for its administration of law to lawmakers.

The case for executive power theory would undergo some significant modifications early in the history of the republic. Thomas Jefferson argued that good administration must reflect the will of the nation—thus the executive branch was entitled to a share of offices commensurate with its electoral mandate. Jefferson used his removal power to attain a proportionate share of offices, turning out many Federalists from office while leaving others in place. Andrew Jackson took office after the party system had become legitimated. He, like Jefferson, linked executive control of removals to the idea that the president's administration must reflect the will of the nation. But the new context allowed Jackson to go further and argue for his principle of "rotation," that is, the president's link to the will of the people and the mechanism for his electoral mandate was his party. The Democratic Party, with Jackson as its leader in the White House, was thus entitled to have its will represented in the very workings of the new administration. Jackson and the Democrats had won; the people had spoken. Their voices should be heard not only from a distance but also from the levers of power embedded within the executive branch.

James Madison and his allies had argued that the president must be responsible to the people—that the people must be able to judge whether or not *they* approved of the manner in which the laws were being executed. Thus, Jefferson and Jackson seized on this *responsibility principle* and then went beyond it: Both argued that the people must be able to judge the conduct of the executive branch and in addition that popular will ought to be reflected within the current administration. Whereas Madison emphasized *accountability*, Jefferson and especially Jackson emphasized *representation*. This transformation of an idea would provoke counterarguments from varied quarters. Noah Webster argued that such "proportionality" would actually foreclose judging removals according to the most important criterion: *merit*. Opponents of the Jefferson-Jackson positions would also argue that it would attract precisely the wrong type of officeholders: crass seekers of power, partisan party hacks seeking their just desserts after a hard-fought electoral victory. Jackson, for his part, argued that rotation would ensure the right people a share of office — ordinary people, decent people, ready to do the simple business of government. Furthermore, such people would never get too comfortable in office. It was people who felt utterly secure and independent in their places who were a danger because they would become indifferent to the public good.

Such arguments for executive power theory — separated from a pure textual interpretation — were addressed by Congress during the 1820s and 1830s. One important position was this: If the will of the people was to be relied upon, and proportionality was important, should not Congress have had its will reflected in the administration? This argument drew upon the advise and consent partisans in 1789 who had argued that Congress was the true representative branch — the branch that most reflected the popular will. Others took a much different angle: Congress's role in removal might be required to check the argument from proportionality. Congressional actions might be justified to ensure that merit would play a meaningful role in appointments and removals. Thomas H. Benton's recommendation that the president must provide reasons for removals appealed to the need for stability and independence — a need perhaps made more acute during the Jacksonian era and the birth of the spoils system, or patronage.

Importantly, even while Jackson heightened Jefferson's extraconstitutional arguments for executive control he also did something Jefferson did not: He made forceful appeals to the same constitutional arguments as the executive power theorists in the First Congress. Jackson's principle of "rotation," coupled with orthodox executive power theory, provoked a strong response from the Whigs. Prominent Whigs made the crucial step of revisiting the Decision of 1789 — arguing that the wrong side had won. Daniel Webster looked back and discovered the soundness of the advise and consent position, and Joseph Story emphasized how Jackson's innovations made executive power theory dangerous. Story linked the removal question to the broader problem of the extent to which the president could control the discretion of his subordinates. He argued that Congress could in fact vest authority in executive officials outside the supervision of the president. Henry Clay made the case that an executive branch entirely responsible to the president was in fact a highly irresponsible government. An executive branch beholden only to the president would result in an administration driven by partial, partisan views likely to put aside the public good as temporary necessity might dictate. In time, Webster came to embrace Clay's argument, perhaps because bicameralism ensured that the House would be reluctant to wholly endorse advise and consent. More generally, Whigs made the case for the position that had been underdeveloped at the First Congress: *congressional delegation*. This seemed to give Congress the widest latitude to counteract Jackson's muscular and popularly grounded version of executive power theory.

The development of congressional delegation would achieve full flower with the passage of the Tenure of Office Act of 1867. President Andrew Johnson asserted executive power theory in the most tense and hostile political atmosphere imaginable. Though designed to counteract Johnson's interference in Reconstruction through removals and then bring about his political demise, Congress's appeal to congressional delegation theory would draw on precedent. The 1867 Tenure Act secured the ascendancy of Congress—particularly the Senate—in the area of appointments and removals, but the executives who came to office during Reconstruction quickly discovered its inconveniences. The Tenure Act was amended in 1869 and was continually challenged by presidents thereafter until full repeal in 1887. Grover Cleveland finally brought Congress to heel after his legendary battles with Senator Roscoe Conkling over removals. Cleveland forcefully made the case for executive power theory, echoing the First Congress and Andrew Jackson. He coupled a unitary vision of executive discretion with an office chiefly accountable to the people.

The United States Supreme Court weighed in on removal and revisited the Decision of 1789 in *Myers v. United States* (1926). Though we find Chief Justice William Taft's argument—that the First Congress did indeed endorse executive power theory—sounder than critics have been willing to admit, we also conclude that the dissent was correct to question the notion that the Decision of 1789 settled the matter in any decisive way. *Myers* is also remarkable for the extent to which it lays bare the constitutional logic of the two predominant positions on the removal question: executive power versus congressional delegation. The case reveals the distinct constitutional resources for each position and the different underlying visions of the place of executive power within the separation of powers scheme.

Justices including Taft, Brandeis, and McReynolds were all driven to ground their positions outside of the confines of the appointments clause and the removal as incident to appointment principle. Taft, like executive power theorists before and since, appealed to the vesting clause and the idea that removal is by nature executive. He also invoked the take care clause and, like presidents such as Jefferson, Jackson, and Cleveland, argued that the president was representative of the whole people, whose unique perspective required unified control of the executive branch. Brandeis and

McReynolds each grounded congressional delegation theory in the necessary and proper clause. Congress's power to create and structure the executive branch as it sees fit must include the power to craft the level of job security enjoyed by executive officers. Without that power, Congress could not direct the administration of federal law in a manner befitting its legislative warrant under Article I.

Myers also revealed the difficulty of assembling the textual puzzle of the removal power in a manner that allows each branch to compete in this domain. In that case, each textual argument was partially driven by broader assumptions about the separation of powers scheme. Thus, executive power theorists did not concede the relevance of the necessary and proper clause, yet the congressional delegation theorists did not concede the legitimacy of the vesting clause of Article II. Corwin's attempt to find a middle ground failed because he could not point to a constitutional foundation that would limit the extent of congressional intervention actions.

Nine years later the Court would again find itself in the middle of the removal power storm. In *Humphrey's Executor v. United States* the Court attempted to secure the place of independent regulatory commissions within its removal power jurisprudence. But by legitimizing a departure from executive power theory as elaborated in *Myers*, the Court seemed to push away the tripartite constitutional separation of powers scheme. According to *Humphrey's*, these new kinds of officers exercised powers that were not executive but partly legislative and partly judicial — thus their protection from at-pleasure removal by the president was both constitutionally and politically sound. By looking through the lens of the political thought of the Progressives as to IRCs, it would seem that the winners in *Humphrey's* were those who were intent upon dramatically altering the constitutional order by securing a place for administrative experts insulated from the political branches. But an examination of the legacy of the Sherman Anti-Trust Act and the statutory origins of the Federal Trade Commission reveals that Congress was not terribly interested in the Progressive vision. Rather, Congress wanted to pass the difficult policy decisions to another body while ensuring that its delegation did not result in the aggrandizement of the executive branch. Ultimately the IRCs, despite the theoretical underpinnings, do not represent a victory for stable, expert, nonpolitical administration but rather for a partial triumph of congressional delegation theory.

By the second half of the twentieth century executive power theory was on the rise, particularly in light of the expectations for popular national leadership under Franklin Roosevelt's reorganization of the executive office in 1939. Limitations on the removal power became an increasingly sensitive liability for presidential accountability as the federal government began to take on a wider array of regulatory issues and programmatic initiatives. This tension culminated in the events of the Nixon presidency, when the branches could no longer find a middle ground upon which they might resolve their disputes over administrative control. As Nixon's case for executive power theory pushed to extreme levels of paranoia, so too Congress's anxiety over presidential domination of the bureaucracy led to another forceful articulation of congressional delegation theory. Congressional power after Nixon would surge with the adoption of new and aggressive statutory controls on presidential administration (including the War Powers Act, the Congressional Budget and Impoundment Act, and the independent counsel provision of the Ethics in Government Act).

In the 1980s, executive power theory was preparing for a second comeback. Lawyers in the Justice Department were looking to restore the integrity of the executive office after the institution's lethargic performance by presidents between Nixon and Reagan. Members of the unitary executive school hoped to sustain their efforts over the long term by winning battles against Congress in the courts. But the Supreme Court was also divided between supporters of executive power theory and congressional delegation and, consequently, handed the Reagan administration a series of wins and losses that failed to settle the debate.

In fact, the scorecard at the Court suggested that the congressional delegation position had taken a lead. Byron White's frank assertion of the congressional delegation position in his dissent in *Bowsher* was eventually adopted by the Court in *Morrison*. The new standard, according to the Court's opinion, is that Congress may impose statutory limits upon the president's removal power even in cases where the officer is clearly executive as long as the legislature does not retain any role for itself. The independent counsel law pushed this point to an extreme by reserving to Congress the power to use a core executive power for its own purposes of checking the presidency. But the Court's decision in *Morrison* is not the end of the story. The investigation of and proceedings against President Bill Clinton during the 1990s under Independent Counsel Kenneth Starr not only thoroughly discredited the institution; it also led to a certain degree of respect for Scalia's lone dissent in *Morrison* — which was premised upon executive power theory. In his dissent, Scalia was the first modern Supreme Court justice to employ the term "unitary executive" in a judicial opinion, and yet again a dissenting opinion may be gaining steam in revolutionizing the Court's jurisprudence. More than a coincidence, Scalia's opinion drew on the argument central to Reagan's legal team. By the 1990s, the unitary executive school was no longer allied with a particular partisan view; rather, its conceptual vision of the presidency would also define many of the institutional reforms of the Clinton administration. And in the 2010 *PCAOB* case, a majority of the Court embraced a doctrine of the removal power held by a single justice in *Morrison*.

Whether the unitary executive school will continue to make its mark in the jurisprudence of the Court remains to be seen. As Breyer's dissent in *PCAOB* indicates, there are too many reservations about the wholesale adoption of this argument for unified accountability. In particular, giving the president the power to remove all executive officials would possibly undermine the expertise and stability required in government generally and in post–New Deal government in particular. Furthermore, the Court's equivocal decision suggests that there are too many political costs involved if one were to apply the logic of the argument consistently across the administration. Given how these arguments have worked in the past, it is likely that opponents of executive power theory will make the case for congressional delegation; still, we can also expect that their arguments will be informed by the case for advise and consent. Perhaps, in the end, all of this confirms the wisdom of James Madison's own judgment of the issue in *The Federalist*, when he answered *no* to the following question: "Will it be sufficient to mark, with precision, the boundaries of these departments, in the constitution of the government, and to trust to these parchment barriers against the encroaching spirit of power?"[1]

Notes

Introduction

1. 177 L. Ed. 2d 706 (2010). Subsequent citations will appear in the endnotes by author and page number.

2. Roberts, 724.

3. Ibid.

4. Ibid., 726.

5. Breyer, 737–738.

6. Ibid., 741.

7. Ibid., 743.

8. Roberts, 725, n. 4.

9. Ibid., 726.

10. Breyer, 737, emphasis added.

11. 295 U.S. 602 (1935).

12. 487 U.S. 654 (1988).

13. Oral argument, 21. The transcript can be found at http://www.supremecourt .gov/oral_arguments/argument_transcripts/08–861.pdf. Accessed August 1, 2012.

14. Ibid., 44.

15. *Youngstown Sheet and Tube v. Sawyer*, 343 U.S. 579 (1952).

16. Stephen Skowronek, *The Politics Presidents Make: Leadership from John Adams to George Bush* (Cambridge: Belknap Press at Harvard University Press, 1993). The "order shattering" metaphor is Skowronek's.

17. Here we rely primarily on the following: For the nonunitarian position, see A. Michael Froomkin, "In Defense of Agency Autonomy," *Yale Law Journal* 96, 4 (1987): 787–814; Froomkin, "The Imperial Presidency's New Vestments," *Northwestern University Law Review* 88 (1994): 1346–1376; and Lawrence Lessig and Cass Sunstein, "The President and the Administration," *Columbia Law Review* 94, 1 (1994): 2–123; For the unitarian position, see Steven Calebresi and Kevin Rhodes, "The Structural Constitution: Unitary Executive, Plural Judiciary," *Harvard Law Review* 106, 6 (April 1992): 1153–1216; Steven Calabresi and Saikrishna Prakash, "The President's Power to Execute the Laws," *Yale Law Journal* 104, 3 (1994): 541–665; and Saikrishna Prakash, "Hail to the Chief Administrator: The Framers and the President's Administrative Powers," *Yale Law Journal* 102, 4 (1993): 991–1017.

18. Calebresi and Rhodes, 1166. See also Gary Lawson, "The Rise and Rise of the Administrative State," *Harvard Law Review* 107, 6 (April 1994): 1244.

19. "The executive Power shall be vested in a President of the United States of America" (Art. II, sec. 1).

20. "He shall take Care that the Laws be faithfully executed" (Art. II, sec. 3); "He may require the Opinion, in writing, of the principal Officer in each of the executive Departments, upon any Subject relating to the Duties of their respective offices" (Art. II, sec. 2).

21. Lessig and Sunstein, 40.

22. Edward S. Corwin, *The President's Removal Power Under the Constitution* (New York: National Municipal League, 1927). Steven G. Calabresi and Christopher S. Yoo, *The Unitary Executive: Presidential Power from Washington to Bush* (New Haven: Yale University Press, 2008).

23. Two book chapters by political scientists are important introductions to the removal power. See Louis Fisher, *Constitutional Conflicts Between Congress and the President*, 4th ed., rev. (Lawrence: University Press of Kansas, 1997), 49–86. See also Richard Ellis, *The Development of the American Presidency* (New York: Routledge, 2012), 295–345.

Chapter 1. The Decision of 1789

1. Charles Thach Jr., *The Creation of the Presidency, 1775–1789: A Study in Constitutional History* (Indianapolis: Liberty Fund, 2007), 124.

2. Ibid., 125.

3. Charlene Bangs Bickford, Kenneth R. Bowling, Helen E. Veit, and William Di-Giacomantonio, eds., *Documentary History of the First Federal Congress*, Volume 16: *Correspondence* (Baltimore: Johns Hopkins University Press, 2004), 890 (hereafter *DHFFC—Correspondence*).

4. Gerhard Casper, "The American Constitutional Tradition of Shared and Separated Powers: An Essay in Separation of Powers: Some Early Versions and Practices," *William and Mary Law Review* 30 (Winter 1989): 233–234.

5. "Federalist No. 77," in *The Federalist*, ed. Jacob Cooke (Hanover, NH: Wesleyan University Press, 1961), 515.

6. Louis Fisher, *Constitutional Conflicts Between Congress and the President*, 5th ed. (Lawrence: University Press of Kansas, 2007), 48. See also David Currie, *The Constitution in Congress* (Chicago: University of Chicago Press, 1997), 36–41; and Saikrishna Prakash, "New Light on the Decision of 1789," *Cornell Law Review* 91 (July 2006): 1021–1077.

7. 272 U.S. 52.

8. Fisher Ames to George R. Minot, 8 July 1789, in *DHFFC—Correspondence*, 978.

9. William Smith (S.C.) to Edward Rutledge, 21 June 1789, in *DHFFC—Correspondence*, 832.

10. Charlene Bangs Bickford, Kenneth R. Bowling, and Helen E. Veit, eds., *Documentary History of the First Federal Congress*, Volume 10: *Debates in the House of Representatives, First Session: April–May 1789* (Baltimore: Johns Hopkins University Press, 1992), 722–723 (hereafter *DHFFC—Debates I*).

11. *DHFFC—Debates I,* 726.

12. "He . . . shall appoint Ambassadors, other public Ministers and Consuls, Judges of the supreme Court, and all other Officers of the United States, whose Appointments are not herein provided for, and which shall be established by law" (Art. II, sec. 2, cl. 2).

13. We adopt the nomenclature of Prakash in "New Light on the Decision of 1789." Most scholars agree that these are the four principle positions taken during the debate. Fisher identifies two more, "judicial review" and "procedural due process," which in our judgment are ancillary to the debate or corollaries to one of the four main schools. See his *Constitutional Conflicts between Congress and the President,* 5th ed., 49–50.

14. See Thach, 128; and Currie, 37.

15. Charlene Bangs Bickford, Kenneth R. Bowling, and Helen E. Veit, eds., *Documentary History of the First Federal Congress,* Volume 11: *Debates in the House of Representatives, First Session: June-September 1789* (Baltimore: Johns Hopkins University Press, 1992), 916 (hereafter *DHFFC—Debates II*).

16. *DHFFC—Debates II,* 928.

17. "He may require the Opinion, in writing, of the principal Officer in each of the executive Departments, upon any Subject relating to the Duties of their respective Offices" (Art. II, sec. 2, cl. 2).

18. "The Congress shall have power to make all Laws which shall be necessary and proper for carrying into Execution the foregoing Powers, and all other Powers vested by this Constitution in the Government of the United States, or in any Department or Officer thereof" (Art. I, sec. 8, cl. 19).

19. *DHFFC—Debates II,* 1028.

20. Thach, 138.

21. *DHFFC—Debates II,* 1027.

22. Ibid., 1030.

23. Linda Grant DePauw, Charlene Bangs Bickford, and LaVonne Siegel Hauptman, eds., *Documentary History of the First Federal Congress,* Volume 3: *House of Representatives Journal* (Baltimore: Johns Hopkins University Press, 1977), 92–95 (hereafter *DHFFC—Journal*).

24. *DHFFC—Debates II,* 1030.

25. Journal of the First Session of the Senate, Volume 1, 41; and Kenneth R. Bowling and Helen E. Veit, eds., *Documentary History of the First Federal Congress,* Volume 9: *The Diary of William Maclay and Other Notes on Senate Debates* (Baltimore: Johns Hopkins University Press, 1988), 109 (hereafter *Diary of William Maclay*).

26. Prakash, 1032.

27. *Diary of William Maclay,* 113.

28. Ibid., 110–111.

29. *The Works of John Adams* (Boston: Charles C. Little and James Brown, 1851), 3: 409, 411.

30. Thach, 141–142.

31. See Charlene Bangs Bickford and Helen E. Veit, eds., *Documentary History of the First Federal Congress,* Volume 4: *Legislative Histories* (Baltimore: Johns Hopkins University Press, 1986), 689 [HR-8, sec. 2]; and Charlene Bangs Bickford and Helen E.

Veit, eds., *Documentary History of the First Federal Congress*, Volume 6: *Legislative Histories* (Baltimore: Johns Hopkins University Press, 1986), 1976 [HR-9, sec. 7], 2028 [HR-7, sec. 2] (hereafter *DHFFC—Legislative Histories I* and *II*).

32. Prakash, 1033–1034.

33. Ibid., 1043.

34. They spoke ten times between them. Smith made speeches on May 19 and June 16, 17, 18, and 22; and Jackson on May 19 and June 17, 18, and 19.

35. Thach, 128–129.

36. Prakash, 1036.

37. *DHFFC—Debates II*, 861, 985.

38. Ibid., 877.

39. Ibid., 985.

40. Ibid., 936–937.

41. Ibid., 912.

42. Ibid., 969.

43. Ibid., 876, 936

44. Ibid., 969–970.

45. *DHFFC—Debates I*, 732; and *Debates II*, 934.

46. *DHFFC—Debates II*, 861.

47. Ibid., 1002.

48. "Perhaps gentleman are so much dazzled with the splendor of the virtues of the present president, as not to be able to see into futurity." Ibid., 862. See also Jackson, ibid., 1001.

49. Ibid., 863.

50. Ibid., 969.

51. See, for example, ibid., 986.

52. *DHFFC—Debates I*, 737. Bland made a motion on May 19 to add "by and with the advice and consent of the senate," which was defeated. See ibid., 738.

53. *DHFFC—Debates II*, 860.

54. Ibid., 1004.

55. Ibid., 928.

56. Ibid., 1022–1023.

57. See, for example, "Federalist No. 47," 323–331.

58. See, for example, "The Address and Reasons of the Dissent of the Minority of the Convention of Pennsylvania to Their Constituents," in Herbert Storing, ed., *The Anti-Federalist* (Chicago: University of Chicago Press, 1985), 217–218.

59. See the remarks of White, *DHFFC—Debates II*, 873.

60. Ibid., 931.

61. Ibid., 930.

62. Ibid., 929.

63. *DHFFC—Debates I*, 737.

64. See White at *DHFFC—Debates II*, 952. It is noteworthy that this is precisely the same argument that Madison would later make as Helvidius: Pacificus looked to British examples rather than to the Constitution to "borrow" his argument that the treaty power was executive in nature, because "the power of making treaties and the power of declaring war, are *royal prerogatives* in the *British government,* and are accordingly

treated as *executive prerogatives* by *British commentators*." See Alexander Hamilton and James Madison, *The Pacificus-Helvidius Debates of 1793–1794*, ed. Morton Frisch (Indianapolis: Liberty Fund, 2007), 63. It is also important to point out that this passage occurs right after Madison denies the applicability of the 1789 removal debate to the 1793 question about neutrality.

65. Ibid.

66. Ibid., 953.

67. Ibid.

68. Ibid., 954–955.

69. "Federalist No. 77," 515.

70. See Alexander Hamilton and James Madison, *The Pacificus-Helvidius Debates of 1793–1794*.

71. John Yoo, for example, argues that Hamilton obscured his views on the treaty power in *The Federalist* No. 69 in order to make the Constitution more palatable to moderates. John Yoo, *The Powers of War and Peace: The Constitution and Foreign Affairs After 9/11* (Chicago: University of Chicago Press, 2005), 121–125. For an account of Hamilton's change of heart, see Jack Rakove, *Original Meanings* (New York: Alfred A. Knopf, 1996), 287.

72. Seth Barret Tillman, "The Puzzle of Federalist No. 77," *Harvard Journal of Law and Public Policy* (2010): 149–167.

73. William Smith (S.C.) to Edward Rutledge, June 21, 1789, in *DHFFC—Correspondence*, 832.

74. "Federalist No. 70," 472.

75. Ibid.

76. "Federalist No. 71," 481.

77. "Federalist No. 72," 488.

78. Ibid., 487.

79. Ibid.

80. Ibid., 488.

81. "Federalist No. 77," 515.

82. Ibid., 515–516.

83. "Federalist No. 72," 488.

84. Harold Syrett, ed., *The Papers of Alexander Hamilton* (New York: Columbia University Press, 1962), 4: 164.

85. *DHFFC—Debates II*, 959.

86. Ibid., 906.

87. Ibid., 909.

88. Ibid., 908–909.

89. Ibid., 960–961.

90. Ibid., 909.

91. Ibid., 1029, emphasis added.

92. Madison to Edmund Pendleton, June 21, 1789, in Jack N. Rakove, ed., *James Madison: Writings* (New York: Modern Library, 1999), 465–466.

93. See in particular Sherman's speech on June 17, *DHFFC—Debates II*, 916–918.

94. *DHFFC—Debates II*, 917.

95. Ibid., 977–978.

96. For this position see, for example, Senator George Wharton Pepper at oral argument in *Myers v. United States*. Particularly revealing is the exchange with Justices Sanford and Stone: "The Power of the president to Remove Federal Officers," 69th Congress, 2nd sess., Senate document No. 174, 175.

97. See *DHFFC—Legislative Histories I*, 689 [HR-8, sec. 2]; and *DHFFC—Legislative Histories II*, 1976 [HR-9, sec. 7], 2028 [HR-7, sec. 2].

98. Gerhard Casper, "The American Constitutional Tradition of Shared and Separated Powers," 240.

99. *DHFFC—Debates II*, 1080.

100. Ibid.

101. Edward S. Corwin, *The President's Removal Power Under the Constitution* (New York: National Municipal League, 1927), viii. See also Lawrence Lessig and Cass R. Sunstein, "The President and the Administration," *Columbia Law Review* 94:1 (January 1994): 1–123.

102. *DHFFC—Debates II*, 867.

103. Ibid., 925.

104. See Ames, ibid., 880.

105. *DHFFC—Debates I*, 734.

106. Ibid., 922.

107. Ibid., 867. See also Benson on June 17, ibid., 932.

108. Ibid., 867.

109. *DHFFC—Debates II*, 880.

110. See above, page 30.

111. *DHFFC—Debates II*, 1004.

112. Ibid., 869.

113. See especially Madison on June 17, ibid., 923.

114. See Vining and Clymer on May 19, *DHFFC—Debates I*, 728, 738, Madison on June 16, *DHFFC—Debates II*, 868, and Ames on June 18, *DHFFC—Debates II*, 979.

115. Ibid., 868.

116. Currie, *The Constitution in Congress*, 40.

117. See Madison, *DHFFC—Debates II*, 922, and Ames, *DHFFC—Debates II*, 979. Prakash points out that this argument would not grant the president the authority to remove the many executive officers who do not execute the law. See his "Removal and Tenure in Office," *Virginia Law Review* 92, 8 (December 2006): 1837.

118. *DHFFC—Debates II*, 924.

119. Ibid., 938–939.

120. Ibid., 973

121. Ibid., 1017.

Chapter 2. From Responsibility to Rotation

1. Bruce Ackerman, *The Failure of the Founding Fathers: Jefferson, Marshall, and the Rise of Presidential Democracy* (Cambridge: Belknap Press at Harvard University Press, 2005).

2. Colleen A. Sheehan, *James Madison and the Spirit of Republican Self-Government* (New York: Cambridge University Press, 2009).

3. Sheehan and Lance Banning argue that Madison's defense of public opinion was consistent and even central to his prior writings. For a summary of the problem see Gordon S. Wood, "Is There a 'James Madison Problem'?" in *Revolutionary Characters: What Made the Founders Different* (New York: Penguin, 2006), 141–172.

4. Todd Estes, *The Jay Treaty Debate, Public Opinion, and the Evolution of Early American Political Culture* (Amherst: University of Massachusetts Press, 2006).

5. Jeremy D. Bailey, *Thomas Jefferson and Executive Power* (New York: Cambridge University Press, 2007).

6. Arthur Schlesinger Jr. offered the most well-known presentation of Jefferson and prerogative, but Lucius Wilmerding seems to have been the first. See Lucius Wilmerding Jr., "The President and the Law," *Political Science Quarterly* 67 (1952): 321–338; Arthur M. Schlesinger Jr., *The Imperial Presidency* (Boston: Houghton Mifflin, 1973); Gary J. Schmitt, "Jefferson and Executive Power: Revisionism and the 'Revolution of 1800,'" *Publius: Journal of Federalism* 17 (1987): 7–25; Oren Gross, "Chaos and Rules: Should Responses to Violent Crisis Always Be Constitutional?," *Yale Law Journal* (2003): 1011–1134; Clement Fatovic, "Constitutionalism and Presidential Prerogative," *American Journal of Political Science* 48 (2004): 434–435; and Jeremy D. Bailey, "Executive Prerogative and the 'good officer' in Jefferson's letter to John B. Colvin," *Presidential Studies Quarterly* 34 (2004): 732–754.

7. See David N. Mayer, *The Constitutional Thought of Thomas Jefferson* (Charlottesville: University Press of Virginia, 1994), 234.

8. Jefferson to Uriah Tracy, January 1806, *Works of Thomas Jefferson*, ed. Paul Leicester Ford, 10 vols. (New York: Putnam's, 1898) 8: 412–413.

9. Jefferson to J. Garland Jefferson, January 25, 1810, *Works of Thomas Jefferson*, 9: 270.

10. Thomas Jefferson, First Inaugural, *Thomas Jefferson: Writings*, ed. Merrill D. Peterson (New York: Library of America, 1984), 498–500.

11. Henry Adams, *History of the United States of American During the Administrations of Thomas Jefferson* (New York: Library of America, 1986), 141.

12. Jefferson to Elbridge Gerry, March 29, 1801, *Writings*, 1089. See also Jefferson to Samuel Adams, March 29, 1801, *Papers of Thomas Jefferson*, ed. Julian Boyd, et al., 36 vols. (Princeton: Princeton University Press, 1950–2005), 33: 487–488.

13. Jefferson to George Clinton, May 17, 1801, *Papers of Thomas Jefferson*, 34: 127.

14. Jefferson to Wilson Cary Nicholas, June 11, 1801, *Papers of Thomas Jefferson*, 34: 309.

15. Jefferson to Levi Lincoln, July 11, 1801, *Papers of Thomas Jefferson*, 34: 547.

16. Carl Russel Fish, "Removals of Officials by the Presidents of the United States," American Historical Association, Annual Report, 1899, Volume 1, 65–86. As cited in Leonard D. White, *The Jeffersonians: A Study in Administrative History, 1801–1829* (New York: Macmillan, 1951), 379. Around the same time, Paul Leicester Ford's collection of Jefferson's writings included a chart by Jefferson documenting the number of removals and appointments by Jefferson, but it is difficult to determine exactly what the table is recording. See *Works of Thomas Jefferson*, 8: 261.

17. Stephen Skowronek, *The Politics Presidents Make: Leadership from John Adams to George Bush* (Cambridge: Belknap Press at Harvard University Press, 1993), 72.

18. Steven G. Calabresi and Christopher S. Yoo, *The Unitary Executive: Presidential Power from Washington to Bush* (New Haven: Yale University Press, 2008), 69.

19. White, *Jeffersonians,* 379.

20. Jefferson to William Duane, July 24, 1803, *Works of Thomas Jefferson,* 8: 255–259.

21. Jefferson to William, May 19, 1807, *Works of Thomas Jefferson,* 9:51.

22. Carl E. Prince, "The Passing of the Aristocracy: Jefferson's Removal of the Federalists, 1801–1805," *Journal of American History* 57 (1970): 563–575.

23. Jefferson to Granger, March 29, 1801, *Papers of Thomas Jefferson,* 33: 493.

24. Thomas Jefferson to Elias Shipman and Others, July 12, 1801, *Writings,* 498–500.

25. Jefferson to William Duane, July 24, 1803, *Works of Thomas Jefferson,* 8: 255–259

26. Jefferson to John Page, 17 July 1807, *Works of Thomas Jefferson,* 9: 117–119.

27. Surprisingly, even though there has been much attention to Madison's defense of presidential removal powers in 1789, scholars have not paid much attention to Madison's post-1789 writings and actions regarding removals. Madison scholars have ignored the question. A good example is Calabresi and Yoo, whose chapter on Madison is less than five pages, with less than one page specifically on removals. In their view, Madison used the removal power to "direct his influence over the departments," even going as far as to remove three department heads. But they also point out that Madison was less "vigorous" than his predecessors in defending removal powers, probably because he succeeded his friend and fellow partisan, Jefferson. Calabresi and Yoo, *Unitary Executive,* 77–82. As we will see in Chapter 3, Madison remained a defender of presidential removal powers into the 1830s, but the scope of his argument changes.

28. Madison to Wilson Cary Nicholas, July 10, 1801, *Papers of James Madison: Secretary of State Series,* ed. Robert J. Brugger, et. al., 9 vols. (Charlottesville: University Press of Virginia, 1986–2011), 1: 393

29. Richard Hofstadter, *The Idea of a Party System: The Rise of Legitimate Opposition in the United States, 1780–1840* (Berkeley: University of California Press, 1969).

30. Noah Webster to James Madison, July 18, 1801, *PJM: Secretary of State,* 1: 436–441. Webster opened his letter demonstrating his credentials as a disinterested observer by pointing to the instances when he had disagreed with Hamilton.

31. Madison to Noah Webster, August 20, 1801 [recorded as not found] in *PJM: Secretary of State,* 2: 58.

32. Madison to Jefferson, 12 August 1801, *PJM: Secretary of State,* 2: 35.

33. Jefferson to Madison, 13 August 1801, *PJM: Secretary of State,* 2: 40–41

34. Noah Webster to Madison, November 30, 1801, *PJM: Secretary of State,* 2: 286–287. Madison's letter to Webster must have been significant, because Webster's reply gratefully acknowledges that Madison's time is precious. Also, Webster opened his letter demonstrating his credentials as a disinterested observer: There were instances when he had disagreed with Hamilton, and in a recent book he had cast himself as different than the leading men of the two parties.

35. Noah Webster, *Miscellaneous Papers, on Political and Commercial Subjects* (New York: 1802; New York: Burt Franklin, 1967). Page numbers are from the 1967 edition.

36. Ibid., 9.

37. Ibid., 18.

38. Ibid., 20, 29.

39. Ibid., 31–33.

40. Ibid., 50–52.

41. Seth Barrett Tillman, "The Puzzle of Hamilton's *Federalist* No. 77," *Harvard Journal of Law and Public Policy* 33 (2010): 166–167. For the traditional view, see the notes in Harold C. Sryett and Jacob E. Cooke, eds., *Papers of Alexander Hamilton*, 27 vols. (New York: Columbia University Press, 1961–1987), 4: 290.

42. Hamilton, "Pacificus" No. 1, ed. Morton J. Frisch, *The Pacificus-Helvidius Debates of 1793–1794: Toward Completion of the American Founding* (Indianapolis: Liberty Fund, 2007), 13.

43. Hamilton, "Letter from Alexander Hamilton, Concerning the Public Conduct and Character of John Adams, Esq. President of the United States," October 24, 1800, *Papers of Alexander Hamilton*, 25: 169, 214–215.

44. Ibid., 214, emphasis added. Notice that this passage undermines Seth Barrett Tillman's argument about Hamilton's use of *displace* in *Federalist* No. 77. It is clear that *displace* cannot mean *replace* here because the president may not replace without the consent of the Senate, precisely the inverse of Tillman's reading of *Federalist* No. 77. See Chapter 1: "The Decision of 1789."

45. This point is reinforced by consideration of the context: Adams did not appoint his own cabinet but instead retained Washington's cabinet; the men Adams fired were Hamilton's cronies and were from Adams's perspective undermining presidential authority.

46. This was itself a departure from another passage in *The Federalist*, where Hamilton had observed that the written opinions clause was a "mere redundancy" because it grew from the right of "the office." *Federalist*, No. 74, Cooke, 500.

47. *Papers of Alexander Hamilton*, 25: 216, 222, 226–227.

48. Lucius Junius Brutus [pseud.], *Examination of the President's Reply to the New-Haven Remonstrance with an Appendix Containing the President's Inaugural Speech, the Remonstrance and Reply; Together with a List of Removals from Office and New Appointments Made Since the Fourth of March, 1801* (New York: George F. Hopkins, 1801).

49. *Papers of Alexander Hamilton*, 25: 418–419.

50. Cooke, *Federalist*, 515.

51. Livy, *The Early History of Rome, Books I-IV,* trans. Aubrey de Séllincourt (New York: Penguin), 108. On Hamilton's pseudonyms, see Douglass Adair, "A Note on Certain of Hamilton's Pseudonyms," *William and Mary Quarterly,* 3rd Ser., 12 (1955): 282–297.

52. *Papers of Alexander Hamilton*, 25: 540.

53. Ibid., 25: 570.

54. Ibid.

55. Ibid., 25: 573.

56. Ibid.

57. Act of May 15, 1820. 3 Statutes at Large 582.

58. Carl Russel Fish, *The Civil Service and Patronage* (New York: Longmans, 1905), 66. White, *Jeffersonians,* 397–389. Annals of Congress, Senate, 16th Congress, 1st

sess. December 16, 1819, 25. John Quincy Adams, *Memoirs of John Quincy Adams*, Volume 8 (Philadelphia: J. B. Lippincott, 1876), 434–435.

59. Fish cites a letter that was privately owned. See Carl Russel Fish, "The Crime of W. H. Crawford," *American Historical Review* 21: 545–556.

60. Jefferson to Madison, November 29, 1820, in *The Republic of Letters: The Correspondence between Thomas Jefferson and James Madison 1776–1826*, ed. Richard Norton Smith, 3 vols. (New York: Norton, 1995), 3: 1825–1826.

61. Madison to James Monroe, December 28, 1820, in *Writings of James Madison*, ed. Gaillard Hunt, 9 vols. (New York: Putnam, 1900–1910), 9:43. See also Madison to Jefferson, January 7, 1821, Hunt, *Writings*, 9: 43.

62. Madison to James Monroe, December 28, 1820, in Hunt, ed., *Writings of James Madison*, 9: 44.

63. Madison to Monroe, September 24, 1822, in Hunt, ed., *Writings*, 9: 111–112. See also Madison's discussion of the definition of "officer" in Madison to Monroe, May 6, 1822, ibid., 9: 91–97.

64. White, *The Jeffersonians*, 387.

65. Peter Zavodnyik, *The Age of Strict Construction: A History of the Growth of Federal Power, 1789–1861* (Washington, DC: Catholic University of America Press, 2007), 123.

66. Skowronek, *Politics Presidents Make*, 124.

67. Mary W. M. Hargreaves, *The Presidency of John Quincy Adams* (Lawrence: University Press of Kansas, 1985), 50.

68. Skowronek, *Politics Presidents Make*, 125.

69. John C. Calhoun to Andrew Jackson, June 4, 1826, in *The Papers of John C. Calhoun, Volume X, 1825–1829*, ed. Clyde N. Wilson and W. Edwin Hemphill (Columbia: University of South Carolina Press, 1977), 227.

70. "Onslow," October 12, 1826, in *The Papers of John C. Calhoun, Volume X, 1825–1829*, Clyde N. Wilson and W. Edwin Hemphill eds. (Columbia, SC: University of South Carolina Press, 1977), 227.

71. Benton's Report, Senate Doc. 88, 19th Congress, 1st sess. (May 4, 1826).

72. "The tenor of Benton's Report bore more directly on elections than on presidential power." White, *Jeffersonians*, 393.

73. White, *Jeffersonians*, 391.

74. This exchange was published by Worthington C. Ford in *Proceedings of the Massachusetts Historical Society*, Third Series, 1 (1908): 361–393.

75. McLean would go on to write a dissenting opinion in *Dred Scott v. Sanford*, and Everett would be the featured speaker at Gettysburg in 1863.

76. Edward Everett to John McClean, August 1, 1828, "Use of Patronage," 361.

77. Ibid.

78. McLean to Everett, August 8, 1828, "Use of Patronage," 365.

79. Everett to McLean, August 18, 1828, "Use of Patronage," 372.

80. McLean to Everett, August 27, 1828, "Use of Patronage," 377.

81. Everett to McLean, August 18, 1828, "Use of Patronage," 372.

82. Ibid., 374.

83. McLean to Everett, August 8, 1828, "Use of Patronage," 367.

84. Everett to McLean, August 18, 1828, "Use of Patronage," 372.

85. McLean to Everett, August 8, 1828, "Use of Patronage," 366.

86. Ibid., 365.

87. Jackson, Protest Message, in James Daniel Richardson, *A Compilation of the Messages and Papers of the President, 1789–1908* (Washington, DC: Joint Committee on Printing, 1908), 2: 438.

88. Andrew Jackson, "Memorandum on Appointments," February 23, 1829, in Daniel Feller, et al., eds., *Papers of Andrew Jackson* (Knoxville: University of Tennessee Press, 2007), 7: 60–61.

89. Ibid.

90. As quoted in Leonard D. White, *The Jacksonians: A Study in Administrative History, 1829–1861* (New York: Macmillan), 307. Original language can be found in Charles Francis Adams, ed., *Memoirs of John Quincy Adams* (Philadelphia: J. B. Lippincott, 1876), 8: 149.

91. Jackson, First Annual, in Richardson, *Messages,* 448.

92. See Bailey, *Jefferson and Executive Power,* chap. 8.

93. Marc C. Landy and Sidney M. Milkis, *Presidential Greatness* (Lawrence: University Press of Kansas, 2000), 99–100.

94. Ibid.

95. Scott C. James, "Patronage Regimes and American Party Development from 'The Age of Jackson' to the Progressive Era," *British Journal of Political Science* 36 (2006): 39–60.

96. White, *Jacksonians,* 5.

97. Ibid., 101.

98. Ibid., 17.

99. Ibid., 301.

100. Ibid., 101, 17, and 301.

101. Ibid., 306–307.

Chapter 3. Jackson to Johnson

1. Leonard D. White, *The Jacksonians: A Study in Administrative History, 1829–1861* (New York: Macmillan, 1954), 41.

2. Ibid., 42.

3. See, for example, Richard Montgomery Young to Jackson, February 14, 1829; John Pope to Jackson, February 19, 1829; and George Hay to Jackson, April 16, 1829, in Daniel Feller, et al., eds., *Papers of Andrew Jackson* (Knoxville, TN: University of Tennesssee Press, 2007), 7: 37–38, 48–51, and 161–162.

4. Mary Chase Barney to Andrew Jackson, June 13, 1829, *Papers of Andrew Jackson,* 7: 281–286.

5. John Quincy Adams, *Memoirs of John Quincy Adams* (Philadelphia: J. B. Lippincott, 1876), 8: 149.

6. Ninian Edwards to Jackson, October 1829, *Papers of Andrew Jackson,* 7: 467–475.

7. Donald B. Cole, *Vindicating Andrew Jackson: The 1828 Election and the Rise of the Two-Party System* (Lawrence: University Press of Kansas, 2009), 146–147.

8. Thomas Ritchie to Martin Van Buren, March 27, 1829, *Papers of Andrew Jackson,* 7: 129–132.

9. Ibid.

10. Ibid.

11. Jackson to Van Buren, March 31, 1829, *Papers of Andrew Jackson,* 7: 132–133. Martin Van Buren, *The Autobiography of Martin Van Buren,* ed. John C. Fitzpatrick (Washington, DC: Government Printing Office, 1920; rpt. New York: Augustus M. Kelley, 1969).

12. Robert V. Remini, *Henry Clay: Statesman for Union* (New York: Norton, 1991).

13. Henry Clay, "Fowler's Garden Speech," May 16, 1829, in Robert Seager II, ed., *Papers of Henry Clay* (Lexington, KY: University Press of Kentucky, 1984), 8: 44.

14. Ibid., 45.

15. Ibid.

16. Ibid., 49–50.

17. Ibid., 47.

18. Michael F. Holt, *The Rise and Fall of the American Whig Party: Jacksonian Politics and the Onset of the Civil War* (New York: Oxford University Press, 1999), 21–23.

19. Charles M. Wiltse, ed., *Papers of Daniel Webster: Correspondence* (Hanover, NH: University Press of New England for Dartmouth College, 1877), 3: 8–9.

20. Hopkinson prosecuted the Alien and Sedition Acts and was on Justice Samuel Chase's defense team in Chase's impeachment proceedings in the Senate. He also argued several notable cases before the Supreme Court.

21. Kent went on to say, however, that he thought it would be very difficult and perhaps imprudent to overturn the precedent. James Kent to Webster, January 21, 1830, in *Papers of Daniel Webster: Correspondence,* 3: 11–13.

22. Joseph Story, *Commentaries on the Constitution of the United States* (Boston: Hilliard, Gray, and Co., 1833), 3: 390.

23. Ibid., 391.

24. Supporters of this position argued from the vesting and take care clauses, that is, that the removal power "was clearly in its nature a part of the executive power, and was indispensable for a due execution of the laws."

25. Story, *Commentaries,* 395.

26. *Myers v. United States* 272 U.S. 52, 205.

27. Story, *Commentaries,* 396.

28. Webster to Warren Dutton, May 9, 1830, in *Papers of Daniel Webster: Correspondence,* 3: 69.

29. White, *Jacksonians,* 107.

30. Holt, *American Whig Party,* 28.

31. Modern textbooks frequently repeat the claims of the Whigs. See, for example, Sidney M. Milkis and Michael Nelson, *The American Presidency: Origins and Development, 1776–2002.* (Washington, DC: Congressional Quarterly, 2003), 123. For the revisionist—and more accurate—view, see Nolan McCarty, "Presidential Vetoes in the Early Republic: Changing Constitutional Norms or Electoral Reform?" *Journal of Politics* 71 (2009): 369–384.

32. Marc Landy and Sidney M. Milkis, *Presidential Greatness* (Lawrence: University Press of Kansas, 2000), 108.

33. Andrew Jackson, Veto Message Regarding the Bank of the United States, July 10, 1832, in James Daniel Richardson, *A Compilation of the Messages and Papers of the Presidents* (Washington, DC: Joint Committee on Printing, 1908), 2: 581–582.

34. Ibid.

35. Ibid.

36. See, for example, Calabresi and Yoo, *Unitary Executive*, 417–418.

37. Bailey, *Jefferson and Executive Power*, 225–230.

38. Abraham Lincoln, "Speech at Springfield," July 17, 1858, "First Inaugural," March 4, 1861, in Roy P. Basler, ed., *Abraham Lincoln: His Speeches and Writings* (Cleveland: World Pub, 1946), 418, 585–586.

39. The statements from Clay and Webster are quoted in Robert V. Remini, *Andrew Jackson and the Bank War: A Study in the Growth of Presidential Power* (New York: Norton, 1967), 84–85. It should be pointed out that the Whigs were correct. The veto is rarely overridden and has become an important negotiating tool for the president.

40. *Register of Debates*, Senate, 23rd Congress, 1st sess., 44.

41. Ibid., 51.

42. Ibid.

43. Story to Webster, December 25, 1833, *Papers of Daniel Webster: Correspondence*, 3: 292–295.

44. Andrew Jackson, "Message Read to the Cabinet on Removal of the Public Deposits," September 18, 1833, in James Daniel Richardson, *A Compilation of the Messages and Papers of the Presidents* (Washington, DC: Joint Committee on Printing, 1908), 3: 7.

45. *Register of Debates*, Senate, 23rd Congress, 1st sess., 84–85. Originally found in Remini, *Jackson and the Bank War*, 138.

46. *Register of Debates*, Senate, 23rd Congress, 1st sess., 386–387. Originally found in Remini, *Jackson and the Bank War*, 141.

47. Ibid.

48. *Register of Debates*, Senate, 23rd Congress, 1st sess., 834–835.

49. Interestingly, Clay explained that the first three resolutions all arose because of the wrong decision in 1789. Clay did not explain the reason for the fourth, but he must have meant that it arose out of patronage.

50. *Register of Debates*, Senate, 23rd Congress, 1st sess., 834–835.

51. Ibid., 893.

52. Ibid., 1187.

53. Holt, *American Whig Party*, 26.

54. Cole, *Presidency of Andrew Jackson*, 208. This Benjamin Butler should not be confused with the Reconstruction-era Republican representative from Massachusetts.

55. Richardson, *Messages*, 90.

56. Webster, "The President's Protest," May 7, 1834, in *The Papers of Daniel Webster: Speeches and Formal Writings*, Volume 2: *1834–1852*, ed. Charles M. Wiltse (Hanover: University Press of New England, 1988), 58–59.

57. Ibid., 65–67.

58. *Register of Debates,* Senate, 23rd Congress, 2nd sess., 361.

59. Ibid., 418.

60. Ibid., 513.

61. Ibid., 514–515.

62. Ibid., 514.

63. Ibid., 517.

64. Ibid., 514.

65. Ibid., 516.

66. Ibid., 518.

67. Ibid., 518–521.

68. Ibid., 478–481.

69. Ibid., 485–488.

70. Ibid., 488.

71. Ibid., 457–460.

72. Ibid., 463.

73. Ibid., 466.

74. Ibid., 469.

75. Charles Francis Adams, *An Appeal from the New to the Old Whigs in Consequence of the Senate's Course and Particularly of Mr. Webster's Speech upon the Executive Patronage Bill* (Boston: Russell, Odiorne, and Company, 1835). The quotation is on page 27.

76. Drew R. McCoy, *The Last of the Fathers: James Madison and the Republican Legacy* (New York: Cambridge University Press, 1991).

77. Madison to Edward Coles, August 29, 1834, in Gaillard Hunt, ed., *The Writings of James Madison,* Volume 9: *1819–1836* (New York: Putnam's, 1910), 536–542.

78. Madison to John Patton, March 24, 1834, *Writings of James Madison,* 9: 534–536.

79. Madison to Charles Francis Adams, October 12, 1835, *Writings of James Madison,* 9: 559–566.

80. Madison to John Patton, March 24, 1834, *Writings of James Madison,* 9: 534–536.

81. Chapter 154, Statutes at Large, 39th Congress, 2nd sess., as reproduced in David O. Stewart, *Impeached: The Trial of President Andrew Johnson and the Fight for Lincoln's Legacy* (New York: Simon & Schuster, 2009), 329.

82. Stewart, *Impeached,* 103–105.

83. Jeffrey K. Tulis, "Impeachment in the Constitutional Order," in Joseph M. Bessette and Jeffrey K. Tulis, eds., *The Constitutional Presidency* (Baltimore: Johns Hopkins University Press, 2009), 229–246. See also Nicole Mellow and Jeffrey Tulis, "Andrew Johnson and the Politics of Failure," in Matthew Glassman and Stephen Skowronek, eds., *Formative Acts: American Politics in the Making* (Philadelphia: University of Pennsylvania Press, 2008), 153–170.

84. Johnson, "Special Message," February 22, 1868, in James Daniel Richardson, *A Compilation of the Messages and Papers of the President, 1789–1908* (Washington, DC: Joint Committee on Printing, 1908), 6: 627.

85. Stewart, *Impeached,* 142.

86. Michael Les Benedict, *The Impeachment and Trial of Andrew Johnson* (New York: Norton, 1973), 48–49.

87. Benedict, *Impeachment and Trial*, 130.

88. Ibid.

89. Stewart, *Impeached*, 117.

90. Keith E. Whittington, *Constitutional Construction: Divided Powers and Constitutional Meaning* (Cambridge: Harvard University Press, 1999), 124.

91. Ibid., 122.

92. Ibid., 126.

93. *Congressional Globe*, 40th Congress, 2nd sess., Supplement, *Trial of Andrew Johnson*, 32.

94. Ibid., 34.

95. Benedict, *Impeachment and Trial*, 52.

96. Ibid., 47, 107–108.

97. Andrew Johnson, "Third Annual Message," December 3, 1867, in Richardson, 570.

98. Andrew Johnson, "Fourth Annual Message," December 9, 1868, Richardson, 673.

99. Ibid., 672.

100. Andrew Johnson, "Third Annual Message," December 3, 1867, Richardson, 570.

101. Ibid.

102. Van Buren, *Autobiography*, 742.

Chapter 4. The Revenge of Executive Power

1. James D. Richardson, ed., *Messages and Papers of the Presidents* (Washington, DC: Bureau of National Literature and Art, 1904), 7: 38.

2. Jean Edward Smith, *Grant* (New York: Simon and Schuster, 2001), 479.

3. Quoted in William Goldsmith, *The Growth of Presidential Power: A Documented History*, Volume 2: *Decline and Resurgence* (New York: Chelsea House Publishers, 1974), 1101.

4. Ibid., 1102. Though there are no firsthand accounts of this meeting, characterizations like that found in the diary of Gideon Welles suggest Grant was bullied. Like Goldsmith, Sidney Milkis and Michael Nelson speculate that "Grant was so popular and respected at the time of his election that if he had asserted himself in favor of repeal, he probably would have prevailed." See Sidney Milkis and Michael Nelson, *The American Presidency: Origins and Development, 1776–2002*, 4th ed. (Washington, DC: Congressional Quarterly Press, 2003), 175.

5. Goldsmith, 1102–1103.

6. Compare 14 Stat. 430, Ch. 154 (March 2, 1867), with 16 Stat. 6, Ch. 10 (April 5, 1869).

7. Wilfred E. Binkley, *The President and Congress* (New York: Alfred A. Knopf, 1947), 151.

8. Ibid.

9. Milkis and Nelson, 179.

10. Quoted in Leonard D. White, *The Republican Era, 1869–1901: A Study in Administrative History* (New York: Macmillan Company, 1958), 33.

11. Goldsmith, 1105.

12. Binkley, 155.

13. Ibid., 157.

14. Goldsmith, 1107–1108.

15. *Messages and Papers of the Presidents*, 9: 4464.

16. Goldsmith, 1111.

17. Quoted in Binkley, 158.

18. Theodore C. Smith, *Life and Letters of James A. Garfield* (New Haven: Yale University Press, 1925), 2: 1109.

19. Quoted in Binkley, 160.

20. Grover Cleveland, *Presidential Problems* (New York: Century Co., 1904), 45–46.

21. Steven G. Calabresi and Christopher S. Yoo, *The Unitary Executive: Presidential Power from Washington to Bush* (New Haven: Yale University Press, 2008), 213.

22. Cleveland, *Presidential Problems*, 26.

23. Ibid., 42.

24. Goldsmith, 1114–1115.

25. Cleveland, 45–46.

26. *Messages and Papers of the Presidents*, 8: 380.

27. Ibid., 8: 381.

28. Ibid., 8: 382.

29. Ibid., 8: 377.

30. Cleveland, 76.

31. Edward S. Corwin, *The President's Removal Power Under the Constitution* (New York: National Municipal League, 1927), v.

32. *Myers v. United States*, 272 U.S. 52 (1926), 114. Subsequent references to this decision will be to page numbers.

33. Opinion of George F. Edmunds, *Supplement to* The Congressional Globe*: The Proceedings of the Senate Sitting for the Trial of Andrew Johnson, President of the United States*, 40th Congress, 2nd sess. (Washington City: F. & J. Rives and George Bailey, 1868), 425.

34. *Myers*, 194.

35. Corwin, 13–14.

36. *Myers*, 285, n. 75.

37. Saikrishna Prakash, "New Light on the Decision of 1789," *Cornell Law Review* 91 (July 2006): 1043.

38. Charlene Bangs Bickford, Kenneth R. Bowling, and Helen E. Veit, eds., *Documentary History of the First Federal Congress*, Volume 11: *Debates in the House of Representatives, First Session: June–September 1789* (Baltimore: Johns Hopkins University Press, 1992), 1028, 1034 (hereafter *DHFFC—Debates II*).

39. Prakash, "New Light on the Decision of 1789," 1048.

40. *DHFFC—Debates II*, 1029.

41. Prakash, 1049.

42. See Chapter 1.

43. Corwin, 23.

44. *Parsons v. United States*, 167 U.S. 324 (1897), 330.

45. See the quotations in *Myers,* at 149–152.

46. Quoted in *Myers,* 151.

47. *Myers,* 211.

48. Ibid., 146. Like Taft, Saikrishna Prakash reads these early statutes as affirming the Decision of 1789. See his "Removal and Tenure in Office," *Virginia Law Review* 92, 8 (December 2006): 1827.

49. *Parsons v. United States,* as quoted in *Myers,* 147.

50. Peter Zavodnyik, *The Age of Strict Construction: A History of the Growth of Federal Power, 1789–1861* (Washington, DC: Catholic University of America Press, 2007), 123.

51. These acts included language like "shall be forthwith removed from office." See *Myers,* 251–252.

52. Cited in *Myers,* 253.

53. *Myers,* 254.

54. "Power of the president to Remove Federal Offices," Senate Document No. 174, 69th Congress, 2nd sess. (Washington, DC: Government Printing Office, 1926), Will R. King, Brief for the Appellant, p. 50. This document contains all the briefs, a transcript of the oral argument, and all the opinions in the *Myers* case. Subsequent references to the briefs and oral arguments will be to this document by page numbers.

55. Senate Document No. 279, 66th Congress, 2nd sess., Conference Report on H.R. 9783, p. 5.

56. Supplement to Pepper Brief, 145–149.

57. Beck Brief, 70.

58. Oral Argument, 204.

59. Ibid., 204–205.

60. Ibid., 205.

61. See *Myers,* 115–118, Beck Brief, 76, and Oral Argument, 194.

62. See *Myers,* 117, Beck Brief, 76, and Oral Argument, 194–195.

63. Oral Argument, 193.

64. Ibid., 194.

65. Beck Brief, 76–80.

66. *Myers,* 119.

67. Corwin, *The President's Removal Power Under the Constitution,* 22.

68. *Myers,* 122.

69. This argument was made by the opponents of advise and consent theory at the First Congress. See Chapter 1.

70. See Vining's remarks at the First Congress, as quoted in Chapter 1.

71. *DHFFC—Debates II,* 1003–1004.

72. Prakash, "Removal and Tenure in Office," 1834–1835.

73. Quoted in *United States v. Perkins,* 116 U.S. 483 (1886), 484.

74. *United States v. Perkins,* 116 U.S. 483 (1886), 484–485.

75. *Myers,* 126–127.

76. Ibid., 161.

77. *Myers,* 162.
78. Oral Argument, 194.
79. Pepper Brief, 119, emphasis added.
80. Oral Argument, 173.
81. Ibid., 175.
82. *Myers,* 180–181.
83. See Chapter 3.
84. Corwin, 45.
85. Ibid., 63.
86. *Myers,* 245.
87. Ibid.
88. Oral Argument, 177.
89. Ibid.
90. *Myers,* 291.
91. Ibid., 294–295.
92. Ibid., 123.
93. See *Kendall v. United States* 37 U.S. 524 (1838).
94. *Myers,* 135.
95. Ibid., viii.
96. Ibid.
97. Ibid.
98. King Brief, 51–60.

Chapter 5. The Progressive Era and Independent Regulatory Commissions

1. Stephen Skowronek, *Building a New American State: The Expansion of Administrative National Capacities, 1870–1920* (Cambridge: Cambridge University Press, 1982), 283, 286–287.
2. Daniel P. Carpenter, *The Forging of Bureaucratic Autonomy: Reputations, Networks, and Policy Innovation in Executive Agencies, 1862–1928* (Princeton: Princeton University Press, 2001).
3. *Humphrey's Executor v. United States,* 295 U.S. 602 (1935). All subsequent references to this case will be to page numbers.
4. Charles Edward Merriam, *A History of American Political Theories* (New York: Macmillan, 1903), 327–329. Woodrow Wilson, *The State: Elements of Historical and Practical Politics* (Boston: D. C. Heath & Co., 1918), 587–612. Also see Herbert D. Croly, *The Promise of American Life* (New York: Macmillan Company, 1911), 24–25.
5. Woodrow Wilson, "The Study of Administration," in *The Papers of Woodrow Wilson,* ed. Arthur S. Link (hereafter *PWW*) (Princeton: Princeton University Press, 1966–1993)5: 378. Emphasis in original.
6. Ibid.
7. Herbert D. Croly and Michael McGerr, *The Promise of American Life* (Boston: Northeastern University Press, 1989), 213–214. David K. Nichols, "The Promise of Progressivism: Herbert Croly and the Progressive Rejection of Individual Rights," *Publius* 1987 17(2): 27-39.

8. *"Federalist* Nos. 70–72," in *The Federalist,* ed. Jacob Cooke (Middletown, CT: Wesleyan University Press, 1982), 471–492.

9. See Jeremy D. Bailey, "The New Unitary Executive and Democratic Theory: The Problem of Alexander Hamilton," *American Political Science Review* 102, 4 (2008): 453–465.

10. *"Federalist* No. 68," 456–462.

11. "A Marriage Made in Philadelphia: Popular Leadership and the Constitutional Presidency," in *Speaking to the People,* Richard Ellis, ed. (Amherst: University of Massachusetts Press, 1998), 16–35.

12. See Theodore Roosevelt, "The Presidency: Making an Old Party Progressive," in *An Autobiography* (New York: Macmillan, 1913), 379–399.

13. Gerard C. Henderson, *The Federal Trade Commission* (New Haven: Yale University Press, 1924), ch. 2; and Robert L. Rabin, "Federal Regulation in Historical Perspective," *Stanford Law Review* 38, 5 (1986): 1189–1326.

14. Geoffrey P. Miller, "Introduction: The Debate over Independent Agencies in Light of Empirical Evidence," *Duke Law Journal* 37, 2/3 (1988): 215–222. Also see John F. Duffy, "The Death of the Independent Regulatory Commission (and the Birth of a New Independence?)" (June 9, 2006) (unpublished manuscript), at http://www.law.georgetown.eduffacultyldocuments/daffy.paper.pdf. Accessed on August 1, 2012.

15. Wilson, *The New Freedom* (New York: Doubleday, Page and Company, 1913), 47. See also Frank J. Goodnow, *Social Reform and the Constitution* (New York: Macmillan, 1911), ch. 1.

16. *The Sherman Anti-Trust Act,* 15 U.S.C. 1 et seq.

17. Arthur A. Ekirch, *Progressivism in America: A Study of the Era from Theodore Roosevelt to Woodrow Wilson* (New York: New Viewpoints, 1974), 158–159.

18. Croly, *Promise,* 274.

19. Marc Winerman, "Origins of the FTC: Concentration, Cooperation, Control, and Competition," *Antitrust Law Journal* 71 (2003–2004), 64, at http://www.ftc.gov/ftc/history/docs/origins.pdf. Accessed on August 1, 2012. See also M. E. McClure, *Earnest Endeavors: The Life and Public Work of George Rublee* (Westport, CT: Greenwood Publishing Group, 2003), 78–81.

20. "Herbert Croly to Learned Hand," December 19, 1911. Quoted in David Levy, *Herbert Croly of the New Republic* (Princeton: Princeton University Press, 1985), 157.

21. *Federal Trade Commission Act,* Pub. L. No. 63–203, 38 Stat. 717 (1914) (codified as amended at 15 USC 41–77 [1994]).

22. Jaenicke, "Croly and the FTC," 481.

23. Martin J. Sklar, *The Corporate Reconstruction of American Capitalism, 1890–1916: The Market, The Law, and Politics* (Cambridge: Cambridge University Press, 1988), 182.

24. *The Sherman Anti-Trust Act,* Pub. L. No. 51–647, 26 Stat. 209 (1890) (codified at 15 USC 1–7 [1970]).

25. Gabriel Kolko, *The Triumph of Conservatism: A Re-Interpretation of American History, 1900–1916* (New York: Simon and Schuster, 1963), chs. 4–5.

26. Naomi R. Lamoreaux, *The Great Merger Movement in American Business, 1895–1904* (Cambridge: Cambridge University Press, 1988), ch. 2.

27. *United States* v. *Trans-Missouri Freight Association*, 166 U.S. 290 (1897).

28. Sklar, *Corporate Reconstruction*, 182.

29. Ibid., 336–338. See also Robert Harrison, *Congress, Progressive Reform, and the New American State* (Cambridge: Cambridge University Press, 2004), 57; and William Henry Harbaugh, *The Life and Times of Theodore Roosevelt* (New York: Oxford University Press, 1975), 295–301.

30. Arthur M. Johnson, "Theodore Roosevelt and the Bureau of Corporations," *Mississippi Valley Historical Review* 45, 4 (March 1, 1959): 576.

31. Roosevelt to John Carter Rose, March 30, 1908, in *The Letters of Theodore Roosevelt*, vol. 6, Elting E. Morison et al., eds. (Cambridge: Cambridge University Press, 1952–54), 983–984.

32. Theodore Roosevelt, *An Autobiography*, 139–140.

33. Ibid., 144–146.

34. Ibid., 395.

35. "Resolution in Opposition to the Hepburn Amendments to the Sherman Anti-Trust Act," quoted in Sklar, *Corporate Reconstruction*, 271.

36. John Milton Cooper Jr., *The Warrior and the Priest: Woodrow Wilson and Theodore Roosevelt* (Boston: Harvard University Press, 1985), 109–111.

37. L. Peter Schultz, "William Howard Taft: A Constitutionalist's View of the Presidency," *Presidential Studies Quarterly* 9, 4 (October 1979): 402–414. See also Rene N. Ballard, "The Administrative Theory of William Howard Taft," *Western Political Quarterly* 7, 1 (March 1954): 65–74.

38. See William H. Taft, *Our Chief Magistrate and His Powers* (New York: Columbia University Press, 1916), ch. 6.

39. See Stephen Skowronek, *The Politics Presidents Make: Leadership from John Adams to Bill Clinton*, rev. ed. (Boston: Harvard University Press, 1997), 256. See also George Edwin Mowry, *The Progressive Era, 1900–1920: The Reform Persuasion* (Washington, DC: American Historical Association, 1958), 247–249.

40. See Wilson's criticism of Taft's prosecutions under the Sherman Anti-Trust Act that left businesses "guessing" about the standards of competition. Wilson, "The Government and Business," March 14, 1908, 18 *PWW*, at 35, 38–39, 42–43, 50.

41. Wilson, "Law or Personal Power," cited in W. Eliot Brownlee, "Wilson's Reform of Economic Structure," in *Reconsidering Woodrow Wilson: Progressivism, Internationalism, War, and Peace*, ed. John Milton Cooper Jr. (Baltimore: Johns Hopkins University Press, 2008), 57–93.

42. Winerman, *Origins of the FTC*, 13–14

43. Ibid., 48.

44. President Woodrow Wilson, "Address to a joint Session of Congress on Trusts and Monopolies" (January 20, 1914), available at http://www.presidency.ucsb.edu/ws/print.php?pid=65374. Accessed August 1, 2012.

45. Ibid.

46. Woodrow Wilson, *The New Freedom: A Call for the Emancipation of the Generous Energies of a People* (New York: Doubleday, Page, 1913), 60.

47. "Address in Minneapolis" (September 18, 1912), in *PWW*, 25: 175. Also see Wilson, "Campaign Address in Detroit," (September 19, 1912), in *PWW* 25: 187–188; and

"Campaign Speech on New Issues in Hartford, Connecticut" (September 25, 1912), in *PWW* 25: 24.

48. *H.R. Document No. 533*, Pt. 1 (April 14, 1914), at 3. An investigation could be triggered, though, at "the direction of the president, the Attorney General, or either House of Congress." *H.R. Document No.15613*, 63rd Cong., 2nd Sess, sec. 10.

49. 51 Cong. Rec. 14,522 (1914). Senator Reed suggested that the state attorneys-general conduct private tort suits for enforcement if the U.S. Attorney General failed to do so.

50. 51 Cong. Rec. 8857 (1914) (remarks of Representative Morgan [R, Oklahoma] upon creation of the Federal Trade Commission).

51. House of Representatives Document No. 15613, 63rd Cong., 2nd Sess., sec. 10.

52. McClure, *Earnest Endeavors*, 90–91.

53. George Rublee, "Memorandum Concerning Section 5 of the Bill to Create a Federal Trade Commission," quoted in Rublee's "Memorandum," in *PWW*, 30: 274.

54. *Federal Trade Commission Act*, 15 U.S.C. 45. The term "unfair method of competition" was kept deliberately vague. While in Rublee's mind the vagueness of Section 5 was its virtue given that he believed that unfair methods of competition could not be defined in law, the Senate was able to quickly marshal the bill through with Section 5 because it avoided raising the highly contentious question among members of Congress regarding what constitutes fair competition.

55. Scott C. James, *Presidents, Parties, and the State: A Party System Perspective on Democratic Regulatory Choice, 1884–1936* (Cambridge: Cambridge University Press, 2000), 179–180. Also see Arnold, *Remaking the Presidency*, 87.

56. 51 *Congressional Record* 11083, 11235, and 12623 (1914).

57. 51 *Congressional Record* 11529 (1914).

58. Jack M. Beermann, "Congressional Administration," *San Diego Law Review* 43 (2006): 103.

59. *Bowsher v. Synar*, 478 U.S. 714 (1986).

60. R. E. Cushman, *The Independent Regulatory Commissions* (New York: Oxford University Press, 1941), 450 (referring to act of June 17, 1930, 46 Stat. at L. 590, 696).

61. Miroslava Scholten, "'Independent, Hence Unaccountable'?" *Review of European Administrative Law* 4, 1 (2011): 17, 21.

62. 51 *Congressional Record* 4239 (1914) (Senator Newlands speaking on difference between this trade commission and the Progressive platform's proposal for a trade commission).

63. 51 *Congressional Record* 12623 (1914).

64. E. W. Kintner, *The Legislative History of the Federal Antitrust Laws and Related Statutes* (New York: Chelsea House, 1978), 4083.

65. McClure, *Earnest Endeavors*, 125. See also George Rublee, "The Original Plan and Early History of the Federal Trade Commission," *Proceedings of the Academy of Political Science* 11 666 (January 1926): 114–120.

66. Marc Winerman and William E. Kovacic, "The William Humphrey and Abram Myers Years: The FTC from 1925–1929," *Antitrust Law Journal* 77 (2011): 701–747.

67. Charlene Bangs Bickford, Kenneth R. Bowling, and Helen E. Veit, eds., *Documentary History of the First Federal Congress*, Volume II: *Debates in the House of Representatives, First Session: June–September 1789* (Baltimore: Johns Hopkins University Press, 1992), 1022–1023 (hereafter *DHFFC—Debates II*).

68. *DHFFC—Debates II*, 923.

69. William E. Leuchtenburg, "The Case of the Contentious Commissioner: *Humphrey's Executor v. US*," in *Freedom and Reform: Essays in Honor of Henry Steele Commager*, Harold M. Hyman and Leonard W. Levy, eds. (New York: Harper & Row, 1967), 280.

70. *Securities Act of 1933*, Pub. L. No. 73–22, 48 Stat. 74 (1933).

71. *Securities Exchange Act of 1934*, Pub. L. No. 73–291, 48 Stat. 881 (1934).

72. Franklin D. Roosevelt, "Message to Congress on Unemployment Relief," March 21, 1933. Available online by Gerhard Peters and John T. Woolley, *The American Presidency Project*, at http://www.presidency.ucsb.edu/ws/?pid=14596. Accessed on August 1, 2012.

73. Ibid., 339.

74. Leuchtenburg, "Contentious Commissioner," 280.

75. Ibid.

76. *Humphrey's Executor v. United States*, 295 U.S. 495 (1935). All subsequent references to this case will be in-text citations.

77. *Myers v. United States*, 272 U.S. 135 (1926).

78. *Humphrey's Executor*, 628.

79. Ibid., 629–630.

80. Ibid., 603, emphasis added.

81. Hadley Arkes, *The Return of George Sutherland: Restoring a Jurisprudence of Natural Rights* (Princeton: Princeton University Press, 1994), 181–185.

82. Arkes, *George Sutherland*, 185.

83. Edward S. Corwin, *The President: Office and Powers, 1787–1957* (New York: New York University Press, 1957), 93.

84. 295 U.S. at 625.

85. Arkes, *George Sutherland*, 185.

86. 51 *Congressional Record* 12861 (1914).

87. 51 *Congressional Record* 12689 (1914).

88. Ibid.

89. Ibid., 12806.

90. Herring, "Federal Trade Commissioners," *George Washington Law Review* 9 (1940): 353. See Leuchtenburg, "Contentious Commissioner," 303.

91. Franklin Roosevelt, Executive Order No. 6166 (June 10, 1933).

92. For similar restrictions imposed by Congress on the Interstate Commerce Commission, see I. L. Sharfman and C. Fund, *The Interstate Commerce Commission: A Study in Administrative Law and Procedure*, vol. 3 (New York: Harper & Row, 1969), 227.

93. Leuchtenburg, "Contentious Commissioner," 303.

94. Skowronek, *Politics Presidents Make*, 303–313.

95. Sidney M. Milkis, "Roosevelt, the Economic Constitutional Order, and the New Politics of Presidential Leadership," in *The New Deal and the Triumph of Liberalism*, Sidney M. Milkis and Jerome M. Mileur, eds. (Boston: University of Massachusetts Press, 2002), 31–73.

96. *Shechter Poultry*, 295 U.S., at 528. Justice Sutherland offered a very similar opinion striking down Congress's delegation of code-making authority to the executive

and a commission of industry experts under the Bituminous Coal Conservation Act of 1935. *Carter v. Carter Coal Co.*, 298 U.S. 238 (1936).

97. *Shechter Poultry*, 295 U.S., at 528.

98. *Securities Exchange Act of 1934*, Pub. L. No. 73–291, 48 Stat. 881 (1934).

99. *Public Utility Holding Company Act*, 49 Stat. 803 (1935).

100. The Economy Act of 1933 gave Roosevelt temporary authority to reorganize some parts of the administration by executive order for purposes of administering emergency relief. The act expired on March 3, 1935, before Roosevelt had been able to employ it very extensively. See Steven G. Calebresi and Christopher S. Yoo, *The Unitary Executive: Presidential Power from Washington to Bush* (New Haven: Yale University Press, 2008), 291–292.

101. Richard Polenberg, *Reorganizing Roosevelt's Government: The Controversy Over Executive Reorganization, 1936–1939* (Boston: Harvard University Press, 1966), 17–20.

102. For a comparison to previous reorganization efforts, see Harvey C. Mansfield, "Federal Executive Reorganization: Thirty Years of Experience," *Public Administration Review* 29, 4 (July 1, 1969): 334.

103. President's Committee on Administrative Management (PCAM), *Report of the Committee with Studies of Administrative Management in the Federal Government* (Washington, DC: U.S. Government Printing Office, 1937). All subsequent citations are to the Brownlow Report.

104. Ibid.

105. Ibid., 7.

106. For an account of the battles between Roosevelt and Congress over the president's attempt to curb patronage, see Arthur M. Schlesinger, *The Politics of Upheaval: The Age of Roosevelt*, 1st ed., vol. 3 (New York: Houghton Mifflin, 1960), 415–421.

107. Brownlow Report, 15.

108. Polenberg, *Reorganizing*, 23–25.

109. The Budget and Accounting Act of 1921, Pub. L. 67–13, 42 Stat. 20 (June 10, 1921).

110. Joint Committee on Government Organization, 1937, Hearings on the Report of the President's Committee on Administrative Management, 75th Cong., 1st Sess., 55.

111. Brownlow Report, 22.

112. The report did make an exception for the quasi-judicial powers of the commission, though it is not clear to us why they accepted this part of the reasoning in *Humphrey's Executor*. Brownlow Report, 10.

113. Brownlow Report, 40.

114. The reorganization plan was proposed in four House bills: H.R. 7730, which provided for six assistants to the president; H.R. 8202, which authorized the president to reorganize the executive departments; H.R. 8276, revising the accounting and audit procedures of the Comptroller General; and H.R. 8277, providing for the extension of the civil-service classification and a Civil Service Administrator. These proposals were consolidated in the Senate into a single bill — S. 2970.

115. Franklin D. Roosevelt, "A Recommendation for Legislation to Reorganize the Executive Branch of Government" (January 12, 1937), in *The Public Papers and Addresses of Franklin D. Roosevelt* (New York, 1938) 5:668.

116. 83 *Congressional Record* 5123–5124.

117. Richard Polenberg, *Reorganizing Roosevelt's Government: The Controversy over Executive Reorganization, 1936–1939,* 1st ed. (Boston: Harvard University Press, 1966), 80–92, 193–194. Also see Barry Dean Karl, *Executive Reorganization and Reform in the New Deal: The Genesis of Administrative Management, 1900–1939* (Boston: Harvard University Press, 1963), 256–257.

118. Joseph P. Harris, "The Progress of Administrative Reorganization in the Seventy-Fifth Congress," *American Political Science Review* 31, 5 (1937): 868.

119. Reorganization of the Government Agencies: Hearings Before United States Congress Senate Select Committee on Government Organization (Washington, DC: U.S. Government Printing Office, 1937), 9.

120. Harris, "Progress of Administrative Reorganization," 869.

121. Elena Kagan, "Presidential Administration," *Harvard Law Review* 114 (2001): 2245. Quoted in Yoo and Calebresi, *Unitary Executive,* 291.

122. Hatch Political Activity Act, Pub.L. No. 76–252, 53 Stat. 1147 (1939).

123. Ramspeck Act of 1940, 5 U.S.C. 3304(c).

124. *Wiener v. United States,* 357 U.S. 349 (1958).

Chapter 6. The New Unitarians

1. James Wilson "preferred a single magistrate, as giving most energy dispatch and responsibility to the office." Randolph, in contrast, "strenuously opposed a unity in the Executive magistracy," which he regarded "as the foetus of monarchy," to which Wilson replied "that Unity in the Executive instead of being the fetus of Monarchy would be the best safeguard against tyranny." Max Farrand, ed., *The Records of the Federal Convention of 1787* (New Haven: Yale University Press, 1966), 64–66.

2. Karl M. Manheim and Allan Ides, "The Unitary Executive," *SSRN eLibrary* (n.d.), at http://papers.ssrn.com/sol3/papers.cfm?abstract_id=943046. Accessed August 1, 2012.

3. Saikrishna Bangalore Prakash, "Hail to the Chief Administrator: The Framers and the President's Administrative Powers," *Yale Law Journal* 102, no. 4 (January 1, 1993): 992.

4. See Douglas W. Kmiec, "OLC's Opinion Writing Function: The Legal Adhesive for a Unitary Executive," *Cardozo Law Review* 15 (1994 1993): 337; Mark Tushnet, "A Political Perspective on the Theory of the Unitary Executive," *SSRN eLibrary* (May 1, 2009), at http://papers.ssrn.com/sol3/papers.cfm?abstract_id=1397746. Accessed August 1, 2012; and Stephen Skowronek, "Conservative Insurgency and Presidential Power: A Developmental Perspective on the Unitary Executive," *Harvard Law Review* 122 (2008/2009): 2070.

5. Sidney M. Milkis, *The President and the Parties: The Transformation of the American Party System Since the New Deal* (New York: Oxford University Press, 1993), 122–124.

6. "The 'Forgotten Man' Speech," Radio Address From Albany, New York (April 7, 1932), at http://www.presidency.ucsb.edu/ws/index.php?pid=88408. Accessed August 1, 2012, emphasis added.

7. Richard Nixon, "Address to the Nation on the War in Vietnam," November 3, 1969. Online by Gerhard Peters and John T. Woolley, *The American Presidency Project*, at http://www.presidency.ucsb.edu/ws/?pid=2303. Accessed on August 1, 2012.

8. Congress rejected Truman's Reorganization Plans No. 1 and No. 2 of 1949, which would have concentrated the control of the executive over the administration in a number of ways.

9. *Wiener v. United States*, 357 U.S. 349 (1958).

10. Beryl A. Radin, *Federal Management Reform in a World of Contradictions* (Washington, DC: Georgetown University Press, 2012), 96.

11. Milkis, *President and Parties*, 142–146.

12. *The Public Papers of the Presidents of the United States: Richard M. Nixon, 1971* (Washington, DC: Government Printing Office, 1975), 51.

13. Richard P. Nathan, *The Administrative Presidency* (New York: Prentice Hall, 1986), chap. 2.

14. Joel D. Aberbach and Bert A. Rockman, "Clashing Beliefs Within the Executive Branch: The Nixon Administration Bureaucracy," *American Political Science Review* 70, 2 (June 1, 1976): 457.

15. Nathan, *The Administrative Presidency*, 49.

16. Aberbach and Rockman, "Clashing Beliefs," 456–468; also see Milkis, *The President and the Parties*, 117–118, 132–134.

17. Cited in G. E. Frug, "Does the Constitution Prevent the Discharge of Civil Service Employees?" *University of Pennsylvania Law Review* 124 (1975): 960.

18. William Safire, *Before The Fall: An Inside View Of The Pre-Watergate White House* (New Brunswick, NJ: Transaction Publishers, 2005), 247.

19. Aberbach and Rockman's 1976 study demonstrates that there is solid empirical evidence supporting Nixon's contention here.

20. As Nixon stated in his 1971 State of the Union Address: "I shall ask not simply for more new programs in the old framework of government itself — to reform the entire structure of American government so we can make it again fully responsive to the needs and wishes of the American people." Quoted in Peri E. Arnold, *Making the Managerial Presidency*, 2nd ed. (Lawrence: University Press of Kansas, 1998), 289.

21. President Richard M. Nixon, *Special Message to the Congress on Executive Branch Reorganization* (March 25, 1971), at http://www.presidency.ucsb.edu/ws/index.php?pid=2951. Accessed August 1, 2012.

22. Charlene Bangs Bickford, Kenneth R. Bowling, and Helen E. Veit, eds., *Documentary History of the First Federal Congress*, Volume 11: *Debates in the House of Representatives, First Session: June–September 1789* (Baltimore: Johns Hopkins University Press, 1992), 922.

23. President's Advisory Council on Executive Organization, *A New Regulatory Framework — Report on Selected Independent Regulatory Agencies* (Washington, DC: Government Printing Office, 1971).

24. Reorganization Plan No. 2 of 1970, 35 Fed. Reg. 7959 (1970), reprinted in 84 Stat. 2085

25. Judith E. Michaels, *The President's Call: Executive Leadership from FDR to George Bush* (Pittsburgh: University of Pittsburgh Press, 1997), 71.

26. James L. Sundquist, *The Decline and Resurgence of Congress* (Washington, DC: Brookings Institution Press, 1981), 201–209.

27. See Louis Fisher, "Impoundment of Funds: Uses and Abuses," *Buffalo Law Review* 23 (1973–1974): 141. See also Ralph S. Abascal and John R. Kramer, "Presidential Impoundment, Part I: Historical Genesis and Constitutional Framework," *Georgetown Law Journal* 62 (1974): 1549–1618; and James P. Pfiffner, *The President, the Budget, and Congress: Impoundment and the 1974 Budget Act* (Boulder: Westview Press, 1979).

28. Deputy Director of the OMB Caspar Weinberger and Deputy Attorney General J. T. Sneed argued before the Senate that the president was required to limit spending under a number of existing statutes, including the Anti-Deficiency Act of 1950, giving the Bureau of the Budget (now the OMB) authority to impound funds in order to effect savings when possible or to provide for contingencies. Weinberger and Sneed defended an administration's broad reading of the law that would permit the OMB to undertake a systematic and aggressive effort to cancel spending. See *Impoundment of Appropriated Funds by the President: Hearings Before the Senate Government Operations Ad Hoc Subcommittee on Impoundment of Funds,* 93rd Congress, 1st sess. (1973).

29. *Anti-Deficiency Act,* 64 Stat. 785 (1950). Sneed also cited the Employment Act of 1946, which mandated that the federal government seek to mitigate the boom-and-bust cycles of the economy that had caused the Great Depression and widespread unemployment. 69 Stat 23 (1946).

30. Steven G. Calabresi and Christopher S. Yoo, *The Unitary Executive* (New Haven: Yale University Press, 2008), 347.

31. Quoted in Andrew Rudalevige, *The New Imperial Presidency* (Ann Arbor: University of Michigan Press, 2006), 58.

32. War Powers Resolution, Pub. L. No. 93–148, 87 Stat. 555 (1976).

33. *The Congressional Budget and Impoundment Control Act of 1974,* Pub. L. 93–344, 88 Stat. 297 (1974).

34. When Sam Ervin proposed in the Senate that Congress pass a bill to require legislative approval for impoundments, the House objected to the Senate's proposal because it would require that Congress acknowledge a limit to spending. Consequently, the Budget and Impoundment act had to address the issue of spending limits first by creating a set of internal procedures designed to curb spending before it could then respond to the problem of executive impoundment.

35. Allan Schick, *The Federal Budget: Politics, Policy, and Process,* rev. ed. (Washington, DC: Brookings Institution, 2000), 250–255.

36. S. 2803, 93d Cong. § 2(c) (1973).

37. United States Senate, Committee on the Judiciary, *Removing Politics from the Administration of Justice: Hearings Before the Subcommittee on Separation of Powers of the Committee on the Judiciary, 93rd Congress, 2nd Session, on S. 2803 and S. 2978* (Washington, DC: U.S. Government Printing Office, 1974).

38. Ibid.

39. Arnold, *Making the Managerial Presidency,* 301.

40. James W. Ceaser, "The Theory of Governance of the Reagan Administration,"

in Lester M. Salmon and Michael S. Lunds, eds., *The Reagan Presidency and the Governing of America* (Washington, DC: Urban Institute Press, 1985), 57–86.

41. Nathan, *The Administrative Presidency*, 74.

42. "There were a number of workshops on the subject of the separation of powers in the Department [of Justice]. On January 9, 1987, the Attorney General chaired a seminar on the subject and invited outside academic participation. I was convinced." Charles Fried, *Order and Law: Arguing the Reagan Revolution, A Firsthand Account* (New York: Simon & Schuster, 1991), 158.

43. *Confirmation Hearing on the Nomination of Samuel A. Alito, Jr. To Be an Associate Justice of the Supreme Court of the United States: Hearing Before the Senate Committee on the Judiciary,* 109th Cong. (2006), 471–472.

44. Steven G. Calabresi, "The President, the Supreme Court, and the Constitution: A Brief Positive Account of the Role of Government Lawyers in the Development of Constitutional Law," *Law and Contemporary Problems* 61 (1998): 61.

45. Douglas W. Kmiec, *The Attorney General's Lawyer: Inside the Meese Justice Department* (New York: Praeger, 1992), 17–47.

46. For an overview of their positions on executive power see Ryan J. Barilleaux and Christopher S. Kelley, *The Unitary Executive and the Modern Presidency* (College Station: Texas A&M University Press, 2010).

47. Edwin Meese, *Towards Increased Government Accountability,* 32 *Federal Bar News & Journal* 406 (1985), 406–407.

48. Peter L. Strauss, "Formal and Functional Approaches to Separation of Powers Questions A Foolish Inconsistency," *Cornell Law Review* 72 (1987): 488.

49. *Bowsher v. Synar,* 478 U.S. 714 (1986). All subsequent references to the case in this section will be to page numbers.

50. *The Balanced Budget and Emergency Deficit Control Act of 1985,* Pub. L. 99–177, 99 Stat. 1038 (1985).

51. Anthony S. Campagna, *The Economy in the Reagan Years: The Economic Consequences of the Reagan Administrations* (Westport, CT: Greenwood Press, 1994).

52. Quoted in Andrew E. Busch, *Ronald Reagan and the Politics of Freedom* (Lanham, MD: Rowman & Littlefield Publishers, 2001), 119.

53. Quoted in Rudelavige, *Imperial Presidency,* p. 146.

54. Statement on Signing H.J. Res. 372 Into Law, 21 Weekly Comp. of Pres. Doc. 1491 (1985).

55. Exec. Order No. 12, 291, 46 Fed. Reg. 13,193 (1981).

56. Ibid. (1981).

57. Fried, 154–155.

58. See Peter L. Strauss, "The Place of Agencies in Government: Separation of Powers and the Fourth Branch," *Columbia Law Review* 84, 3 (April 1984): 573–669.

59. Ibid. 592–593.

60. *Bowsher,* 715.

61. Transcript of Oral Argument at 51, Bowsher, 106 S. Ct. 3181 (1986).

62. *Bowsher,* 725.

63. Ibid., 944, n. 4.

64. Ibid., 749.

65. Ibid., 761–762.

66. Ibid., n. 13.

67. Ibid., 763.

68. Ibid., 762, internal quotation marks omitted.

69. Ibid., 763.

70. Ibid., 764.

71. Section 274(f)(1), 99 Stat. 1100.

72. *Synar v. United States,* 626 F. Supp. 1374 (D.D.C. 1986), 1400.

73. David K. Nichols, *Myth of the Modern Presidency* (College Park: Pennsylvania State University Press, 1994), 82.

74. Bernard Schwartz, *Decision: How the Supreme Court Decides Cases* (Oxford, UK: Oxford University Press, 1997), p. 130.

75. Quoted in Schwartz, *Decision,* p.132.

76. Schwartz, *Decision,* 132–133.

77. For an excellent and exhaustive study of the independent prosecutor act, see Katy J. Harriger, *The Special Prosecutor in American Politics,* 2nd ed. (Lawrence: University Press of Kansas, 2000).

78. 28 U.S.C. 591 (1978).

79. 28 U.S.C. 592(a), (b), and (c) (1978).

80. 28 U.S.C. 593(b) and (c) (1978).

81. 28 U.S.C. 596(a) (1978).

82. M. E. Kraft and N. J. Vig, "Environmental Policy in the Reagan Presidency," *Political Science Quarterly* 99, 3 (1984): 415–439.

83. Lloyd N. Cutler and David R. Johnson, "Regulation and the Political Process," *Yale Law Journal* 84 (1975): 1405.

84. Kevin M. Stack, "The Story of *Morrison v. Olson*: The Independent Counsel and Independent Agencies in Watergate's Wake," in Christopher H. Schroeder and Curtis A. Bradley, eds., *Presidential Power Stories* (New York: Foundation Press, 2009), 416.

85. See Mark Rozell, *Executive Privilege: Presidential Power, Secrecy, and Accountability,* 2nd ed. (Lawrence: University Press of Kansas, 2002), 16–17.

86. Ethics in Government Act of 1978, Pub. L. No. 95–521, 92 Stat. 1824 (codified at 28 U.S.C. secs. 49, 591–599 (1994) (Title VI).

87. Alexia Morrison, *In re Theodore B. Olson and Robert M. Perry: Report of the Independent Counsel* (December 27, 1988), 9.

88. Stack, "The Story of *Morrison v. Olson,*" 419.

89. In order to avoid directly challenging the law, at least until the administration could find a case that would not cause Reagan to lose political credit even with a legal victory, Attorney General Meese had offered a number of "parallel" appointments to the independent counsel lawyers that retained all of the protections afforded by the law but would not actually fall under the law. This way, the defendants could not challenge the constitutionality of the independent counsel act in court. Meese also offered such an arrangement to Alexia Morrison, who rejected the offer. See Stack, "The Story of *Morrison v. Olson,*" 419–422.

90. For Olson's position on separation of powers, see Theodore B. Olson,

"Separation of Powers and the Supreme Court: Implications and Possible Trends," *Administrative Law Journal of the American University* 6 (1992/1993): 266.

91. See Constitutionality of Statute Requiring Executive Agency to Report Directly to Congress, 6 Op. Off. Legal Counsel 632, 632 (Nov 5, 1982), cited in Stack, "The Story of *Morrison v. Olson*," 412.

92. Fried, 160.

93. *Immigration and Naturalization Service v. Chadha*, 462 U.S. 919 (1983).

94. *In re Sealed Case*, 838 F.2d 476 (1988).

95. President Reagan, Statement on Signing the Independent Counsel Reauthorization Act of 1987, Independent Reauthorization Act of 1987, 2 Pub. Papers 1524 (December 15, 1987).

96. Justice Stevens did not participate in *Morrison*. Chief Justice Rehnquist joined the majority in *Bowsher*. Justices Sandra Day O'Connor and William Brennan joined the majority but expressed strong reservations about any decision that might imply that the independent regulatory commissions were unconstitutional. See Schwartz, *Decision*, 125–129. Justice Thurgood Marshall joined Stevens's concurrence in *Bowsher*, which argued against clear demarcations of legislative and executive power. Justices Harry Blackmun and Byron White separately dissented from *Bowsher* majority, arguing that Congress should be free to limit presidential power in any way so long as it does not undermine the executive's ability to do his assigned task.

97. "Congress is only given power to provide for appointments and removals of inferior officers after it has vested, and on condition that it does vest, their appointment in other authority than the President with the Senate's consent." *Myers v. United States*, 272 U.S. 52, 56.

98. *In re Sealed Case*, 838 F.2d 476 (1988). See also *Bowsher* (White, dissenting, n. 3); *FTC v. Ruberoid Co.*, 343 U.S. 470 (1952), 487–488 (Jackson, J., dissenting).

99. *Morrison v. Olson*, 487 U.S. 654 (1988), 707.

100. Robert Jackson, "The Federal Prosecutor," Address Delivered at the Second Annual Conference of United States Attorneys, April 1, 1940. See *Morrison*, 728.

101. *Morrison*, 703.

102. Ibid., 703.

103. *In re Sealed Case*, 511.

104. Stacks, 438.

105. *In re Sealed Case*, 488.

106. Brief for Appellee at 18, *Morrison*.

107. Brief for Appellant at 50, *Morrison*.

108. *Morrison*, 658.

109. *Nixon v. Administrator of General Services*, 433 U.S. 425 (1977).

110. *Nixon v. Administrator of General Services*, 433 U.S. 477, 443. Internal quotation marks omitted.

111. *FTC v. Ruberoid*, 343 U. S. 488 (1952).

112. *Morrison*, 699, emphasis added.

113. Nick Bravin, "Is Morrison V. Olson Still Good Law- The Court's New Appointments Clause Jurisprudence," *Columbia Law Review* 98 (1998): 1104.

114. Marianne Means, "An Idea Whose Time Has Gone," *Times Union* (Albany),

December 1, 1997, at A6, quoted in Lee S. Liberman, *"Morrison v. Olson*: A Formalistic Perspective on Why the Court Was Wrong," *American University Law Review* 38 (1989): 313.

Conclusion

1. *"Federalist* No. 48," in *The Federalist,* ed. Jacob Cooke (Middletown, CT: Wesleyan University Press, 1982), 332–333.

Index